Project Planning for the Stage

Project Planning for the Stage

Tools and Techniques for Managing Extraordinary Performances

Rich Dionne
Foreword by Bonnie J. Monte

Southern Illinois University Press
Carbondale

Southern Illinois University Press
www.siupress.com

Printed in the United States of America

21 20 19 18 4 3 2 1

Cover illustrations: photo (*top*, by John Underwood) of set and actors in a Purdue University production of *Cabaret*; model (*middle*) and sketch (*bottom*) of set designed by Ivana Vukomanović. Production directed by Amy Lynn Budd, costume design by Stephanie Nguyen, and lighting design by Megan Turnquist.

Library of Congress Cataloging-in-Publication Data
Names: Dionne, Rich, author. | Monte, Bonnie J., writer of foreword.
Title: Project planning for the stage : tools and techniques for managing extraordinary performances / Rich Dionne ; foreword by Bonnie J. Monte.
Description: Carbondale : Southern Illinois University Press, [2018] | Includes index.
Identifiers: LCCN 2018007364 | ISBN 9780809336890 (paperback : alk. paper) | ISBN 9780809336906 (ebook)
Subjects: LCSH: Theater management. | Project management.
Classification: LCC PN2053 .D52 2018 | DDC 792.02/32—dc23
LC record available at https://lccn.loc.gov/2018007364

Printed on recycled paper. ♻

This paper meets the requirements of ANSI/NISO Z39.48-1992 (Permanence of Paper) ♾

Contents

Illustrations

Foreword

In the twenty-first century, it is almost impossible to imagine that there is not a "how to" book on every imaginable subject. But until this book came into being under the sure hand of Richard Dionne, there had been no complete resource on the elusive and often misguided process of physically mounting a work of living art—whether stage play, opera, dance piece, or any presentation that requires the collaboration of artists and artisans to create a visual and aural landscape in which a piece of art can reside.

There are books, or chapters in books, that define—for students or amateur thespians—the basic, step-by-step process of building flats, platforms, and other basic components of a set. And there are many books that contain information on aspects of production—how to create costume patterns, for example. But those are descriptions of specific functions within the scope of a larger project.

This book does not address specific functions but, more importantly, attempts to define the steps and philosophies that guide the process in which collaborators must engage if they are to meld specific functions to create a successful project that is convivial, resourceful, inventive, and inspired.

I was pleased and honored when Rich asked me to write the foreword to this book, in part because I have the greatest respect for him as a colleague and fellow artist, in part because it is always satisfying when someone you have mentored asks you to do something like this, and in part because I enjoy Rich so much as a fellow human being. Most importantly, it is deeply satisfying to me that he has evolved into such an exemplary man of the theatre.

I first met Rich when he came to work for us at the Shakespeare Theatre of New Jersey as a guest sound designer for a production of Ionesco's *Rhinoceros*—not an easy show. He did a splendid job, and we asked him back repeatedly. Eventually, when the need arose, I asked him to sign on with us as our production manager and resident sound designer. Happily, he accepted and performed those roles admirably for almost four years.

Rich continued to design for us after he moved to Purdue University, when his schedule allowed. What probably focused his attention so acutely on *process* was the fact that when Rich was our production manager, we had recently moved into our newly renovated and expanded facility, and myriad aspects of the process had to be reexamined or newly invented for our new performance space. So, we were not only creating a system for all our project work but were also creating systems and processes for the very space and institutional spine that supported the work. Many of the systems and processes that Rich implemented are still in use at our theatre today.

The efficacy of the process Rich outlines in this book speaks for itself, but what I find most heartening and admirable in these pages is Rich's attempt to capture the most elusive and intangible aspects of what we do as theatre artists; Rich's *process philosophy* demands vigilance—constant reassessment, subsequent reexamination and regrouping, a willingness to change course, to think out of the box to invent creative solutions, and to always remember that necessity is the mother of invention. He reminds us that that kind of ongoing assessment and agility of thought is part of our job and our specialty, and that in itself is something to be excited about, not something to resist or resent, which is too often the response to creative change. We did not go into this field to perform functional work. We went into it because we love the thrill of invention, and *how* we invent changes project to project. If we forget this along the way, we might as well work on an assembly line.

Last but not least, Rich stresses the importance of well-articulated communication at every juncture. Not only do I heartily agree with and endorse this point, but I feel that if we all did this more—in our lives outside the theatre, as friends, as family members, as citizens—the world would be a better place, and would, perhaps, be more often as magical as the worlds we create on stage.

Bonnie J. Monte
Artistic director of The Shakespeare Theatre of New Jersey

Project Planning for the Stage

Introduction

I managed my first live production in 1978 or 1979. It was a Christmas play. I don't remember the title—in fact, I don't remember much about the production at all—but my family assures me that I wrote, cast, directed, designed, and built the whole thing. I, of course, was the star at four years old—playing old Kris Kringle himself—and my aunts and mother played reindeer and probably elves. I can't say for certain that my interest in managing live productions began that winter, but claiming it did makes for a good story, so I'll stick with it.

Years later, when I was in college, I produced plays with middle schoolers in a local community center (with a good friend who now runs a nonprofit theatre and shared arts space in Oakland, California); in graduate school, I helped found an all-student performance company, producing shows in our theatre department's black box and in found spaces around campus. After working at a number of smaller and regional theatres in different capacities after graduation, I found myself asked to take on the responsibility of production manager for a mid-size regional theatre. When I left that theatre four years later, I landed at Purdue University, where I am now, working as a technical director and production manager.

In other words, whatever my other interests—writing, teaching, control systems, sound design, what have you—I keep coming back to managing productions.

I came to theatre with a passion for stories, a love of tinkering, a tendency to look at the big picture as well as the niggling details, and a desire to create exciting and moving live performances. I've been working professionally for almost twenty years, and wherever I go, I find the same truth: a production managed well provides the audience with an incredible experience, regardless of the amount of resources available, the size of the organization, or the goals of the production.

What does it mean to manage a production well? I've spent most of my professional career trying to figure that out. Much of my early career I relied on advice my father told me over and over again growing up: I trusted my gut. And I watched what those around me were doing, trying to pick up what to do from the best, and what to avoid from those who weren't. This worked well: during my time as production manager at the Shakespeare Theatre of New Jersey, we improved the size and skill of the staff working in production. We opened a second performance space, and added a second leg of our educational touring company. And our work pushed boundaries even as the quality of our production elements increased dramatically.

Unfortunately, because I was often working on instinct, I couldn't explain what I was doing or why I was doing it. I spent many hours that, in retrospect, I can see were wasted on figuring out processes, methods, and systems—to streamline our production department, to try to balance the desires of our artists, the needs of our staff and technicians, and our fiscal responsibilities—that already existed, that others, smarter than I, had developed and practiced and polished.

When I came to Purdue in 2004, one of the first tasks I set for myself was to research what was known about production management. I found a handful of texts, but none that focused on the big picture processes in the way that I was looking for. As I dug deeper into the management library, however, I discovered a treasure trove of texts on the field of project management. These books, while specifically focused on large-scale construction projects or fast-paced software development projects, described many of the processes and techniques I had been intuitively feeling my way through during the process of managing a production.

Among the books I discovered there are some standouts, deserving specific acknowledgment here. First among them: *Project Management Step by Step: How to Plan and Manage a Highly Successful Project*, by Richard Newton. In many ways, this book was the white rabbit that led me to wonderland; it was one of the first I pulled off the shelf, and it led me deeper into the stacks. Admittedly, the book is a basic introduction to the philosophy of project management—there are many others that go into greater depth and detail—but the language is clear and simple, and the explanations are accessible and understandable. It is well worth a read if one has the time.

Project Management, by Dennis Lock, and the identically titled book by Gary Heerkens were instrumental in the development of this book, providing in-depth explanations of things like precedence diagrams, Gantt charts, and the critical path. Heerken's *Project Management* provides a good overview of the project life cycle, and provides some good insights into understanding how to be a project manager. Lock's text is in its tenth edition, and is exceptionally comprehensive (as well as incredibly heavy). In particular, Lock covers in detail finances, stakeholders, and planning and scheduling resources; these latter two tasks can be quantified in interesting and complex ways, and anyone who has an affinity for understanding the world through mathematics should enjoy these chapters immensely.

The McGraw-Hill 36-Hour Course: Project Management, by Helen S. Cook and Karen Tate, is another good book on project management concepts. Their text is as much a guide to understanding project management as a process as it is a clarion call for increased implementation of project management techniques and project managers in today's corporate and industrial worlds. While sometimes the language assumes a foundational understanding of management practices, skills, and techniques, the explanation of project management concepts is clear. Additionally, the authors include a number of helpful templates in the appendixes.

Team-Based Project Management, by James P. Lewis, deliberately focuses on the people- and team-management aspects of project management; as Lewis states, "Project management is not just scheduling." While much of the text you hold focuses on the mechanics of estimating and scheduling (the planning parts of the project life cycle), Lewis's exhortation to remember that without taking care of your team the project will fail informs much of the rest of it. He explores how leadership impacts team performance—how to build trust, gain buy-in, and support team members who need it. Additionally, he discusses decision-making, team building, teamwork, and managing interpersonal conflict.

Visualizing Project Management, by Kevin Forsberg, Hal Mooz, and Howard Cotterman is another text worth reading—in part because it deliberately comes to describing the project management process sideways. Forsberg, Mooz, and Cotterman include—as one might expect—an almost dizzying number of visualizations of the project management process. In contrast to many authors on the subject, they talk about project management as four elements: vocabulary, teamwork, the project cycle, and management essentials. Of particular interest in their discussion of the project cycle is the importance they place on "control gates"—milestones at which a project is assessed to determine whether the project should proceed. The authors also describe ten "management elements" that are essential for project success: project requirements, organization options, project team, project planning, risks and opportunities, project control, project visibility, project status, corrective action, and project leadership. Most of these elements, in some way, are reflected in the organization of the book you are holding.

While the United States Department of Labor website can be a bit of a slog to wade through, the wage and hour division (www.dol.gov/whd) proved invaluable for chapter 3 of this book. It is definitely worth your time to read through the materials here to gain a deeper understanding of the labor law that governs wages, overtime, and seasonal work.

Anyone interested in project management should explore the Project Management Institute (www.pmi.org) and the resources available there. This group works to push the envelope of the practice of project management, and has numerous publications and documentations available, and offers the opportunity to become certified in a number of project management skills. There are others texts to pick up and resources to read—too numerous to call out individually—and I strongly recommend finding a management library and browsing the stacks on project management to find the volume(s) that speak best to you.

Finding a way to translate the tools so familiar to project managers into the language of the "typical" (i.e., American regional theatre) production process for my students was the birth of this book some thirteen years ago. In these pages, I've tried to lay out the philosophical underpinnings of thinking about productions as projects; additionally, I've tried to provide a foundation for understanding some of the processes, methods, procedures, and tools common to project management. This book is primarily geared toward those interested in production management—particularly those working in small- to mid-size regional theatres. Many of the references used to contextualize material will be far more recognizable to people working in these environments than, perhaps, those working in cruise-line entertainment, themed parks, or large-scale for-profit theatre. Further, I can't pretend that my background hasn't been primarily in technical direction, and many of the examples and references reflect this bias. However, the philosophy and the tools presented here are useful for technicians and craftspeople working in live entertainment of any size and scope—even if some additional translation may be necessary for some live entertainment environments.

Additionally, the material in this book is essential for any technical manager in live entertainment. Technical directors, costume shop managers, properties masters, master electricians, video supervisors—anyone managing even a portion of a production should understand concepts like clearly defining the project expectations, knowing the boundaries of authority and responsibility, parametric and bottom-up estimates, and precedence diagrams. They are incredibly useful and powerful tools that allow any technical manager to provide the best possible work for a production.

I've tried to organize the book somewhat chronologically, based on a typical life cycle for a production project. In many ways, I think that's a logical way to read the material. However, that may not be the most efficient for every reader. There's no reason one can't hop from chapter to chapter, reading about estimating time and scheduling resources before reading about managing team members and labor law. Each chapter begins with an outline of the topics covered in it, which should provide some guidance for the reader looking for specific material.

In the end, use the book in whatever way you find it most useful. If nothing else, it is sure to provide a reference for when, like me, you know there must be a way to do something better in your production process, but you just can't figure out how.

I would be remiss if I did not include some acknowledgments here. First, I need to recognize the many students who have been generous enough to explore this material with me—both in class and out—during the years I have been developing it. Additionally, a number of friends and colleagues agreed to read all or at least portions of this book and contribute their wisdom and experience. Heath Hansum, Jeremy Jenkins, Ashley Bishop, Chuck Meacham, Jean Burch, Beth Martell, and Ted Kraus generously gave of their time to read early drafts of this book, and each of them made insightful suggestions that led to significant improvements in the manuscript. My colleagues Rose Kaczmarowski and Kristine Holtvedt came in at the eleventh hour to provide insight and wisdom from their experiences in costumes and in performance and directing—areas where my skills are, at best, weak. To all those who have aided me along the way, my eternal gratitude; this book may not be perfect, but it is immensely closer to that goal thanks to your help.

PART I

Productions as Projects

Bringing a live-entertainment project to fruition is an ambitious task. So many questions come into play when trying to shepherd a creative project from conception to realization. How do we maintain the integrity of the initial vision? How do we figure out how to make it real? Whom do we need to bring on board to make it happen? How do we make sure we have the resources to accomplish our goals? What happens if we don't?

These questions can be daunting, whether we are a production manager hired to help realize a large-scale, for-profit production destined for Broadway or a technical director for a small summer-stock theatre in the middle of the Kansas plains. Fortunately, theatrical events have been produced for millennia, and we can draw on previous experiences in live entertainment, replicating production processes that have worked before and avoiding those that have been unsuccessful. We can also do what theatre does best—borrow and steal the most successful ideas from other fields, and apply them to the live-entertainment production process. In some ways, the live-entertainment industry has already done that. Design deadlines, production meetings, budget meetings—these are all examples of best practices from other major industries that have found their way into the live-entertainment production process.

This text aims to introduce a process for managing live-entertainment production in a more comprehensive manner, drawing on management and planning techniques used for running long-term and large-scale projects in a number of other industries, from software development to traditional construction. In the chapters that follow, you will be introduced to ways of thinking about decision-making and responsibility, to ways of organizing a production team, to methods of estimating costs and scheduling tasks in a project. All of these are drawn from the rich field of project management.

Project management, as a field, is far too broad and deep to be examined fully in a single book. The following chapters, instead, introduce tools, techniques, and processes common to project management, and place them within the context of a traditional live-entertainment project. Hopefully, in the following pages, you'll find helpful tools and techniques for thinking about a production process as a project, and for applying those tools to any live-entertainment project you have the privilege of working on.

Part 1, "Productions as Projects," looks at what it means to think about a production as a project. Part 2, "Planning the Project," explores planning tools for estimating and scheduling a project. Part 3, "Executing and Managing the Project," examines tools for tracking project progress, for determining how to respond when progress deviates from the plan, and how to respond to changes in the scope of the project. Part 4, "Closing Out the Project," talks about the importance of reviewing the production process after opening has been reached, and how to document the production and the production process.

Chapter 1, "Projects," introduces foundational concepts about projects, including the differences between traditional, functional work, and project-based work; project-based organizational structures; project-management approaches; and the four stages of a project's life cycle, from conception to closeout.

Chapter 2, "Project-Definition Phase," will explore in more depth the first stage of any project: the project-definition phase. It is during this part of the project that the goals and scope of the production are defined, the team is gathered, and the overall objectives of the production and the resources available to complete it are fleshed out.

Chapter 3, "Gathering the Team," examines putting together a production team, including basic hiring principles and key labor law considerations in the live-entertainment industry.

Chapter 4, "Leading the Team," explores what it means to manage a team, including the differences between managing and leading, the importance of strategic thinking, and understanding principles of organizational communication, including the relationships among authority, responsibility, and accountability.

1. Projects

What is a project? What work makes up a project, and what parameters define its completion? How does the concept of a project relate to the work we do in theatre, particularly as production managers (and technical directors, costume shop managers, and other technical supervisors and managers)?

According to the Project Management Institute (an organization dedicated to advancing the science and practice of project management), a project is a group activity designed to produce a unique product or result, with a defined beginning and end and defined scope and resources. Any production we embark on can be thought of as a project. Every production is a planned undertaking. Every production is intended to tell a particular story in a particular way at a particular time. Every production has a defined scope and defined resources: it has a definite beginning (the play's selection as part of a season, or the first time the director reads it) and a definite ending (opening night, performances, and strike). Every production has elements designed to create a unique, never-seen-before world specific to the artistic team's interpretation of the story being produced. Because a production can be thought of as a project, regardless of the specifics of the production, we can identify a set of procedures or processes that allow us to successfully complete the project.

By thinking about a production as a project—as a unique product that needs to be managed and ushered into being on its own terms—we open up possibilities in the creation of a live production that can be missed if we simply do it the same way we always did. The project itself—the goals and intent behind producing this particular show at this particular time in this particular space will inform and define the process we use to bring it to fruition. By going through a systematic and consistent process that answers the questions, what needs to be done, who needs to do it, and how we accomplish it, we are better prepared to avoid the pitfalls and limitations imposed by a rigid, traditional, "we always do it this way" process. Once we define and utilize a consistent process, we are better prepared to see opportunities for efficiency, innovation, and imagination in the production process that might otherwise have been missed.

> Often, the production process can take on a kind of rote sameness: read the play; design specific elements in discrete silos (scenery, costumes, lighting, sound, video), build/create those elements, rehearse and open. This sameness is helpful: we can fall back on assumptions dictated by the process to define the production's scope and boundaries, identify responsibilities and areas of authority for the stake holders, and provide a kind of automatic understanding of how to get from the beginning to the end of "making a play," all without having to do so explicitly. However, by allowing these assumptions to drive an implicit understanding of the process, we may miss the opportunity to focus on creating a truly *unique* project.

Project management incorporates and integrates a broad range of practices into a process for thinking about the progression of a project from inception to completion. These practices have been developed, honed, and improved by thousands of practitioners through application on projects large and small; as a result, these practices have a proven track record for shepherding projects effectively and efficiently. A savvy manager working in technical theatre can take advantage of this wealth of experience and leverage project management practices not only to more effectively execute the work of each production, but also to shepherd imaginative and innovative productions to the stage.

Topics covered in this chapter:

- Functional work versus project work
- Organizational structures
    - Functional organizational structures
    - Project-based organizational structures
    - Hybrid/matrix organizational structures
- Project-management methodologies
- The project life cycle
    - Define the project
    - Plan the project
    - Execute the project
    - Close the project

Functional Work versus Project Work

Most of us, when we talk about working in theatre, refer to our experience in terms of titles—for example, actor, director, carpenter, stitcher, welder, electrician, mixer, engineer, or draper. These titles reflect the skills we demonstrate in our jobs; unfortunately, they also—intentionally or not—tend to suggest that our work is *functional*: that we show up in the morning, stitch on a machine all day, go home at the end of the day, and complete work that rarely changes from day to day, week to week, or production to production.

> *Functional work.* Work that is organized primarily around skill and experience that is typically consistent, requiring the same skills applied in the same manner day after day.
>
> *Project work.* Work that is organized primarily around expected outcomes that requires specific skills and experience that can change scope and expectations based on context and goals.

While it is true that in many ways our work does require consistent application of similar skills—stitching a seam or building flat framing doesn't change much from production to production after all—our work *isn't* functional. We're not churning out shirt after shirt to get bagged, boxed, and shipped to the local big-box store for people to purchase. Rather, each garment, flat, wagon, or light hang is specifically designed as part of an individual project. For example, a production may require a rain curtain that spans ten feet and that must have variable rates of rainfall. It is unlikely that there is an existing unit (or design for a unit) that fulfills all the requirements of the particular rain curtain for this particular production; the work on this element will all be prototypical and specific to this one use. This is *project* work, not functional work.

Managing project work is different from managing functional work. Consider an assembly line in an automotive plant. One station in the shop might be for inspecting and sorting parts; another might be responsible for installing seats, and another for bolting on wheels. A fourth station might be the place where windshields are installed. A fifth might be quality-control inspection, and a sixth packaging units for distribution to vendors. Each of these stations would represent a functional area, and the employees in each area would have a set of duties, responsibilities, tools, and resources related to the work performed in that area. Managing these areas would likely entail things like training employees, ensuring they are performing up to expectations, and overseeing the maintenance of equipment and tools.

Managing project work in a theatrical production shop, like a scene shop, is different. Because the work produced in the scene shop may vary moment to moment in terms of the skills required; the time on task; the number of people, resources, equipment, and materials required; and innumerable other factors, keeping the work moving forward becomes more complicated. A manager can't simply check off on a list that Johnny Carpenter has manufactured the three hundred pieces of eight-foot crown molding he was expected to make during his shift, or know that on Thursdays, when the shop is working at a typical pace, another pallet of materials needs to be ordered for the following week's work. Rather, a manager of project work needs to be able to assess and control myriad dynamic elements while working with directors, designers, actors, and other stakeholders as the project evolves and changes through the rehearsal process.

Consider the Dorset Theatre Festival, a small summer-stock theatre in Dorset, Vermont, where the difference between functional work and project work is constantly on display. The company mounts four productions over twelve weeks, with a small scene-shop staff comprised of the technical director, an assistant technical director, a scenic artist, two carpenters, and a handful of interns. The schedule means the shop often works on two shows at once, stacking scenery wherever they can find a place for it. For one production in particular, I recall the shop had to create a sandy, rocky beach structure for the apron of one show while also preparing a low-profile platform to support three actors that hung over a truss for another show. The technical director needed to harness basic construction skills (cutting plywood and adhering extruded polystyrene foam panels together); foam carving and forming skills (to form the contours of the sand on the beach); carpet-laying skills (to apply sandy-colored carpet to the foam); foraging skills (to gather reeds, twigs, moss, and other foliage to add splashes of organic realism); scenic art skills (to use paints and scenic treatments to marry all of the disparate elements into a cohesive hole); welding skills (to build the platform); prototyping skills (to test and perfect methods for "hanging" the platform on rented truss safely and securely without marring the truss); and Tetris skills to store and sort the eight-foot-long beach panels and platform in a small shop with minimal storage space. Only a handful of these skills would be considered essential for doing the typical functional work of "building scenery." However, the project was dependent on them for completion.

The truth is, suggesting that the work done by anyone in live entertainment can be sorted into either of two categories—functional or project—is a false dichotomy. The two categories are somewhat arbitrary, but they provide a convenient framework for talking about how to manage live entertainment projects. The task of managing an organization is often easier in the context of functional work; it is one of the reasons the assembly-line approach to manufacturing is so efficient. Consequently, it can be tempting (though erroneous) to think about the work done by team members working on a live entertainment project as solely functional. The management process can focus on what changes might improve efficiency, speed up production, maintain tooling, and the like.

However, this idea—that the work done in theatre is project work, not functional work (which extends through all areas of work on a production, from the carpenters and stitchers, to the designers, engineers, actors, and director)—forces managers to consider that each project is different. Each project has its own unique requirements, driving the allocation of resources and materials, and consequently each must be managed differently.

It may not always be obvious, but clinging to a production process model that is based in traditional, functional-work silos can limit what we choose to do; it can leave us trapped in traditional modes and less able to adapt to new ideas, new approaches, and new trends in specific areas of production. It is important, then, to examine how theatre has traditionally organized the work in production, and how we might think about that differently. If we start thinking about productions as projects, we can focus on how we organize the people involved in the production process and how we organize the process itself.

The focus of this text is primarily on the production project; however, many live entertainment projects happen within existing producing organizations. Consequently, much that is included in this and the following chapters assumes that a live entertainment project is situated within an organization that is staffed along traditional functional-work lines. Certainly, this is the case for most summer-stock and regional theatres; it reflects, as well, the organization of many academic programs that teach theatre. The first part—*organizing the people*—is about how we structure authority, responsibilities, and accountability within our producing organization. How do we think about who does what, and how do we optimize that structure to harness the efficiency of functional work and the flexibility of project-based work to create innovative, exciting, and powerful work on stage? The second part—*organizing the project*—is the process of defining, driving, and managing the production from inception to closing night.

Organizational Structures

Every organization has a way of understanding how all of the parts and people work together, who is in charge of what, who reports to whom, and what the rules are for. Whether tacitly understood or expressly laid out in a formal manner, these *organizational structures* define the organization, the responsibilities, and the scope of work undertaken. The term "organizational structure" is a complex one, with multiple layers of meaning; for our purposes we will use the term to define the lines of authority and responsibility for an organization and the rules and procedures for interaction within the organization. Understanding the relationship between responsibility and authority in an organization and the related concept of accountability is discussed in more detail in chapter 4.

Typically, organizational structures are grouped into three major types: functional, project-based, and hybrid models that combine elements of both functional and project-based models.

Organizational structure. A system used to define the scope of work and goals of an organization; the allocation of resources; distribution of authority and responsibility; and lines of communication that provide for an organization's achievement of its goals.

Functional Organizational Structures

Often, theatres have been represented using functional organizational structures. Consider the typical organizational chart of a regional theatre as taught in many undergraduate theatre programs (figure 1.1).

Each design area is represented as an individual functional group: for example, scenery under the scenic designer, costumes under the costume designer. These functional hierarchies group together employees with similar skills. This is one of the major advantages of a functional organizational structure: all the carpenters are together in the scene shop, doing carpentry work. There are also very clear, though not absolute, lines of communication: the carpenter reports to the scene shop foreman, who reports to the technical director, who reports to the scenic designer. (This communication hierarchy also suggests a career progression—that stitchers can generate enough experience to promote to cutter/draper and cutter/drapers can generate enough experience to promote to costume shop supervisor. Realistically, though, this career progression isn't always possible: the skills required for becoming a set designer aren't necessarily learned or honed by working in the scene shop, for example.)

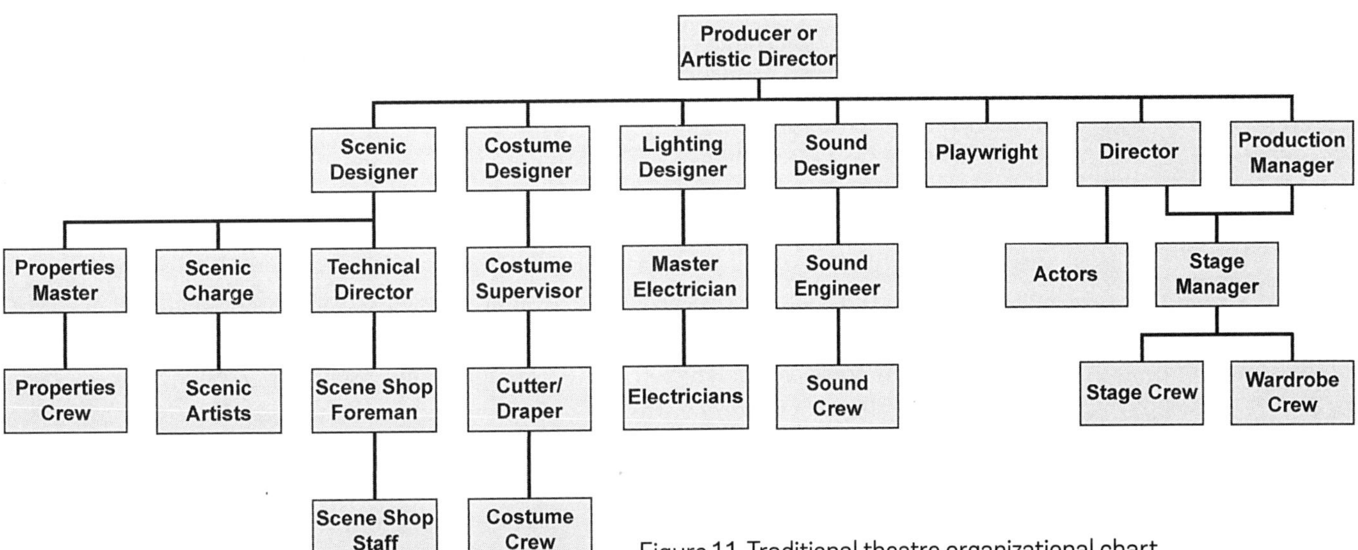

Figure 1.1. Traditional theatre organizational chart

However, for all its strengths, a functional organizational structure like this one also has drawbacks when applied to the kind of project work required to realize a typical production. One drawback is that each functional area can become isolated from other functional areas, limiting or hindering cross-functional collaboration. This can lead to significant inefficiencies. For example, the sound area may need a new tech table and may put audio engineers to work building one, while the carpenters in the scene shop are enjoying a slow build day. Or, the scene shop may purchase a suite of electrical tools (such as soldering irons, wire strippers, and crimps) that both the electrics department and the sound department may already own.

In addition, elements of a production tend to span functional disciplines, requiring collaboration among multiple people. Consider a period radio that needs to sit on a shelf on a moving piece of scenery from which sound must be played. Building the period radio probably falls to the properties department. Ensuring the unit has enough structural integrity to support the prop falls to the scenic department. And making sound come out of it falls to the sound department.

Further, a functional organizational structure such as this can insidiously stifle imaginative approaches to a production. A production divided into rote functional areas becomes difficult to envision in a way that doesn't suit some preconceived process. Straying from traditional functional divisions—envisioning, for example, a production that features video projections as scenery, with costumes as sources of illumination, and actors that provide stimulus for the soundscape—will likely result in frustration within the constraints of the traditional model. Further, by becoming entrenched in these divisions, it is possible that a production like the one described above *may never even be dreamed up.*

Project-Based Organizational Structures

The advantages of thinking about a production team as a functional organization are seductive. Consistency in structure, process, lines of communication, and divisions of authority theoretically allows effort to be spent on the production, not on "how we do the production." However, that consistency can trap artists and practitioners in familiar modes and methods. In contrast to the functional organizational model stands the *project-based organizational model.* In a project-based organizational model, an organization is broken into distinct groups based on projects being undertaken, each of which contains all the staff and resources to fully realize each project assigned to it.

For example, a large architecture firm may create architectural designs by using specialists in structural engineering, HVAC systems, electrical systems, interior design, drafting, and fire-protections systems. Organized functionally, each of these specialists would be grouped together, and the project might progress in sequence from the interior designers, to the structural engineers, to the electrical systems engineer, to the draftspeople. In contrast, a project-based organization may have an interior designer (or interior design team), a structural designer (or team), and an HVAC system designer for a specific project (for example, a new university theatre arts building). These specialists work as integral participants in the new-building project, with opportunity to provide input throughout the process, rather than being confined to just their functional area.

Corporate or for-profit theatre may often be organized on this project-type basis, as in figure 1.2: producers (or a producer) gather(s) a group of artists, technicians, engineers, and managers who have training, background, and emphases in areas specific to the project (such as set designers, composers, musical directors). These collaborators work on a project, from beginning to end, and then depart for other projects and other collaborations. (This is often how staffing of "artistic" personnel is handled for regional, academic, or summer-stock productions: directors, designers, and actors are often brought in on a project basis, whereas production staff are hired as part of functional departments.)

There are a lot of advantages to a project-based organizational structure: everyone is committed to the specific project they have been brought together to complete; resources can be swiftly reallocated from one part of the project to another; there are fewer functional barriers to communication about project elements. Additionally, when the focus of all collaborators is on the specific needs of the project and not on day-to-day functional work, innovative ideas and approaches are far easier to envision and bring to fruition.

However, because different productions require different combinations and levels of skills, materials, and resources, staffing and supplying each project based on the needs of the project can be challenging, particularly for producing organizations that present multiple productions during any given production season. Ensuring there are enough staff members with sufficient skills and training to be ready for whatever requirements may come with a production can be expensive and inefficient (particularly when management finds they are paying wages for employees whose skills are not required on any productions currently under way). Additionally, in most regional, summer, or academic theatres, project timelines overlap: one show is being built while another is loading in and in technical rehearsals, for example. Fully staffing each project would require that both projects have a full suite of staff and resources available—another way of increasing costs and inefficiencies.

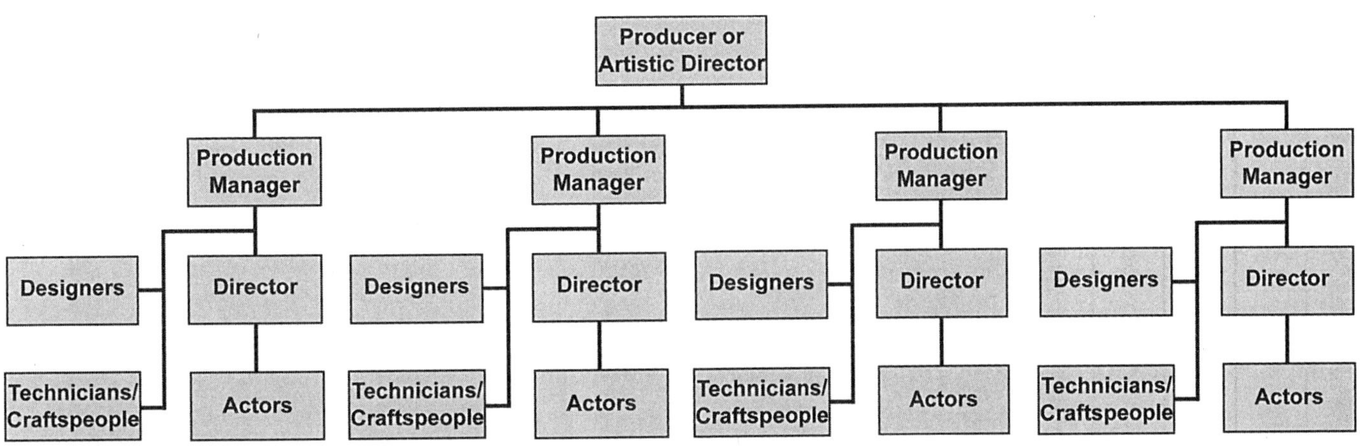

Figure 1.2. Project-based organizational structure for a producing organization

Hybrid Organizational Structures

Striking a balance between the efficiency of a functional structure and the focus and innovative qualities of a project-based structure is the challenge of any production manager in theatre. A *hybrid/matrix organizational structure* combines the efficiency of a functional structure—with clearly delineated areas of responsibility and groups of people with similar skill sets completing similar tasks—with the flexibility of a project-based organizational structure. In a hybrid organizational structure, staff in an organization may be grouped by functional skills and responsibilities, but may be assigned to specific projects that are overseen by project managers who have significant decision-making authority.

To keep labor costs down and increase efficiency, theatres are often staffed in *functional areas* such as the scene shop, the costume shop, and the marketing department. As indicated above, this is partly because this kind of organization of labor can increase cost-efficiency and reduce superfluous labor. However, as we have also pointed out above, theatres tend to produce work that is more like projects—whose scope and requirements change on a regular basis. Because of this, theatres are best served by an organizational model that blends the best parts of a functional organizational structure with the best parts of a project-based organizational structure, in a *matrix structure.*

If we think about a theatre company in this way, we might imagine a structure where project specialists (such as technical directors, costume directors, lighting designers, and directors) are assigned to consider the needs of specific productions, while each functional area is supervised by a functional manager (such as scene-shop foreman or costume-shop manager). In a structure like this (figure 1.3), a production project would be managed by a production manager who supervises a team of specialists in many different areas. Each of these specialists would be assigned labor from functional areas as needed by the functional area supervisors based on the needs of a specific production balanced against the overall needs of the functional area in the context of the whole production season.

If we accept this matrix organizational structure—a structure that combines elements of a functional approach with a project-based approach—production managers gain a large amount of freedom to efficiently manage resources and labor in the realization of a production as well as the ability to encourage innovation in production and design.

Take, for example, a dance project that incorporates embedded sensor technology in costumes, which are also designed to light up in various ways and in different colors. The embedded sensors provide data to the lighting system to control some automated lighting-fixture parameters, and to a computer running an algorithm composing music to be played while the dancers dance. A project like this, produced by a traditionally organized theatre venue, would be ill served by a traditional functional-work organizational structure, given the ways in which many of the production elements live outside or span traditional theatrical disciplines. Similarly, a project-based organizational structure might serve the project well as a stand-alone event, but such a structure would make it exceptionally difficult to effectively manage other projects in an ongoing production season. In this situation,

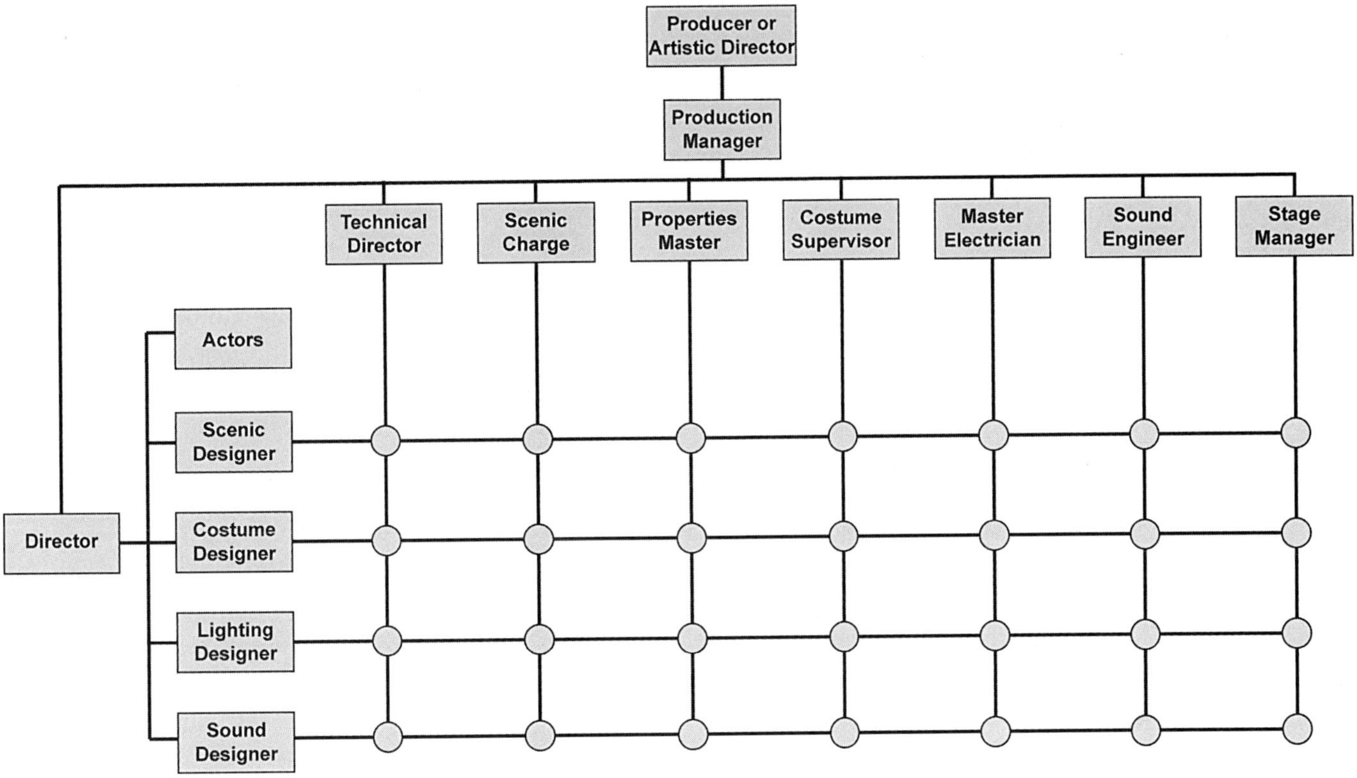

Figure 1.3. Matrix or hybrid organizational structure for a producing organization

such a project would be well served by the hybrid/matrix structure shown earlier.

Working within a hybrid structure to mount a production like this, a production manager can streamline communication and maximize resources. At the same time, she can provide a framework in which exploration of these nontraditional approaches to costumes, lighting, and sound, for example, can be used to create a compelling experience on stage. The production manager might assign to the costume-shop manager a stitcher, a draper, and an electrician (who has experience with electronics) to work on the costume construction; she might assign electricians and sound technicians with experience in control systems to the master electrician and sound engineer to install the lighting, sound, and control systems. A hybrid structure provides a manager flexibility and agility in allocating resources and labor.

Successful use of the hybrid organizational structure relies on a production manager who is granted responsibility for framing the scope of the project, organizing the resources required for the production, and overseeing its progress. Organizing the people is only the first step; managing the rest of the project requires a production manager who understands and communicates equally well with designers, artists, technicians, and engineers; who is facile with terms, technology, and techniques specific to many different areas of specialization, from acting, to visual composition, to textual analysis, to millinery, and welding; and, most importantly, who is comfortable not just managing a production but leading the production team from inception to closing night. "Being facile" does not imply being skilled in all of these areas; this would be beyond almost anyone's capacity. Rather, what is referred to here is having gained enough knowledge to be able to understand and converse with artists and craftspeople in an intelligent way.

Project-Management Methodologies

Thinking about productions as projects is the first step to managing them effectively. The next step is finding a model to follow for managing them. There are many methodologies for managing projects that a production manager can turn to for structuring and organizing the work of a live-entertainment project. Different kinds of projects are better managed by some methods than others, and an important skill for a project manager is to know which approach to turn to when managing a project or kind of project. A common and traditional project-management methodology is the waterfall model (figure 1.4); this model comprises four phases (project definition, project planning, project execution, and project closeout). The name "waterfall" reflects a visualization of the flow of a project managed in this way, in which one phase of the project cascades or waterfalls into another, with little opportunity to iterate or circle back and make changes.

The waterfall methodology makes a lot of sense as a way of managing live-entertainment projects—at least on the surface. Live-entertainment projects typically have a rigidly defined deadline—opening night—and there are tight labor and resource constraints on the rehearsal and build processes. This generally means that a live-entertainment project must have a clearly defined scope from the outset of the project—designs must be completed

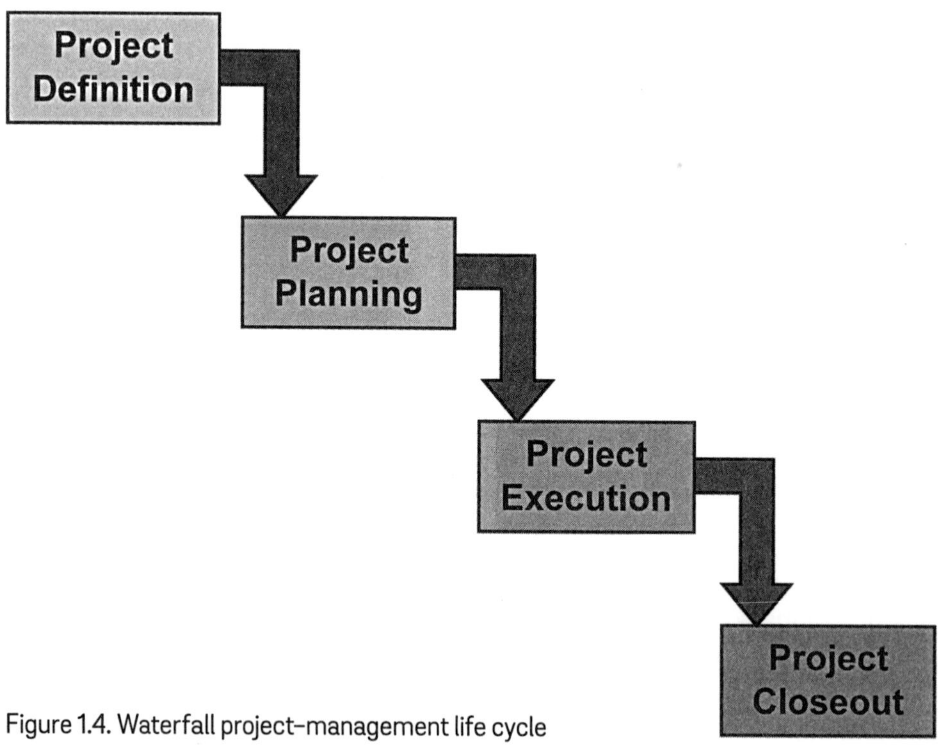

Figure 1.4. Waterfall project-management life cycle

and approved before costume and scenery construction begins, for example. Once defined, a live-entertainment project will need to be estimated and scheduled before the construction and rehearsal processes begin to ensure each design can be achieved. This stepped approach is exactly what the waterfall project management method is designed to accomplish.

However, the waterfall method presents a significant downside: it is not designed for managing projects whose scope is not fully designed at the outset. Theatre projects often don't fully realize their scope until just before opening, when rehearsals and the integration of technical and design elements have been completed. While the design process for some elements (scenery and costumes, for example) may conclude prior to construction or realization, the rehearsal process often does not. And, while it is tempting to believe that the rehearsal process is simply "practicing the play," anyone with any experience in live entertainment knows that is not the case: rather, the rehearsal process is an opportunity for a director and actors to make discoveries about how best to tell the story—and these discoveries can often lead to the need to make changes to elements that have already been designed, are being built, and may even already be completed. Technical rehearsals only add to this lack of definition, as this is the time when many intangible design elements—lighting, sound, and projections, for example—are folded into the project. The traditional waterfall method—with its emphasis on moving cleanly from one phase of the project to another, without iterating or circling back to revisit earlier decisions—is ill equipped to manage these discoveries.

Many "agile" project-management methodologies have arisen to better manage projects that have a less well-defined scope at the outset, or that require a more flexible development process. Agile project-management methodologies allow for iteration and adaptation throughout the life cycle of a project (figure 1.5). Often—as is the case for software or technology-development projects, for example—this serves to accommodate rapidly changing resources and technologies. In other situations, agile approaches can be used to promote flexibility on a project whose outcomes and goals may change during the process. Management methodologies like Scrum, Spiral Model, Six Sigma, and the Adaptive Project Framework, are examples of agile project-management approaches. What they share is an ability to respond to changes in scope and resources relatively quickly.

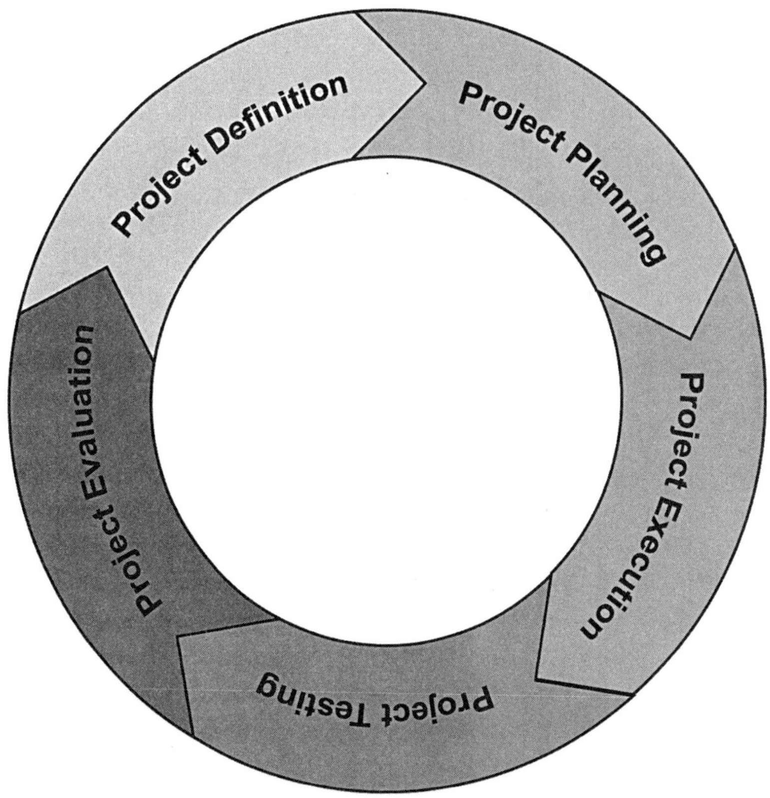

Figure 1.5. Agile project-management life cycle

An agile approach like the one pictured earlier allows for testing, evaluation, and iteration back through the process. However, if a major downfall of the waterfall approach is an inability to effectively deal with changes and adaptations during a project, more agile methods tend to be ineffective for managing live-entertainment projects, with their combination of limited resources, limited time, and (relatively) time- and resource-heavy design elements like scenery and costumes.

Clearly, managing live-entertainment projects requires an approach that combines the ability of the waterfall method to effectively manage projects that have relatively limited time and resources with more agile methods that leave room for the scope of the project to continue to be refined throughout the project life cycle. Consequently, this text presents a version of the waterfall method that has been adapted to include mechanisms for responding to changes in the scope and goals of a live-entertainment project during its life cycle (figure 1.6). This adapted approach preserves the benefits of the waterfall method for projects with limited time and resources by maintaining a set of cascading phases with approvals and gateways between each. At the same time, it provides methods for accommodating change and development of a project throughout its life cycle by defining processes for returning to earlier phases in the project's life cycle.

The Project Life Cycle

In the waterfall approach, every project—and every production—has four distinct phases: project definition, project planning, project execution (which includes

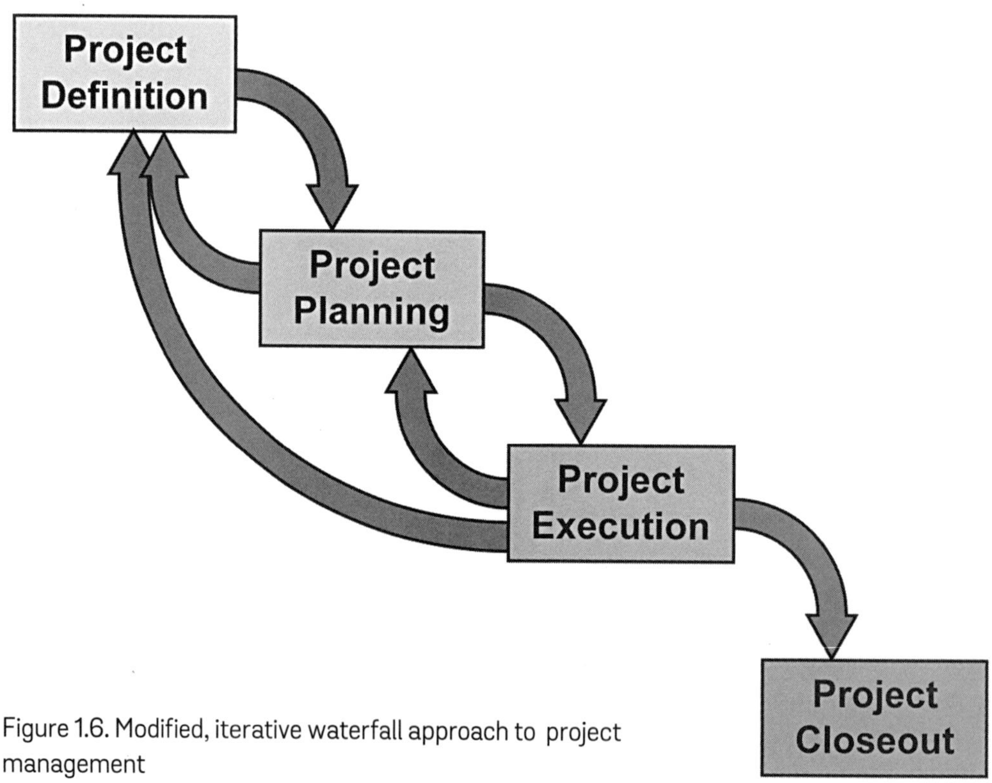

Figure 1.6. Modified, iterative waterfall approach to project management

monitoring progress and controlling for variance), and project closeout. Understanding what work needs to be completed during each phase, and how best to manage the staff completing the work in each phase, is essential for any project manager. This is especially true in theatre, where time and resources are often limited, and rapid feedback concerning feasibility is essential to the overall completion of the project to the satisfaction of all involved.

Define the Project

Before anyone can manage a project, she needs to know what the project is and who is involved in the project. This happens during the project definition phase of a project's life cycle. This is the time when the project's purpose and function are determined, and how much money will be spent completing it. Other parameters, such as who has authority to make certain kinds of decisions, how long the project will take, and the overall schedule of the project is determined during this time as well. Designers, artists, technicians, and craftspeople will be hired during this time, and a performance calendar might be finalized, among other things.

The project definition phase will be examined in more detail in chapters 2, 3, and 4.

Plan the Project

The project-planning phase is when, well, the planning of the project happens. Project management tasks during this phase would include overseeing the development of the design of the project (e.g., set design and costume design); generating cost and labor estimates and detailed construction and installation calendars; creating construction and installation drawings (if required); and determining required labor and resources. (These tasks may be performed directly by a production manager, or by technical managers under the supervision of the production manager.) The project-planning phase will be examined in more detail in chapters 5, 6, and 7.

Execute the Project

During the project execution phase, the project is realized and the planning brought to fruition. This usually involves, in a theatrical project, things like the build process, rehearsals, fittings, load-in and technical rehearsals, and opening. During this time, the project manager should be focused on tracking progress, reporting changes in the schedule or the cost estimate, and revising plans based on the evolution of the project (through rehearsal discoveries, for example). The project execution phase will be examined in more detail in chapters 8 and 9.

Close the Project

Project closeout is probably one of the most overlooked parts of the project life cycle in theatre. During project closeout, a project manager reviews the entirety of the project life cycle to determine what went well in the project and what areas present opportunity for improvement. Methods for tackling project closeout will be examined in chapter 10.

Summing Up

Functional Work versus Project Work

Functional work is work completed every day, without an expectation of change. A classic example of functional work would be the assembly line worker whose job is to install door panels on sedans at an automotive plant, or the attendant of the mail sorting machines at the post office. The work these people complete is similar day in and day out, regardless of what car is on the line or what mail is being sorted.

Project work is work that varies depending on the specific item, unit, or product being produced. Theatre production is almost entirely made up of project work: each production has a unique design, a unique schedule, and unique resources, all of which make every production—even multiple productions of the same play—unique.

Managing project work is different from managing functional work.

Organizational Structures

Companies organized along functional lines have difficulty adapting to the requirements of project work; those organized along project-based lines have a hard time completing functional work efficiently. Most theatre work combines a fair amount of functional work (e.g., stitching and carpentry) in the service of projects. A theatre organized in a manner that combines the best elements of a *functional organizational structure* and a *project-based organizational structure* uses a hybrid, *matrix structure.*

Project Management Methodologies

The waterfall methodology is the most common project-management approach seen for live-entertainment productions. The name reflects the flow of a project, in which one phase of the project cascades or waterfalls into another, with little opportunity to iterate or circle back and make changes. Most live-entertainment projects need to be more flexible however, as scope and goals can change as the project progresses (most often because of discoveries made during rehearsal). A more agile methodology for managing live-entertainment projects merges the traditional waterfall approach with mechanisms that provide for opportunities to effectively incorporate changes to the scope of the project while it is ongoing.

The Project Life Cycle

Project-definition phase. When the project manager determines the parameters of a production project: for example, how much time is available, what resources can be applied, and how complex or simple the project will be.

Project-planning phase. When the project manager oversees the design, costing, and scheduling of the project.

Project-execution phase. When the design is realized, during which process the project manager is tracking and reporting on progress and responding to change.

Project-closeout phase. When the project manager reviews the entire life cycle of the project with the project team to learn from successes and opportunities for improvement.

2. Project Definition Phase

During the definition phase of any project, a project manager determines who the personnel involved in the project are, the scope of the project, the expectations that determine "successful completion," the resources available for completion of the project, and the general schedule of the project. This information in many industries is combined into a "project charter," a document detailing the project team's understanding of the parameters of the length and breadth of the entire project. In theatre, project managers don't often generate a project charter—sometimes called a mission statement—per se, but coming to agreement about these elements is essential for effectively guiding a project from conception to completion. This is especially true in theatre, as the overall scope of the project is refined during the rehearsal and build process; clearly stating the understanding of the project at the outset provides a touchstone to refer to when making revisions and changes as the project progresses.

Topics covered in this chapter:

- Project charter
- VIPs: project personnel
    - Client
    - Contractors
    - Stakeholders
- Project team
- Project objectives
    - Project scope: What is the end product?
        - Load-in
        - Tech
        - Opening night
        - Strike
    - Project resources: What resources are available?
        - Project budget
        - Labor
        - Equipment
        - Materials
        - Space
    - Project schedule: How long do we have?
- Change management

Project Charter

A project charter or project brief is a document that sums up the objectives and expectations at the start of a traditional project. It is a summation of all of the information described in this chapter, presented in a way that is specific to the project being undertaken. A project charter provides a reference point for the client, team members, and stakeholders alike; it contains an understanding of the scope, labor, time, and budget agreed to for the project.

A formal, written project charter is rare in live entertainment. (Some information that is normally included in a project chart may find its way into individual contracts for team members: an actor's contract will indicate the rehearsal and performance dates, for example, and a set designer's will typically indicate design deadlines, the dates of load-in, technical rehearsals and performances, as well as the budget for the scenic elements on the project.) A written charter provides more accountability for the team; however, even an informal discussion and meeting to come to agreement about the parameters and scope of the project is a good step toward ensuring team members are all on the same page. Ideally, this agreement would be reported in meeting notes or minutes distributed to team members.

VIPs: Project Personnel

When managing a project, knowing whom to turn to with questions about scope, quality, cost, or scheduling enables a project manager to navigate the design and execution processes of the project and production, as well as the inevitable changes and challenges that arise during the life cycle of the project. The key people to consider when defining the project are the *client*, the *contractors*, and the *stakeholders*.

On a typical, nontheatrical project, the *client* is the person (or group) who has launched the project; it is the source of funding—the reason the project exists at all. Depending on the context, the client may also be referred to as the customer. On some projects, the client may be part of the organization that is creating a project—an internal client. In all cases, the client provides the funding and receives the finished project when it is completed. In a regional, summer-stock, or academic-theatre project, the client will vary based on the organizational model; usually the artistic director, producer, or executive director are identified as the client. For a commercial production, the client is the producer (or producers) who provides the funding and vision, and who brings together the production team.

The client on a project has the ultimate authority for all aspects of the project; it is, after all, paid for by them. At any moment, the client is the person who can determine if additional funding is available, or if funding needs to be cut. Additionally, the client has authority to demand changes to the scope of the project. The client also determines the quality-control expectations for the project: what deliverables are acceptable, and what are not. However, on any given project the amount to which the client wields that authority may vary, and, certainly, on many projects in live entertainment, the client—whether artistic director, producer, executive director, or some other person—generally defers to the director for most decisions.

> *Client.* The person (or persons) who sets a project in motion. Often, in live entertainment, this is a producer, artistic director, or executive director, for example.
>
> *Deliverable.* Anything that is expected to be delivered to a client at the conclusion of a project. For a live-entertainment project, these would include design elements and performances from actors, for example.

The amount of authority wielded by clients on theatrical productions is similarly variable. Some regional or academic theatres have artistic directors or producers who are involved in every aspect of a production, requiring that every design choice be approved before it can be implemented. In others, the producer or executive directors take a more hands-off approach to scope, but remain deeply invested in issues of cost and scheduling. On large commercial productions, the producers may be intimately involved in questions of scope and cost, or may outline expectations in broad strokes and permit the team to "sweat the details."

The concepts of authority and responsibility—and the related concept of accountability—are deeply interconnected facets of how people work together on any project. Authority refers to the ability to make decisions about an aspect of a project; responsibility refers to the degree to which one will be answerable for successes and failures on part of a project; accountability refers to taking personal ownership for actions. These concepts are discussed in more detail in chapter 4.

In any project, it is important that a project manager understand to what degree the client will be involved in the decision-making process. This can be as simple as asking questions such as: How involved are you in the design process?; or—Will you want to go over construction techniques and materials with me? A project manager may determine this information through conversations with other members of the company as well. However it is gleaned, understanding both the expectations of the client on a project and their level of involvement in the decision-making process is essential. This is just as true with a theatrical-production project as with any other type of project. A production manager should become very familiar with the level of involvement the client—artistic director, producer, executive director—will want to have on the production. This level of involvement should be clearly stated and forms a fundamental part of the project definition.

You're probably asking yourself an important question: Aren't the theatre patrons the clients of a production? In some ways, yes—they pay (usually) to watch the performance. However, the patrons of a production generally don't determine the scope of the project, the artistic goals of the project, or the overall funding of the project—at least not directly. Indirectly, the scope of the project is informed by audience preferences (as reflected typically by ticket sales), but decisions about scope and goals are often also led by the mission of an organization. Consequently, it may be helpful to consider theatre patrons as stakeholders (discussed in more detail below).

Contractors

What about the director? Many approaches to the production process position the director as the ultimate authority—the person who defines the artistic vision, who directs the design team, who tells the actors what to do. Wouldn't this make her the client? Certainly, she has been engaged to oversee the overall aesthetic approach of the production and to lead the team of designers, technicians, and performers. However, except in rare cases, directors are not supplying the funding for the production, nor are they responsible for financial considerations, resources, or labor management. (In the end, if an aesthetic desire put forth by a director would cause a theatre company to go broke, there is no doubt that an artistic director/producer/executive director will force a change in aesthetic—except in those cases where a director has significant popularity and wields exceptional clout.) The director, therefore, isn't the client, but is more appropriately considered one of the *contractors* (albeit typically an incredibly powerful one).

Contractors are traditionally defined as people or organizations that are contracted to complete a project. For a theatrical project, the term would be used a little more broadly, to refer to all the people—some of whom may be contracted, some of whom may be employees of the theatrical organization mounting a particular production—who execute the work of creating a production project. This definition will extend from the director to the designers; from the actors to the electricians, stitchers, and carpenters working the shops; from the stage manager to the stage crew that keep the production running while it is on stage. Each of these individuals make up part of the team of contractors that create the production.

In this text, to reflect the more collaborative approach that most theatrical projects embrace, the term "team members" will be used in place of "contractors." Just as any project may require a specific team of contractors to get from vision to realization, each production may require a different composition of team members. A musical, for example, will require a musical director, a choreographer, musicians, singers, and dancers, while a straight play likely will not. A production incorporating large-scale puppets will require puppet makers and puppeteers; a production that calls for a dog onstage will require a dog and a dog handler. We'll take a closer look at defining the *project team* below.

> *Contractor.* The individuals and groups hired to complete a project. In live entertainment, some of the individuals who complete the work for a project might be hired on a contract basis, while others may be staff members of a producing organization. To avoid confusion, this text will refer to anyone involved in completing the work of a live-entertainment project as "team members."
>
> *Stakeholder.* Any individual or group that may affect or be affected by the decisions, activities, and outcomes of a project.

Stakeholders

In any project, there are people for whom the success or failure of the project will have an impact. These people—people who have some "stake" in the success or failure of the project—are called *stakeholders*. Of course, the client is obviously included in this list: she wants to see the project succeed, and see her investment provide some kind of return. The client is usually the primary stakeholder, although some productions may have investors and other financial backers who might have as large a financial stake as the primary producer. Of course, the patrons who attend the live performance have an interest in the project; typically, they have paid to observe the live event.

Projects often have other, not-so-obvious stakeholders; these are people who have an interest in the decisions made during the life cycle of the project and in its completion, but who don't have much or any authority to impact those decisions. Team members—actors, technicians, crew members, technical managers, designers, directors, choreographers, and the like—are all stakeholders in this way. They have far less authority over certain decisions that must be made as the project progresses, but are impacted by the project; actors are usually affected by decisions about how the set functions, but rarely have any authority to make changes to those functions, for example. The costume designer may have a stake in how ladders are constructed on a production in which everyone is wearing heels, for example, or a set designer may have a stake in the colors the lighting designer intends to use.

We can distinguish between two types of stakeholders: active stakeholders, who have authority to affect changes to the project, and passive stakeholders, who have little to no authority. Active stakeholders would include the producer, as mentioned above; other active stakeholders are typically the director, the designers, and technical managers, for example. Passive stakeholders might include the patrons who pay to see the production, artists and craftspeople working in the various shops producing the designed elements, and the crew members making the production happen live on stage. Because all the various stakeholders may have an interest in any of the many decisions made during a project's life cycle, identifying them becomes an important part of managing any production project. Knowing who has a stake in a decision makes it possible to bring their concerns and perspectives into the conversation when decisions need to be made.

Project Team

Who comprises the project team? The project team is the group of key personnel required to define, envision, and oversee the realization of a project. Obviously, a key member of the project team is the project manager; other members of a project team might include experts in different fields related to the successful realization of the defined project—depending on the project, anyone from structural engineers to computer programmers to database designers. Typically, a theatrical project team comprises a director and designers, technicians and managers, crew members and actors—all the people required to create the production project.

Traditionally, project teams have reflected the functional organization of many theatres, comprising at the top a director and designers from the four "major" design disciplines (scenery, costumes, lighting, and sound); depending on the production, this group may be expanded to include a choreographer and a musical director, or increasingly a projections designer. As noted above, defining the project team using these "default" categories can lead the design of the project down predetermined paths, and is a good reason to define the project and its scope before determining the makeup of the project team.

It would be better, in an ideal world, to allow the development of the production aesthetic to define the makeup of the production team—this would prevent any predetermination of aesthetic based on the categories of people involved. However, this introduces a bit of a chicken-and-egg scenario: if we don't define the people until we define the aesthetic, who defines the aesthetic? If we define the people before we define the aesthetic, preconceived notions of categories of work may inadvertently impact the design process. (This tension persists the more detailed we get: do we hire welders in case we have metal work to do, or do we decide not to do metal work because we don't have welders?)

A savvy production manager will recognize that there's no good answer to this conundrum, and will go ahead and put together a project team anyway, trusting in good team leadership to avoid the pitfalls of predetermined assumptions about aesthetic paths. Because the skills required by team members may not become clear until the project designs have been fleshed out, this makeup must, of course, be flexible, as will the individuals that comprise that makeup. For many productions, this may mean starting with a traditional design team (e.g., director, set designer, costume designer, sound designer, and lighting designer) and production team (e.g., technical director, costume director/shop manager, sound engineer, and master electrician/lighting director). As the project objectives and scope become more defined, this team could change.

With the team defined, we can move to defining the project objectives: What is the *project scope*? What are the *project resources*? And what is the *project schedule*?

Project Objectives

"You can have it good, fast, or cheap: pick two." This truism reflects the very real balancing act any project presents among the competing pressures of time, cost, and quality, and has an impact on the *project scope*. A project manager's primary responsibility is to guide the project team during the life cycle of the project to achieving the scope of the project within the limitations of the available time and money and to the level of quality expected by the client. Defining the scope of the project requires a solid understanding of these four things prior to embarking on the project: What is the end product, how much can we spend on it, how long do we have to do it, and what is the expected level of quality control?

The relationships between cost, time, scope, and quality are often represented as the "iron triangle" (figure 2.1). The sides of the triangle represent cost, time, and scope, while the area of the triangle represents the overall quality of the project. On any project, there is an ideal balance among the scope of the project, the time and money spent on the project, and the level of quality expected by the end user.

Normally, the requirements of the project will constrain one of these sides. For live-entertainment projects, the side with the tightest constraints is time: the show must go on, after all. With one side of the triangle constrained, the other two sides vary in proportion to each other. If time is

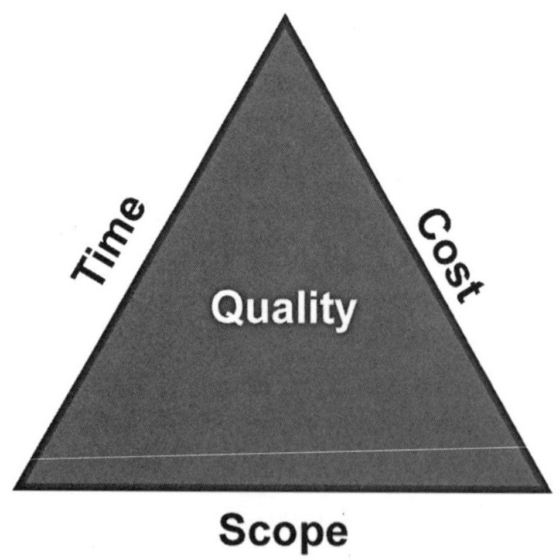

Figure 2.1. Iron triangle

two equally important goals of training cast and crew and getting all the elements working smoothly together can be challenging. As with many other aspects of project management for live entertainment, determining early in the project life cycle how this time will be managed is the best recipe for success.

In truth, in many live-entertainment productions—usually because of time constraints—technical rehearsals aren't only a time when the cast and crew are trained on the technical elements and fine tuning their interaction. Often, the tech process is also the first time the lighting, projection, and sound designers have an opportunity to develop their aesthetic contributions. (It is difficult, at best, to create the lighting looks for the production without both a sense of the timing of each moment of the production as well as the cast available on stage to see how the light plays on them.) The need to make time for this work to happen during tech adds another level of complication to an already complex balancing act.

Opening Night

If there were a self-evident end to any production project in live entertainment, it would be opening night. By opening night, all of the scenic and costume elements have been created, installed, and polished; the lighting, video, and audio systems have been installed and checked, and cues have been finalized; the storytelling choices of staging and acting work have been determined and set. Indeed, the production has been delivered to its first audience.

Of course, in most situations, the production continues after opening—sometimes for a long time. This requires a handoff of materials to a team responsible for—and with authority over—the production during its run. The specifics of this team and its organization vary from production to production, but it is important to understand them and how they impact the final deliverables of the project if it is to end at opening. In some cases, the project manager responsible for the initial project will continue to be responsible for it after opening, and will need to be prepared to manage the handoff from one team to the next.

Strike

Strike is that time after the last performance of a live-entertainment project when all the design elements for the production are removed and the space is returned to a neutral state. For some venues and organizations, strike can be scheduled to come just before load-in for a subsequent production. Like performances, strike is a project in and of itself, often with its own team and specific constraints. Like load-in, the constraints on time, labor, and resources that affect the planning for strike have an impact on the project that is being struck. These constraints should be included in the original production-project definition, as they will play a role in determining the scope of the production.

Project Resources: What Resources Are Available?

Project resources refers to the total of all materials, equipment, labor, and funding available to complete the project. In order to effectively plan how to complete a project, a project manager needs to know what resources are available to make that happen.

Project Budget

The project budget represents the total amount of funding available for the project and the projected expenses that funding will be spent on. Depending on the venue or producing organization, some budgeted expenses may be clearly delineated for projects, while others may be folded into organizational operating costs; typically, this happens with labor expenses, but may also be true for other expenses, such as venue, equipment, and vehicle rental costs, for example.

Consider a typical regional theatre that employs a year-round production staff but hires actors and artistic staff (designer, directors, and choreographers) on a per-show basis, owns their own venue, rents their production shops, and typically rents a large truck to transport items from the production shops for load-in. The project budget for a production might include funding allocated for materials (such as scenery, costumes, and lighting equipment), actor and artistic staff contracts and transportation, and truck rental. The project budget likely would not include funding for the mortgage on the performance space, the rent on the production shops, or the labor expenses of the annual production staff (but might include additional funds for over-hire labor—technicians and craftspeople hired on a per-production basis). In contrast, a project produced independent of a regional theatre would have to plan for funding to cover labor expenses, venue rental expenses, and a myriad of additional expenses over and above materials.

A clear determination of available funding is essential for developing a project budget. As the scope of the project is refined, the project manager can determine how those funds should best be allocated for a project (analogous estimates, discussed in chapter 5, can be a helpful tool for this process). As the project definition is finalized, so, too, should the project budget, in consultation with the appropriate stakeholders. (Some projects may require a highly detailed and large set but a smaller commitment to costumes. This would mean a larger allocation of the budget for scenery and a smaller one for costumes. A different artistic team might determine, as the project gets defined, that a project will require a greater emphasis on video and projection equipment, necessitating a larger allocation of the project budget for those elements.)

Labor

When defining the available labor for a project, it is beneficial to determine the range of skills each person involved in the project may bring to the table. At this stage of the production life cycle, the intent is to determine what resources are *available*, not what resources are *needed*. For a production project taking place at an established organization that employs people based on a traditional functional-organizational model, such labor may be readily available. For other projects—for example, a small, experimental project that is dreamt up by two artists over coffee, or a large, for-profit project proposed by a freelance producer—there may be no labor yet attached, or no associated venue. It can be helpful to identify alternative sources of labor—local scene shops or costume shops, for example, or a known community of artists willing to participate in the project—and the range of skills available from those sources.

One method for cataloging the skills a team can bring to bear on a project is to make a list of the different kinds of skills typically called upon for completion of a similar project, and then ranking each person available to contribute to the project as to their level of competence in each skill area. A common list of skills required for the completion of set projects, for example, would include:

- Drafting
- Costing
- Scheduling
- Rough carpentry
- Finish carpentry
- Metal fabrication
- Plastic fabrication
- Sewing/working with fabric
- Scenic art (foam shaping and papier-mâché, for example)
- Scenic painting
- Rigging (traditional)
- Rigging (nontraditional/arena/spot)
- Electrical
- Pneumatics/hydraulics
- Automation/control systems
- Lifting/strength
- "Being squirrelly" (getting into tight spaces)
- Climbing/work at heights

One might rank each person available to work on a project as being unskilled, novice, skilled, or advanced in each of these skill areas (figure 2.2). These rankings—and the associated picture of available labor for the project—become essential when assessing the project during the planning phase of the project life cycle. This information will inform labor and schedule estimates, the allocation of team members from and among functional areas for the project (for projects produced in more traditional organizations), and the distribution of authority and responsibility.

	Rough Carpentry	Finish Carpentry	Metal Fabrication	Plastic Fabrication	Sewing/Fabric	Scenic Art	Scenic Painting	Rigging (traditional)	Rigging (arena)	Electrical	Pneumatics	Control Systems	Lifting/Strength	Squirrely	Heights
John	4	4	2	1	1	1	1	4	3	4	2	1	4	1	4
Emily	4	2	4	4	1	2	1	3	3	1	1	1	3	4	4
Scott	4	2	1	1	3	2	2	4	4	2	4	4	2	2	4
Annie	2	1	1	1	1	4	4	2	1	1	1	1	1	4	4

Figure 2.2. Labor skill-set chart, with individuals ranked 1–4 for each skill (1 for unskilled, 2 for novice, 3 for skilled, and 4 for advanced)

Equipment

Knowing what equipment is available to complete a project is essential. For example, a project that requires steel work cannot be completed by a shop that doesn't have a welder or other metalworking tools. A simple list of the available equipment and facilities can be enough to inform a project manager about what can and cannot be done in a venue. It can be helpful, as with labor above, to annotate an equipment list with an indication of the various ways that equipment may be used. For example, a table saw may have self-evident uses; it isn't particularly useful in cutting fabric, but is really good at cutting lumber. However, many laser cutters may be used to cut multiple materials: fabrics, paper, wood, foam board, and acrylic, and often can be used for engraving work on many of the same materials; an industrial sewing machine in the costume shop can be useful for sewing soft scenery or leather props.

Materials

Are there stock flats available somewhere in storage? Did a board member replace all the windows in her home and donate the old windows to the theatre, or donate a wardrobe full of period garments from her time in the Society for Creative Anachronism to costume stock? Knowing what materials are available means a project manager and her team won't inadvertently pay for new materials that they already have. Generating and maintaining a complete list of stock materials can be time consuming and tedious, but the benefits to any project far outweigh the time spent. This can be especially true if it allows for organizations to purchase items in bulk when on sale or when prices are low, and internally "resell" them to projects or functional areas.

Space

Building a unit that is fourteen feet tall and ten feet wide in a space with doors only seven feet tall and three feet wide is probably not the wisest choice; it's usually best to figure out that a unit won't fit through the doors before you build it and attempt to move it during load-in. Some venues have on-site production spaces adjacent to the performance space; others do not. Some projects need to tour from venue to venue, and be broken down to fit into vans or trucks. A project manager—and her team members—needs to know as much about the spaces available to her for completion of the project and in which the project will be presented. When thinking about spaces related to scenery, this list might include:

- Floor area (Room to paint a full-stage drop? Set up a trial-fit of a complex deck?)
- Build-area height
- Work tables (How many different units can be under way at once?)
- Storage (Can the entire lumber order for the project be stored on-site?)
- Material lengths and equipment placement (Can someone crosscut a sixteen-foot board on the chop saw, or is there only room for eight-foot boards?)
- Door sizes
- Loading access
- Stairways, elevators, lifts
- Vehicle sizes

Project Schedule: How Long Do We Have?

The *project schedule* refers to the broad set of *milestones* that define the life cycle of the project. The major milestones on most theatre productions are similar:

preliminary design deadlines, final design deadlines, budget meetings, first day of build or rehearsal, hang, load-in, focus, level set, technical rehearsals, dress rehearsals, previews, opening, closing, and strike. (Milestones and schedules will be explored more fully in chapter 7.)

Change Management

During the life cycle of any project, of course, change happens. In live-entertainment projects, discoveries are made in rehearsal (and, sometimes, in various production shops and processes) that will require altering the scope and objectives of the project. As mentioned in chapter 1, the traditional waterfall approach to managing a project does not allow for adapting well to changes in scope as a project progresses. At the outset of the project, when defining the scope and objectives, is a good time to discuss and agree upon methods for managing change during the life cycle of any live-entertainment project. A project manager should encourage an open and frank conversation about how much change there might be during the development of the project, as well as how much change can be accommodated based on the project schedule and project resources, and how changes will be discussed and acted upon. Managing change is a complex but important part of managing any project, and is discussed more fully in chapter 9.

Summing Up

Project Charter

The project charter comprises the comprehensive statement of the project, detailing personnel, objectives, and change management processes. In many live entertainment projects, the project charter is an unwritten agreement; however, documenting these essential project elements can make managing the project through its life cycle immensely simpler.

Project Personnel

The *client* is the person (or persons) who set the project in motion, and typically is the final arbiter of all questions related to scope, cost, and time. In theatre, this person is usually called the artistic director, producer, executive director, or other similar title.

The *stakeholders* are people who hold an interest in decisions made about the project, but who may hold little authority or responsibility related to the project. For example, the lighting designer's work on a production is affected by the color choices used on the set, but the lighting designer may not have any authority to determine what those colors are.

Project Team

Anyone whose work will contribute to the completion of the project is a member of the project team. Project team members often come primarily from related functional departments (i.e., scenic construction laborers from the scene shop), but are also pulled from other functional departments as the needs of a project dictate (i.e., seconding an electrician to the scene shop for a week to electrify practical lighting fixtures for the set).

Project Objectives

Project scope refers to the overall purpose of the project and the level of quality expected of its completion.

Project resources refer to all the tangible elements that impact the completion of the project, and include:

- Project budget (What funding is available and how is it allocated?)
- Labor (What people are available, and what skills do they have?)
- Equipment (What tools are available to complete the project?)
- Materials (What existing stock units or supplies can be applied to the project?)
- Space (What are the physical limitations dictated by space?)

The *project schedule* is the series of milestones that have been set for the project, including design deadlines, rehearsals, load-in, technical rehearsals, and opening.

Change Management

The project definition should include clear statements about how much change can be accommodated and how change will be discussed and acted upon during the project's life cycle.

3. Gathering the Team

Knowing the ideal makeup of your team is only part of the battle when managing a project; the real work begins with hiring and recruiting the right people for the project and leading them through the full life cycle of the project. This aspect of managing a project comprises different kinds of skills and knowledge, from hiring practices to elements of ever-changing labor laws related to hiring and firing of personnel, from mentoring practices to communication techniques. The study and mastery of this material can take a lifetime (a good project manager will constantly seek to improve his skills and knowledge throughout his lifetime), but the next two chapters will provide some introductory information for project managers in live entertainment.

> Labor law is complex, laws vary from state to state, and laws change—sometimes frequently. Additionally, it is not uncommon for theatres—particularly smaller theatres and summer stocks—to live in the gray areas of what is legal in terms of labor practices. This book is by no means an exhaustive examination of labor laws related to theatre, and should not be used as a legal resource. It is merely intended to provide a general overview of the topic.

This chapter will examine hiring practices and aspects of employment law that typically apply (or may be misapplied) to live-entertainment organizations and practices.

Topics covered in this chapter:

- Hiring
  - Job descriptions
  - Interviews
    - Portfolios
    - Legal dos and don'ts
  - Evaluating candidates
  - Hiring offers and employment law
    - FLSA minimum wage requirements
      - Young workers
      - Seasonal employment
    - Overtime
      - Nonprofit theatres and the FLSA
  - Union contracts
- Internships and apprenticeships

Hiring

Hiring staff seems like it would be a simple task; however, as with any iceberg, there are unseen depths lurking below the surface. Hiring isn't so much a task as a process, with multiple steps and considerations to make for it to be successful. First and foremost, it's important to consider what we're looking for. Once we've determined that, we can begin seeking out and vetting potential applicants. This step will, ideally, culminate in an offer of employment to a good candidate, who will accept and then be introduced to the team. Each of these steps is far more complicated than a simple one-sentence description would suggest, and will be examined more deeply in the following sections.

Job Descriptions

Consider the following actual job description (with the venue name changed to the fictional East Barn Playhouse): "East Barn Playhouse, a small regional theatre, seeks carpenters to assist with the load-in of our upcoming show. Ideal candidates will have carpentry experience. Rigging experience is also a plus." This description seems straightforward and clear: the potential employer is looking for people with carpentry experience. Except, what does that mean? Even assuming the context is "theatrical carpentry," this casts a wide net: Does a potential carpenter need to be able to use traditional power tools? Pneumatic tools? Have experience with fine carpentry (including joinery, finish work, and the like)? Must he or she know how to weld? These questions don't even begin to discuss the potential candidate with "rigging experience."

Of course, descriptions in job advertisements must necessarily be short. Almost certainly, the employer who posted the ad has a (relatively) clear idea of what they are looking for, and intends to use the resume-reviewing and interviewing process to match applicants to their needs. However, determining what those skills are can take some time—particularly when staffing an organization that must be mindful of both functional work and project-specific work.

There's an anecdote that's told about staffing a scene shop; it's said that every shop should have at a minimum a tall person with long arms (to reach into enclosed scenery, to reach that piece of trim *just* out of reach of everyone else); a skinny person (to shimmy under decks and into other tight spaces); and a large, Hulk-like person (to do the heavy lifting). It's funny because it's true: in that load-in situation where you need to shim a piece of scenery at a spot most people can't reach under the stage, you want that long-limbed and/or skinny person—and that situation almost always happens at least once every load-in.

Of course, hiring someone on the basis of body shape has serious legal and ethical implications, and you're likely never to see "must be petite with long limbs" on any job description for any crew position anywhere. However, the anecdote serves well for thinking about job descriptions in hybrid functional/project-based shops like those in many theatres. It behooves a manager to look for employees with the traditionally expected functional skill set but who also individually bring a variety of other skills to the table that could be required by as-yet-undefined projects in the future.

Remember the labor skills chart from chapter 2 (figure 3.1)?

Not every carpenter in the shop needs to be excellent at all these skills. Rather, a project manager should identify which skills are day-to-day requirements for the typical function work in the shop, and which skills might possibly be called upon on a project-by-project basis in the future. The former skills comprise those skills all potential applicants must have, while the latter list might define a diversity of skills some potential applicants must display at some level of skill.

For example, for a large summer-stock or small- to mid-range regional theatre, it is reasonable to expect all carpenters in the scene shop to be well practiced in the following skills:

	Rough Carpentry	Finish Carpentry	Metal Fabrication	Plastic Fabrication	Sewing/Fabric	Scenic Art	Scenic Painting	Rigging (traditional)	Rigging (arena)	Electrical	Pneumatics	Control Systems	Lifting/Strength	Squirrely	Heights
John	4	4	2	1	1	1	1	4	3	4	2	1	4	1	4
Emily	4	2	4	4	1	2	1	3	3	1	1	1	3	4	4
Scott	4	2	1	1	3	2	2	4	4	2	4	4	2	2	4
Annie	2	1	1	1	1	4	4	2	1	1	1	1	1	4	4

Figure 3.1. Labor skill-set chart, with individuals ranked 1–4 for each skill (1 for unskilled, 2 for novice, 3 for skilled, and 4 for advanced)

- Rough carpentry
  - Pneumatic tools
  - Basic stationary tools (e.g., table saw, jig saw, drill press)
  - Common hand and power tools
  - Traditional theatrical construction techniques and materials
- Rigging
  - Traditional rigging equipment (e.g., shackle, aircraft cable, turnbuckle, hanging irons)
  - Counterweight systems
  - Basic rigging knots (e.g., bowline, clove hitch)
- CNC technologies
  - Router
  - Laser cutter
- Able to lift 50 pounds unassisted
- Practiced at heights

It would be necessary for at least one—but not necessarily all—of the carpenters to be experienced in the following:

- Finish carpentry
  - Fine joinery
  - Molding and shaping
  - Turning
- Welding and metalworking
- Arena rigging
- Sewing and soft scenery
- Pneumatic and hydraulic actuators
- Control systems
- Electrical systems

In many summer-stock or small- to mid-size regional theatres, these skills may be used far less often than on a day-to-day basis; therefore, it wouldn't be necessary for all applicants to be skilled in all these areas. However, when a project comes along that requires any of these skills, it will be vital to have them available in the shop, so finding applicants who represent a healthy diversity of these skills is important.

The more complete a description of skills a manager has for each position, the better the chances the hiring process will culminate in a good fit. To generate these descriptions, a manager should spend time looking at the typical functional work expectations as well as a broad collection of examples of previous productions. This will help determine the kinds of skills required to complete each project (and the kinds of skills that might have resulted in a more successful completion), and allow a manager to derive a comprehensive list of skills—both functional and project-based—that members of the team should have. (This list can then be pared down as needed to fit into the small amount of space typically allotted for job advertisements.)

> *"Equal Opportunity Employer."* This phrase, or the sentence, "All qualified applicants will receive consideration for employment without regard to race, color, religion, sex, sexual orientation, gender identity, national origin, disability or veteran status," is often included in job descriptions and advertisements. Federal executive orders require that government contracts not discriminate on the basis of any of the categories listed above. Consequently, hiring advertisements include these or similar statements to indicate their compliance with nondiscrimination orders. It is not uncommon for other, nongovernmental organizations to include them as well.

Interviews

Portfolios

Much has been written elsewhere regarding best practices in interviewing techniques. Rather than rehash what others have already covered well, this section will focus on portfolio evaluation. A portfolio review or evaluation is a typical part of an interview for theatre, but not as common in other fields. Therefore, it is often overlooked in other discussions of the interviewing process and is worth focusing on here. At the end of this section, however, can be found some basic dos and don'ts for anyone engaging in interviewing potential candidates.

Portfolios can shed light on many different facets of a potential employee. Portfolios can reveal (from the most surface-level examination to deeper abstraction):

- Breadth of experience in the field
- Depth of experience in specific skills
- Attention to detail and quality control
- Sense of visual composition and aesthetic
- Self-reflection
- Degree of engagement in lifelong learning and continuing growth

When reviewing a portfolio with a potential applicant, the portfolio can be both a lens through which to view the applicant and a springboard for deeper conversations about him or her. Evaluating a portfolio during an interview requires both in-depth examination of each artifact in the portfolio and using the overall collection of materials to generate a broader perspective on the candidate.

Each artifact in a portfolio can provide insight into both what skills an applicant has (and at what level of depth), as well as what skills the applicant thinks are important and how she feels about her level of experience in specific skills. For example, two applicants for a stitcher position might show portfolios of costume photos. One applicant—let's call him Brian—might include production photos for many shows on which he served as a stitcher; these photos might be relatively close-up, revealing quality construction and attention to detail.

The other stitcher, Lisa, might include photos taken in process, with very close-up shots of specific sewing techniques and technologies.

At first blush, one might assume Lisa is the better candidate; her portfolio demonstrates both depth and breadth of skills quite effectively. Brian's portfolio, on the other hand, reveals less detail about his work. However, that does not mean he is a lesser candidate (although perhaps he is less adept at building a portfolio); rather, Brian's portfolio requires more in-depth analysis during the interview process. Ask for more detail; encourage Brian to talk about specific stitching techniques and his comfortability with them. Use the lack of information revealed in a portfolio as an opportunity to dig deeper during conversation.

The way a portfolio is put together can also reveal a lot about a potential candidate. Brian's paper portfolio includes clear labels and is free of typographical errors. His photos are all mounted neatly, and the photos are of high quality. Lisa's portfolio, on the other hand, looks hastily thrown together: her labels—when present—are handwritten. Occasionally, they omit important information, like the name of the director or the producing organization. Brian's portfolio demonstrates a consistent visual aesthetic that is carried throughout; he uses similar colors, fonts, and other visual elements in each part of his portfolio. Additionally, his portfolio is arranged to demonstrate a clear progression of skills and techniques. Lisa's portfolio, like Brian's, is mostly free of typographical errors, but it is hard to navigate; the sheer number of photos, put together in a generally disorganized fashion, is overwhelming, and it is difficult to get a sense of her work as a whole. Brian's portfolio shows signs of attention to detail and pride in one's work—good qualities for a potential candidate. While Lisa's badly labeled and disorganized portfolio may not signal that Lisa would be a poor candidate, it may indicate that additional questions need to be asked of her during the interview.

While the differences between Brian's and Lisa's portfolios might not reveal any actual difference in breadth and depth of skill attainment, they could reveal something else, however: a lack of experience or comfortability with self-examination and self-assessment of skills. Theatre, at its best, is an art form that pushes its own boundaries, and often asks the artists involved in its creation to experiment, to learn new skills, and to apply old techniques in new ways. In this milieu, artists and craftspeople that are comfortable assessing their own skills and pursuing new ones make the difference between "OK" productions and exceptional ones. How a potential candidate demonstrates her skills in a portfolio can say a lot about her ability to examine her own work and assess her own development. A good manager will use a portfolio evaluation as an opportunity to assess this in a potential employee.

Legal Dos and Don'ts

Many regulations cover employment practices in the United States, and consequently there are a lot of things an interviewer can and cannot do during the interview process. These regulations generally protect the rights of potential employees from discrimination of various kinds, and not following them exposes the interviewer and the company he represents to the risk of litigation.

DON'T

- Ask someone's age
- Ask someone's gender or sexuality
- Ask if someone is pregnant, or is planning to get pregnant
- Ask someone's family status (i.e., "Are you married?" or "Do you have children?")
- Ask someone's weight or height
- Ask someone's race or ethnicity
- Ask about disabilities or health history
- Ask about citizenship or national origin
- Ask about arrest records
- Ask about records of military service
- Ask about social or religious affiliations
- Ask questions about financial history, educational background not specifically related to the job, language proficiency, or anything else not directly relevant to the job

DO

- Establish a rapport and a comfortable atmosphere
- Ask every candidate the same set of questions
- Ask open-ended but direct questions, building from information on a resume and portfolio or from previous answers
- Keep the conversation focused on the applicant, not on yourself
- Share information about the position and the theatre or organization
- Indicate the time frame for the rest of the hiring process

Remember that the interview process is your opportunity to learn more about the candidate than has been or even can be revealed through a resume, cover letter, and a portfolio. Use this opportunity to ask questions that reveal intangibles such as work ethic, problem-solving ability, growth potential, attitude, and suitability for the theatre organization and position. Some theatres have a rapid pace; others do not. Some theatres leave room for experimentation; others prefer to stick to the tried and true. The interview is your opportunity to gauge a candidate's ability to fit into the way your organization functions. Additionally, be prepared to answer questions from the candidate pertaining to the company and job-specific expectations that cannot be surmised from the brief advertisement. We often forget that the interview process is a two-way street, and that the candidate is also, in many ways, interviewing the company. A successful interview may not be the interview that leads to that candidate being hired (though typically this is the case), but to both candidate and company finding their way through the labyrinth that is the hiring process in a manner that best serves both parties.

Evaluating Candidates

Once the interviews and portfolio reviews are done, it's time to decide whom to hire. Easy, right? Just select the person who has the skills you're looking for.

Except it's never that easy. Occasionally, a candidate will be an obvious perfect fit; she has a greater depth of experience in the required skills for the position, she has a breadth of skills that can widen what kinds of work the theatre organization is capable of, she has a stellar attitude, attention to detail, can work independently as well as collaboratively, and is a good problem solver. In that situation, the next step is obvious: hire her. But when it is not that cut and dried—

which is far more often—how to evaluate each prospective candidate and determine who is the best choice?

Maybe there is one candidate who has a lot of depth of experience in the foundational skills required for the job, but doesn't have a whole lot of breadth beyond that. There is another who has a wide variety of skills, but not a lot of depth of experience in most—including the skills you have identified as essential for the job. A third has a little more depth in multiple skills than the second candidate but not as much as the first, and a greater breadth than the first but not as much as the second. Selecting any one of the candidates will come with advantages, but also some disadvantages.

Choosing among a variety of less-than-perfect candidates is, in the end, a balancing act. Does the candidate with less depth of experience seem willing and able to learn on the job? Do you have enough depth of skill in the rest of the team members to cover the gap in this person's skills for a time while he gets up to speed? Can you get by without the breadth of skills one candidate presents, because depth of experience is essential given the kind of project or functional work you foresee in the future?

Personality, attitude, attention to detail, self-reflection, and other intangible traits can be the thing that sets a candidate apart. This is why establishing an interview process that draws out these skills in a candidate can be so essential. Don't be afraid to call in a handful of candidates that are neck and neck for second interviews; bring additional company members to the table whose judgment you trust, and seek their perspective on the candidates. In the end, though, a good manager trusts her instincts: All other things being equal, who is the best "fit"?

Hiring Offers and Employment Law

The laws covering employment are complex. Regardless of anything written here, it is best that any contract or hiring offer you make be reviewed by an attorney who specializes in labor law, and who is familiar with the complexities of the live-entertainment industry, including not-for-profit organizations, union contracts, and seasonal employment, as any or all of these may be relevant. This section will point out some key considerations and common misconceptions about employment in the live-entertainment industry, but should not be taken as legal guidance in any way.

FLSA Minimum Wage Requirements

The Fair Labor Standards Act (FLSA, https://www.dol.gov/whd/flsa/) governs minimum-wage requirements in the United States. Similar laws exist in most states; in the case of conflict between state law and FLSA, the employer must follow the requirements that provide the greater protection for the employee.

In short, FLSA states that no one can be paid a wage that amounts to an hourly rate less than the minimum wage established by law (federal or state, whichever is higher). This applies to anyone receiving payment for work done, regardless of whether he or she is paid "hourly" or "on salary." For employees who "punch a clock" or keep an hourly timesheet and are paid by the hour, determining whether they are being paid at least the minimum wage is simple. For those employees who are paid on a salary basis, their hourly rate is determined by dividing their weekly pay by the number of hours worked per week; this rate must be no lower than the minimum wage. (Overtime considerations make this calculation somewhat more complex. More on overtime below.)

FLSA includes exemptions to minimum wage that may be applicable in some situations, particularly in summer-stock and smaller regional theatres with shorter seasons, and on short-run productions not affiliated with an established producing venue.

YOUNG WORKERS

According to FLSA (https://www.dol.gov/whd/childlabor.htm), workers under twenty years of age may be paid a minimum wage of $4.25 per hour (as of this writing) during the first ninety consecutive calendar days of their employment as long as their work does not displace other workers. After ninety days, or if they reach age twenty, they must be paid the minimum wage of all workers.

The minimum wage exemption for young workers only applies when no other workers are "displaced." In other words, if a company would normally hire someone who doesn't qualify for the exemption for a position, they cannot hire someone who does qualify simply to save money on wages.

SEASONAL EMPLOYMENT

FLSA provides an exemption to the minimum wage requirements for an employee of "an amusement or recreational establishment." According to the FLSA, an "amusement or recreational establishment" is one that does not operate for more than seven months in a calendar year or whose average receipts for any six months of the previous calendar year were not more than one-third of its average receipts for the other six months of that year (https://www.dol.gov/whd/regs/compliance/whdfs18.htm). What this means, in practice, is that a seasonal organization must pass one of two tests to determine if employees might be exempt from minimum-wage requirements under FLSA: the seven-months test, or the one-third test.

The seven-months test specifically relies on the phrase "does not operate." For theatres and other producing entities that present shows (i.e., "operate") fewer than seven months a year (even if employees are engaged in "off-season" work during the rest of the year), this exemption *may* be applicable.

The one-third test requires that an organization compare the average of the highest six months of receipts against the average of the lowest six months. If the lower average is less than a third of the higher average, this exemption *may* be applicable.

Overtime

In addition to determining the federal minimum wage, the FLSA states that any employee working over forty hours in a work week must be paid a rate of not less than one and one-half times his regular rate of pay for all hours worked over forty (https://www.dol.gov/whd/overtime_pay.htm). It is important to note that FLSA does not limit the number of days in a week an employee can work, the number of hours in a day an employee can work, or the number of hours above forty an employee can be scheduled—only that he or she be paid the overtime rate for any hours worked beyond forty in a work week. (Some state laws do limit some of these things.)

A common misconception about overtime is that salaried employees are exempt from overtime pay. This is not correct;

except for employees who meet specific exemption criteria (the most common to theatre are detailed below), all employees—regardless of whether they are paid on an hourly or weekly basis (or otherwise)—are subject to overtime protection. This means that all employees who are not exempt should have their work hours tracked, and should be paid the appropriate overtime rate should their work exceed forty hours in each week.

Consider, for example, Suzie Carpenter, who works in the scene shop. She gets paid a salary of four hundred dollars per week. During a normal workweek, she works forty hours, and gets paid four hundred dollars. During a load-in week, however, her work schedule flexes up to sixty-five hours. For that pay period, she would receive $775 in pay: her base pay of four hundred dollars plus $375 in overtime pay. Suzie's overtime was calculated by taking her base salary, four hundred dollars, and dividing it by forty hours, to determine her base hourly rate of ten dollars per hour. Her overtime rate was calculated as 1.5 times her base rate, or fifteen dollars per hour; her overtime pay was calculated by multiplying her overtime rate by the number of hours she worked beyond forty, or twenty-five. Twenty-five hours of work at a rate of fifteen dollars per hour comes out to $375, which gets added to her base salary of four hundred dollars, for a total of $775 for that week.

FLSA provides exemptions from overtime and minimum-wage requirements for employees who perform certain specific kinds of work: so-called executive, administrative, learned-professional, and creative-professional employees. For an employee to be considered exempt from minimum-wage requirements, he must pass three tests: the salary-level test, the salary-basis test, and the duties test.

To pass the salary-level test, an employee must earn more than a minimum salary level per week mandated by law, set at $455 per week. To be considered exempt from minimum-wage requirements, an employee must be compensated the equivalent of at least $455 per week; employees may be paid weekly, biweekly, semimonthly, or monthly, provided that the total wages are at least the equivalent of $455 per week.

The Department of Labor's "Final Rule." In 2016, the Department of Labor issued a new rule focused on updating salary and compensation levels needed for employees to be considered exempt from minimum-wage and overtime requirements. Among other things, the rule increased the salary threshold for exemption from $455 to $913 per week, and established a mechanism to automatically increase this threshold every three years. The rule was set to go into effect on December 1, 2016. On November 22, 2016, the US District Court granted an injunction against implementation of the new rule. On December 1, 2016, the Department of Justice on behalf of the Department of Labor filed an appeal against this injunction. On August 31, 2017, a US District Court ruling held that the new salary thresholds exceeded the Department of Labor's authority to set; on October 30, 2017, the Department of Labor appealed this decision; and on November 7, 2017, the US Court of Appeals for the Fifth Circuit granted the US government's motion to hold the appeal in abeyance while the Department of Labor undertook additional rulemaking actions.

What all this means is that currently the "Final Rule" is not in effect, leaving the salary threshold for exemption at $455 per week. However, this may change, depending on the outcome of the Department of Labor appeal, and discussions about the threshold level won't go away any time soon.

To pass the salary-basis test, an employee must be paid on a salary basis. The employee must receive a predetermined amount of compensation each pay period, and that compensation cannot be reduced because of variations in the quality or quantity of work performed. (This test does not preclude an employer from tracking an employee's hours, or maintaining a regular work schedule for employees.)

The requirements to pass the job-duties test are different for each classification of employee. Depending on the specific work to be performed, there may be employees of a theatrical project that satisfy the requirements for any of the four classifications of exempt employees.

For an employee's duties to be classified as "executive":

- The primary duty of the employee is the management of the whole organization, or a customarily recognized department or subdivision. (This would include positions such as technical director, production manager, costume shop manager, or properties master).
- The employee must regularly direct the work of two or more full-time employees.
- The employee must have the responsibility for hiring or firing other employees, or their recommendations about hiring, firing, and advancement of employees must be given particular weight.

For an employee's duties to be classified as "administrative":

- The primary duty of the employee must be the performance of office or nonmanual work directly related to the management or business operations of the employer or their customers. (This might include buyers in a shop; an employee responsible for accounting; an employee who handles costume or prop rentals full-time.)
- The primary duty of the employee must include the exercise of discretion or judgment.

For an employee's duties to be classified as "learned professional":

- The primary duty of the employee must be the performance of work requiring advanced knowledge in a field of science or learning. (This would include positions such as on-staff engineer or similar position. An argument can possibly be made that any position *requiring* an MFA or equivalent degree may qualify for this exemption.)
- Advanced knowledge must typically be acquired by a prolonged course of specialized intellectual instruction.

For an employee's duties to be classified as "creative":

- The primary duty of the employee must be the performance of work requiring invention, imagination, originality, or talent in a recognized field of artistic or creative endeavor. (It is tempting to try to apply this exemption to anyone working in theatre. However, the exemption is written such that work that depends on diligence and accuracy—most carpentry, lighting, and stitching work—is not exempt. However, a scenic charge, a props artisan, and a draper might fall under this exemption.)

The federal Department of Labor website (www.dol.gov) has extensive documentation to assist in determining whether a position can be considered exempt from minimum-wage requirements. The federal Department of Labor, the Department of Labor in the state where one is hiring, and an attorney who specializes in labor law all should be consulted before making any determinations about the exempt status of a specific position. The exemption status of a position should be clearly presented to potential applicants during the interview process, as well as part of any hiring offer.

NONPROFIT THEATRES AND FLSA

Another general misconception about employment law (specifically about minimum-wage and overtime requirements) is that nonprofit arts and theatre organizations are not covered by the law. According to the FLSA, only organizations doing more than five hundred thousand dollars per year in sales or business are covered by the FLSA; nonprofit organizations are not covered unless they engage in commercial activities—such as selling tickets to a performance.

What this means in practice is that any theatre—nonprofit or commercial—that sells tickets with a total from ticket sales (or a combination of ticket sales and gift-shop sales, for example) more than five hundred thousand dollars is covered by the FLSA. Therefore, its employees are subject to all the minimum-wage and overtime requirements of any other business.

Union Contracts

Many theatres and producing organizations operate under collectively bargained employment contracts for various categories of employees. These might include agreements for actors and stage managers (covered by agreements with Actor's Equity Association, or AEA), designers (United Scenic Artists, or USA), stagehands and technicians (International Alliance of Theatrical Stage Employees, or IATSE), directors and choreographers (Stage Directors and Choreographers Society, or SDC), musicians (Theatre Musicians Association of the American Federation of Musicians, or AFM-TMA).

Agreements between these collective bargaining unions and producing organizations vary. For example, AEA alone includes dozens of contracts for different kinds of theatres. Three of the most common agreements, the LORT, CAT, and Production agreements, provide employment rules and policies for many regional and resident theatres, theatres in and around Chicago, and Broadway productions (respectively). These rules cover everything from wages to auditions to photo calls, from safe and sanitary workplaces to the steepness of raked stages to the length and frequency of breaks during rehearsal.

Because each agreement and each venue and organization is different, there isn't enough space in this book to examine each and every one. However, a production manager must be aware of what agreements govern their venue or organization. Further, they must familiarize themselves with the rules and policies set forth in each agreement when hiring new employees covered by it.

Internships and Apprenticeships

Because the idea of an internship or an apprenticeship is a ubiquitous one in theatre, internships and apprenticeships deserve some special attention. Internship and apprenticeship programs have very specific definitions that govern how they interact with the regulations contained in FLSA (https://www.dol.gov/whd/regs/compliance/whdfs71.htm). To qualify as an internship or an apprenticeship program, and to take advantage of the ways these programs alter the regulations of FLSA, programs need to follow these definitions. Otherwise—even if called internship or apprenticeship programs—for the purposes of FLSA, they are not; therefore, those participating are considered employees, entitled to all the protections described in FLSA.

To be considered an internship in an organization, the federal Department of Labor provides a six-point litmus test, all six points of which must be satisfied to consider the internship exempt from FLSA requirements:

1. The internship, even though it includes actual operation of the facilities of the employer, is similar to training that would be given in an educational environment.
2. The internship experience is for the benefit of the intern.
3. The intern does not displace regular employees, but works under close supervision of existing staff.
4. The employer that provides the training derives no immediate advantage from the activities of the intern, and on occasion its operations may actually be impeded.
5. The intern is not necessarily entitled to a job at the conclusion of the internship.
6. The employer and the intern understand that the intern is not entitled to wages for the time spent in the internship.

By these rules, an "internship" in which an "intern" works as a carpenter, stitcher, electrician, or in some other position on a production that relies on that person's contribution to complete the project, is technically not an internship. Consequently, the "intern" must be paid a minimum wage and is entitled to overtime wages. A good rule of thumb when considering whether an organization "derives immediate advantage" is to ask: Does having the intern do the work take longer or put the production at greater risk? If so, he or she can probably be safely called an intern.

Of course, there's nothing stopping anyone from volunteering his services to a nonprofit. However, many factors must be considered to determine if a person's activities qualify as "volunteerism" (https://www.dol.gov/whd/regs/compliance/whdfs14a.htm):

- If the organization receiving the services is a nonprofit
- If there is any compensation provided (including room and board or stipends)
- If there are any expectations of benefits in the future
- If the activity is less than a full-time position
- If regular employees are displaced
- If the services are offered freely (i.e., without pressure or coercion)
- If the services are a type usually associated with volunteer work

By these considerations, if a "volunteer" works a regular workweek, and the work she does is required to complete the work of the project (i.e., an organization could reasonably expect a hired carpenter or hired scenic painter to do the same work for pay), the work is not truly volunteerism.

Consequently, the volunteer should be hired as an employee, and be entitled to a minimum wage and overtime pay.

Some theatres, producing organizations, or commercial production shops with internships that do meet the requirements laid out by the Department of Labor opt to provide some form of stipend. A stipend is a small fee or compensation to cover an intern's (or volunteer's) expenses while doing the work of the internship (or while completing his or her volunteerism). This can be a risky proposition, as it may send a mixed signal to the Department of Labor about whether the work provides wages. Strictly speaking, a stipend cannot exceed 20 percent of what a worker would normally be paid to perform those services, and cannot be tied to productivity or hours worked (FLSA Opinion Letter 2005-51, https://www.dol.gov/whd/opinion/FLSA/2005/2005_11_10_51_FLSA.pdf). In other words, a stipend is really intended to cover out-of-pocket expenses. This includes the value of any room and board provided by the organization.

Apprentices are a worker classification that may be exempt from minimum-wage and overtime regulations. According to the Department of Labor (https://www.doleta.gov/oa/history.cfm#amendments): "An apprentice is a worker, at least sixteen years of age . . . who is employed to learn a skilled trade through a registered apprenticeship program. Training is provided through structured on-the-job training combined with supplemental related theoretical and technical instruction."

To qualify as an apprenticeship, a program must be validated and registered through the Department of Labor. Many theatres and related organizations employ "apprentices," though these are not part of registered programs, and are consequently employees entitled to minimum wage and overtime pay as indicated by FLSA.

Summing Up

Job Descriptions

Hiring the right people requires knowing what skills you need. Create clear job descriptions listing the full breadth of skills required for a position, and be specific about the depth of experience in each skill. Balance skill sets across an organization and a project, and plan for the future by diversifying some less-common skills throughout the members of the team.

Interviews

Portfolios

Portfolios can provide key insights into the breadth and depth of a candidate's experience, as well as into fundamental "soft skills," such as the ability to learn new skills, attention to detail, and self-reflection. Use the interview and portfolio-review process as an opportunity to explore these aspects of a candidate that aren't as easily displayed in a resume or revealed in a traditional interview.

Legal Dos and Don'ts

Remember that asking questions that suggest the possibility of making hiring decisions based on anything other than the ability to do the job should be avoided.

Evaluating Candidates

Finding the perfect candidate is rare. When evaluating candidates, balance breadth and depth of experience against the needs of the organization and project, but also against a candidate's ability to learn and explore new skills. Sometimes a candidate with less depth of experience in some skills but a greater breadth across skills is more desirable, especially if she demonstrates the potential to develop greater depth through practice.

Hiring Offers and Employment Law

Know what the law says about employment practices, particularly as related to minimum wage and overtime, and consult with those experienced with labor law when making offers and generating contracts. The Fair Labor Standards Act is the federal law that mandates the minimum wage and who must be paid at least that minimum, as well as how overtime wages are calculated and who is exempt from being paid overtime. Broad categories of exemption that may be applicable in live entertainment include:

- Young workers
- Seasonal employees
- Executive, administrative, professional, and creative employees (paid over a specified weekly amount and on a salary basis)
- Employees in organizations that do less than five hundred thousand dollars in annual sales

Union Contracts

Some organizations operate under collective bargaining agreements (union contracts). Be aware of any applicable agreements, and what those agreements require when hiring new team members.

Internships and Apprenticeships

Though many theatres operate internship and apprenticeship programs, these terms have specific guidelines related to minimum-wage and overtime practices. In essence, to qualify as an "internship" (and therefore be exempt from minimum wage and overtime requirements), the work completed must be for the purpose of education or training, must not provide any advantages to the employer, and must not provide wages for the intern. To qualify as an "apprenticeship," an organization must be validated through the federal Department of Labor.

4. Leading the Team

You've gathered your team. You've established the scope of the project, defined the resources available, and created a team charter. Now what?

Now you lead your team.

This chapter will examine the differences between managing a team and leading a team, and why both are important in live entertainment. Most of this book will cover management skills and practices in detail; this chapter will focus primarily on leadership: what it means and how to practice it.

Topics covered in this chapter:

- Managing and leading
    - Setting clear expectations
        - Authority, responsibility, and accountability
    - Job evaluations: mentoring and coaching
        - Letting people go
    - Personal time management
    - Conflict management
        - Project- or organization-related conflicts
- Strategic thinking
- Organizational communication
    - Direct reports
    - Decorum
        - Meetings
        - Emails
        - Phone calls and text messages

Managing and Leading

It's been said that there is a difference between managing and leading. But what is the difference? The internet offers any number of memes or tropes. "Leaders inspire, managers require." "You manage things, you lead people." "Management is doing things right, leadership is doing right things." "Managers push where leaders pull." Like any good meme, these statements all contain some small kernel of recognizable truth; they resonate with our own previous experiences. Can we more clearly define the difference between management and leadership, however? Can we definitively say one is better than the other? Can we find ways to be better at one than the other?

Management, it can be argued, comprises skills that focus on *administration* of a task or project. Think resources: time and money, spaces and vehicles, tools and equipment. Vendors must be paid. Trucks must be available for load-in. Actors cannot rehearse on stage while the electricians are hanging a light plot. "Managing a project" means wrestling with resource allocation—everything from initial budgeting and planning, to tracking progress, staffing, and problem solving along the way. Often, this means adhering to structures and methods, to plans, processes, and procedures.

Leadership is different. Leadership focuses on people—specifically people *as people*, not as labor resources in a project calendar. Leaders do inspire, as suggested above: good leaders gain the trust of those they lead, and use that trust to elicit action and commitment. Great leaders encourage initiative; they inspire outside-the-box thinking; they promote risk-taking and challenging the status quo.

The drives of management and leadership, obviously, can often be at odds with each other.

There are many who would suggest that being a leader is far more important than being a manager. You can inspire good work better than you can demand it, for example, and if the project gets done, that's all that matters in the end—regardless of how messy the journey to get there was. There are many theatres that operate under this mode of thinking. To be sure, there are theatre artists who respond to the idea of "managing the process"—time tables, schedules, budget plans, and the like—as being antithetical to the artistic process.

Conversely, there are those who adhere to the notion that any good project must be managed: that charts and schedules and deadlines are the only way in which a project can be completed within the cost and time allocated, to the degree of scope and quality required. There are theatre projects that operate this way as well, focusing heavily on the mechanical steps of achieving the product.

It may seem obvious to some, but both approaches outlined above—valuing vision and leadership at the expense of management processes, or valuing a mechanical process at the expense of vision—have the potential to suffer from a lack of balance. The truth of the matter is that every project needs leadership, trust, and inspiration—especially a theatrical project. Further, every project needs structure and management—especially a theatrical project. A production manager's job, then, is to provide both: to be the leader of a project management structure that inspires people while dealing with tangible (and sometimes intangible) resources.

Setting Clear Expectations

One of the key elements of leadership is trust. When members of a team trust the leader of that team, they are more likely to not only meet expectations, but to exceed them. And one of the most fundamental means of establishing trust is by setting clear expectations. Nothing damages trust between team members and a leader more than feeling that the bar keeps shifting. A team member needs to know what is expected of him or her in terms of responsibilities, time-on-task, and deliverables.

All too often, unfortunately, expectations are communicated on the fly on an "as-needed" basis. This is generally not helpful to the team member, and can have an effect that is the opposite of what is intended: instead of clarifying expectations, these kinds of "oh, yes, you need to do this, too" moments can appear to team members as having expectations change unexpectedly. Better, instead, to have expectations outlined clearly at the beginning of a project or when a team member joins the project.

One approach to consider for clearly communicating expectations: work orders. Work orders are formal, written forms that detail specific job requirements used in many industrial and contracting situations, including some larger theatrical scene shops. In environments that are averse to heavy "management" practices, these might be seen as a little too formal; weekly or daily "work lists" that detail job expectations and posted in the shop can be an effective and less formal approach.

Of course, expectations can change from time to time; different projects may require different goals. It is important to be clear about changes in expectations—how they are changing, the reasons for the changes, and how those changes will impact a team member's work. Additionally—especially with new hires, or when embarking on new projects—expectations tend to be in flux. This is because however clearly we communicate the expectations of a position or a project to a team member, the team member brings her own perspective to bear. This can usually be a good thing, and a good leader will harness what might otherwise be seen as errors in understanding as opportunities to bring new perspectives to the table. This is a fantastic way to earn the trust of team members; if they see a leader attempting to see a project or position through their perspective, it can build rapport.

Authority, Responsibility, and Accountability

When it comes to setting expectations with team members, establishing an understanding about each member's areas of accountability, responsibility, and authority is essential (figure 4.1). How a team leader balances them can make all the difference between inspiring a team and managing one.

Accountability refers to the willingness (and obligation) to answer for the specific actions, choices, and decisions one makes. A carpenter who chooses not to follow directions when building a scenic unit, for example, is accountable for that decision, and whatever ramifications may result. A stitcher who decides to use a hand-sewing technique that results in a higher quality product (though it may have taken more time) is also accountable for that decision, and whatever trade-off of time may be the result.

Accountability is, in many ways, highly correlated with one's value system. Being timely, taking care of your colleagues, and

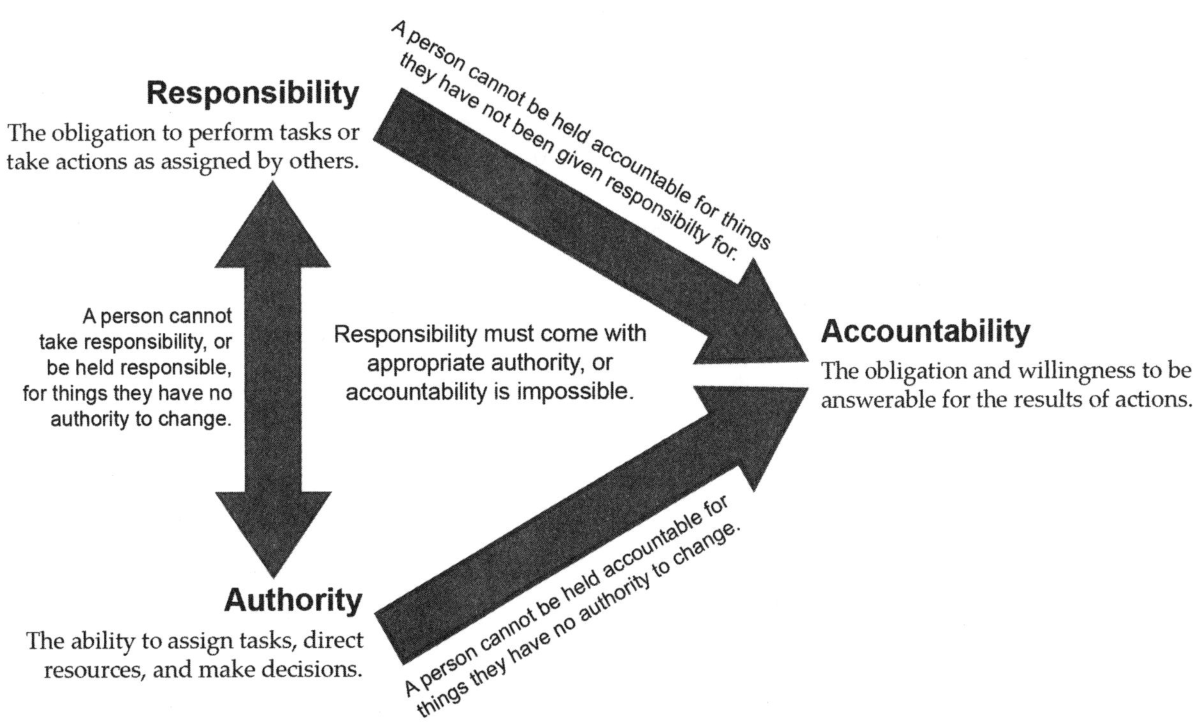

Figure 4.1. Accountability, responsibility, and authority triangle

taking pride in your work are all examples of values that represent ways in which one can be accountable for one's own work. A team leader may establish clear expectations and attempt to hold team members accountable for the actions they take that either lead to fulfilling or failing to fulfill those expectations. However, no amount of accountability *assigned* by someone else will have the same impact as a person's own *self-accountability.* An effective leader will take steps to encourage the development of self-accountability in team members to support a project's expectations.

> Many theatre artists have an intrinsic commitment to "the work": a desire to achieve the best "show" possible. This can be a strong motivator if tied clearly to expectations, encouraging team members to hold themselves accountable. This can also be a detriment to efficiency, if it leads to building a Corvette when the project calls for a Yugo.

Responsibility refers to the obligation to perform tasks or to take actions assigned by others. For example, a scenic designer may be responsible for designing the overall aesthetic of the physical environment on stage, the development of the drawings and renderings that communicate that environment to the rest of the team.

Assigning responsibility is more than saying "design the costumes," for example. It means defining the scope of the task, the expectations related to any deliverables (including quality, style, and material) and the timeliness by which it needs to be completed. For example, if a team leader assigns responsibility to Johnny Costumer for the costume design for a production, she should also include details about:

- What the play is
- Who the rest of the team is (and how the costumes fit with their work)
- The overall aesthetic desires (period, style, and color)
- The amount of money available to spend on costumes
- The size and makeup of the inventory of stock costumes
- The size and makeup of the personnel in the costume shop
- Whether a research presentation is expected (and, if so, what comprises such a presentation)
- What the deadlines are, and what deliverables are expected at each
- What the expectations are during the build related to hands-on work, shopping, fabric selection, fittings, and the like

This is not a comprehensive list, of course, but it demonstrates the point: one can't simply be "responsible for the costumes," rather, one is responsible for an explicit set of expectations that can be clearly outlined.

Authority refers to the ability to assign tasks, direct resources, and make decisions related to a project. For example, a technical director may be provided a set budget for a production and be given the authority to spend those funds as she deems appropriate to achieve the design provided by the set designer. A more nuanced example: a set designer may indicate on a drawing about a sash window in a flat that it must open and stay in place, but that she is leaving it to the technical director to determine how to construct the window so that is possible. In this example, the set designer has *granted authority* to the technical director for engineering the functional aspects of the window.

In highly collaborative projects—such as live-entertainment productions—the boundaries between areas of authority can get quickly blurred. An effective team leader will be attentive to when this may be happening, and will clarify whenever necessary who is responsible for what. In many stage productions, properties can be an area where this happens often. For example, stage practicals—chandeliers, wall sconces—cross many boundaries of authority and responsibility. In most situations, the set designer has authority over what the practical looks like; the properties master has authority over how it is procured; the master electrician is responsible for how it is electrified; the lighting designer for how it is lamped and how it is cued; and the technical director has responsibility for how it is mounted in the space. Clearly outlining these expectations of authority is key to ameliorating confusion—and, quite possibly, frustration—down the line.

The relationship between authority, accountability, and responsibility can often result in tension for team members. Someone might find herself responsible for something on a production, but not feel she has the authority to act to complete the task. (Consider a properties master who's being asked by the set designer to buy three hundred more books to pile in the ramshackle study on stage, but who has been told by the production manager not to spend any more money.) Or, someone might find himself held accountable for something over which he has no responsibility. (Consider the master electrician who is asked by a stage manager to clean up the mess on stage that was left by the carpentry crew that just left for lunch.) Or—something not uncommon in the performing arts—someone may find herself responsible for creating something over which she has no authority. (Consider the technical director tasked with building a kitchen cabinet that is not architecturally accurate, but who wants everything she builds to be made *right.*)

A good leader will recognize these tensions and make efforts to alleviate them. This can be as simple as a conversation. "I know it's not how that cabinet should be built, but remember, that's not your job. Everyone knows that it was Rob's design choice, and I need you to support his choice." Other times, this may require a meeting or a discussion, to ensure that all parties involved are clear about the distribution of responsibility, accountability, and authority. "I know you want Rachel to buy more books, but I've told her she can't spend any more money. If she can find books for free, that's fine." Or, "Allan, Brad had to clean up the mess your shop left onstage today. Let's talk about how to make sure that doesn't happen again."

In an ideal world, a team leader or project manager could distribute accountability, responsibility, and authority among team members such that there would never be these kinds of conflicts. Because we don't live in an ideal world, a project manager must both be clear about differentiating for each team member the bounds of his or her accountability, responsibility, and authority, and be diligent about encouraging, supporting, and arranging opportunities for clear communication among team members about the fuzzy boundaries involved in every project.

Job Evaluations: Mentoring and Coaching

The above discussion about accountability, responsibility, and authority leads nicely into a discussion about evaluating team members' performance. Although sometimes intimidating—particularly for inexperienced leaders—the job evaluation process doesn't have to be painful, and is an important part of leading a team. Team members need to know how they are doing, if they are meeting expectations (or not), if they are fulfilling their responsibilities, taking enough accountability for their actions, and making effective choices within the authority they have been given. Leaders provide this feedback in two ways: just-in-time coaching and mentoring through regular performance evaluations.

Coaching through just-in-time feedback should be *frequent, actionable, specific,* and *timely*—FAST. When feedback is frequent, team member and leader are engaged in an ongoing conversation about job performance, engendering trust from both parties. By providing feedback that is actionable, a leader makes clear to team members exactly how they can perform better and how improvement can be measured. Leaders who provide specific feedback make clear to team members exactly what behaviors, decisions, or actions need improvement. And, by providing feedback when the behaviors, decisions, or actions that need to be corrected happen, leaders give team members an opportunity to avoid making similar mistakes in the future. Letting someone know that how they prepared a cost estimate was incorrect after three months without much contact is not helpful. Telling an employee immediately after he has submitted a cost estimate that it would be better to include contingency estimates as an individual line item for clarity is much better.

Mentoring through regular performance reviews provides an opportunity for leaders to build rapport and develop trust with team members by developing an understanding of their journey as professionals. A good leader will find out if Suzie Carpenter's career goal is to become the best carpenter she can, or to move into rigging, become a technical director, or if the whole "carpentry thing" is simply to pay the bills while she auditions for roles. Further, a good leader will use this knowledge to support and encourage team members along their journey. During an evaluation of Suzie Carpenter, for example, one might discover that her goal is to become a true "master carpenter." Subsequent evaluations should include feedback—positive and negative, as necessary—specific to Suzie's growth along that journey. In this way, a good leader nurtures the growth of her team members.

Leading a team, however, means more than providing feedback about what team members did well and what they didn't. One powerful way a leader gains the trust of her team is by soliciting feedback *from*

> Building trust through feedback of team members is really a two-part process. The first step is actively seeking their comments, concerns, and suggestions. The second part is engaging in a process that validates those comments, concerns, and suggestions, and that finds ways to incorporate or address them whenever possible. Failure to follow through on the second step will lead to a significant decrease in trust—the opposite of the desired effect.

Although regular performance evaluations are an important part of developing trust and leading a team, they are also part of *managing* a team. Performance evaluations should be documented with dates and details related to where an employee needs improvement and the steps that both the employee and the organization will take to make those improvements. This written documentation is essential if stronger steps need to be taken by either the employee or the organization in the future.

them: asking what is working and what isn't, what helps and what hinders, from their point of view. A regular performance evaluation is an opportunity to solicit this information.

How often should "regular" performance reviews happen? Typically, management resources suggest after the first ninety days or so, and then annually. Of course, that only works when team members are involved with an organization for longer periods of time; many live-entertainment organizations and projects don't operate on time frames long enough for annual performance reviews to be effective. Therefore, a leader must determine an appropriate time frame for performance reviews within the constraints of the organization or project. A good rule of thumb for this is to have reviews often enough to allow for timely intervention regarding a team member's areas of improvement, but not so often that there's no opportunity to see changes in that team member's behavior and work.

For example, a typical summer-stock theatre may hire people for a twelve- to fourteen-week contract. It's been said that one day of summer theatre is like a week of "real time," given the pace of work; one might consider, then, that an initial performance review might happen after about two weeks of employment, with subsequent reviews at about six weeks and twelve or fourteen weeks. For team members brought in to work on a single project for, say, five weeks, an initial review might happen after only a few days, then at about two weeks, and then a final review at the end of the project.

Additionally, a leader should work to encourage a culture of periodic informal review and mentoring of team members. Team members with authority over the work of others should be coached to provide suggestions, encouragement, and correction to those they supervise; similarly, they should be encouraged to solicit and receive feedback from those they supervise as well. When implemented with thoughtfulness, a culture of consistent and constant constructive feedback and growth can cause team members to forge bonds of great trust among one another.

Remember: it is trust that a leader leverages to elicit action. The stronger the bonds of trust among members of the team, and between the team and its leaders, the more that team can accomplish. In some situations, taking time to "break bread" together can increase levels of trust among team members. From bringing in donuts for the shop to a once-a-month team lunch outings, food and conversation can do a lot to bring a team together.

Letting People Go

One challenge for any leader is recognizing when no amount of coaching, mentoring, encouraging, training, reward, or punishment will improve a team member's work. When all efforts seem to have failed to generate an improvement in a team member, it is important to ask the following key questions:

- *Is he holding himself accountable for actions related to his lack of success?* As discussed above, it is difficult to hold someone accountable for actions if he doesn't hold himself accountable. Sometimes, the solution is as simple as making it clear that particular values are important for an organization or project; for example, it can be important to inform a stitcher that the hand sewing he is doing will be visible and a key element in the overall aesthetic on stage, and consequently he will need to value patience, precision, and care.
- *Is she responsible for the duties she is being measured against?* It can sometimes be easy—particularly in the complexity of overlapping responsibilities that is live entertainment—to incorrectly ask someone to improve on something for which she is not directly responsible, or that she did not think was her responsibility. For example, the master electrician may not have been responsible for hanging a specific set of practicals on a set, or may not have realized that she was responsible for doing so because that responsibility was never clearly expressed.
- *Does he have the authority to do better?* It is possible that a team member may not have the authority to improve upon those things he has been encouraged to improve upon during performance reviews. For example, a welder in the scene shop may need to replace the tank of welding gas to improve his welds, but the scene shop manager won't approve the purchase. No amount of encouraging the welder to complete prettier welds will solve the problem until someone with the authority to purchase more gas does so.
- *Does she have the skills required to do better?* As opposed to not having the will to improve, some team members simply don't have the skill to do so. Suzie Carpenter, for example, may be an incredibly inept stitcher; doing better at sewing soft scenery items may not be as simple as "trying harder." She simply doesn't have the requisite skills to complete the work; finding a way to train Suzie in the stitching skills expected of her is necessary.
- *Can she learn the skills required to do better? And, does she want to?* If Suzie Carpenter doesn't have the stitching skills required to improve her soft-scenery construction, can she learn them? This isn't the same as asking, "Will she learn them?" This is asking quite directly, "Is Suzie capable of learning specific new skills?" Some people don't naturally possess the manual dexterity for hand sewing, for example, without an incredible amount of practice. Additionally, Suzie Carpenter may not see the utility in learning a new skill.

When all is said and done, any of the above questions might pose an insurmountable challenge to a team member improving in the ways that would be most desired. For example, convincing a team member to take accountability for things he doesn't value can sometimes be impossible. In some circles, this is known as a "will" problem: this team member just may not care about improving the actions or choices at issue. For example, it may be necessary for the electricians on a call to tie cable runs neatly along a batten; an electrician may not see the utility in wasting his time on this detail-oriented task, no matter how it has been explained to him. If a team member disagrees about the value of specific actions, and cannot be convinced, this represents an impasse.

If such an impasse is reached, it is worth asking, "Is this team member responsible for the right duties?" In other words, is he the right person for the job? It can be challenging for a leader to reach the conclusion that a person isn't the right team member for certain responsibilities, but doing so is an important part of a *leader's* responsibilities. Keeping the wrong person in the wrong position can result in poor work results and, perhaps more problematically, a corrosion of trust among other members of the team. A leader needs to recognize when someone isn't in the right position, and take steps to quickly rectify the situation.

On an agile and flexible project, a team leader can and should identify where a person's skills and temperament best fit a project and move him to where he would be most appropriate. When a team member needs to be let go completely, however, it should be handled in a timely manner, and with care and respect. Being not right for a project doesn't mean a person should be treated badly, spoken harshly to, or otherwise mistreated—regardless of how high tensions may have gotten while discovering a team member wasn't suited to the responsibilities he was assigned.

Of course, firing an employee can be a complex issue, particularly when contracts and collective bargaining agreements come into play. Additionally, some states have laws requiring that certain standards be met in the process of relieving a person of his job. It is imperative, when it starts to become likely that a person will need to be let go, to research that employee's contract, any governing union rules, and applicable laws. How does his contract read? Are there stipulations governing termination? What conditions do any collective bargaining agreements stipulate? What state laws govern termination? However, in most cases, if an employee has been given multiple opportunities to improve—and these opportunities have been documented—and he has not done so, there is enough legal standing to relieve an employee of his duties.

Doing so will generally mean one final performance evaluation. During this meeting, the employee should be presented with a clear, verifiable, and documented rationale for his termination. Remember that this conversation isn't a debate or an opportunity to be proven incorrect about the decision—though many employees will want to take an opportunity to assert how they might do better or might change if given a chance. Further, an employee may say that being terminated will impact his finances, his family, his life. This is an attempt to argue for remaining in his position using emotion. If a leader has done due diligence in mentoring, coaching, and providing opportunities for improvement, there should be no reason to reconsider the decision to terminate an employee. Be sensitive to the employee's frustration, sadness, fear, or even anger at being terminated, but do not allow that to change the decision to terminate the employee.

Sometimes, these conversations are handled best with an additional person in the room, who can provide a buffer between the team leader and the employee being terminated. An additional person may also be able to point out that additional discussion is no longer warranted, and call an end to the conversation. A third party can also provide helpful feedback to the team leader about how he or she handled the situation. This can be an important aspect of maintaining trust among members of the team, as the termination of a team member—even when justified—is sure to have an impact on the rest of the team.

Personal Time Management

Leading a team can mean being pulled in many different directions; even more so when leading many different teams on multiple projects whose schedules overlap. Consider the production manager at an average regional theatre, for example. She may be observing strike for one production while organizing a schedule for the load in of the next. Later during that same day, she may be attending a preliminary design presentation for a third production. In the next few days, she may also attend a budget meeting for a fourth production, and a production meeting and first rehearsal for a fifth. (And, of course, she will probably be sending emails introducing designers and directors to each other for a sixth.)

The seemingly constant stream of emails, phone calls, text messages, and meetings can be overwhelming. Add to that the pressure to produce financial statements, contracts, strategic planning documents, job advertisements, and any number of other management-oriented tasks, and a project leader can find it next to impossible to find time to lead in between the managing he or she must do. A good leader finds a way to balance the competing pressures for

> Why "good life balance"? What about "work/life balance"? Using the latter phrase implies that life and work are somehow separate but equal. In reality, work is a part of life, not separate from it: life is a balance of work, of family and friends, and of mental, physical and emotional health. In any seven-day period, an average adult needs to sleep for approximately fifty-six hours. An additional forty hours of that week are typically given over to work. This means that a total of ninety-six out of 168 hours in a seven-day week is given over to sleep and work—almost 60 percent of the whole week. Add to that about three to four hours per day for eating, showering, getting dressed, and other personal hygiene needs (going to the bathroom alone takes up an average of almost two hours per week!), and that leaves only about forty-four hours per week for everything else—housecleaning, unwinding, exercise, reading, playing games with the family, grocery shopping, what have you. That's only about 25 percent of the whole week. Finding a good life balance is more than organizing the time spent on "life stuff"; rather, it is about finding a way both to minimize the time and attention work takes when not at work, and to use the personal-time opportunities that a workplace provides. This means making sure that lunch hours are nonworking periods; that personal days, sick days, and vacations days are used when they are available.

her time. Additionally, a good leader finds a way to balance these pressures in a way that models *good life balance*: that demonstrates to the team that as important as the project and the organization are, every individual is important as well.

One effective approach to time management is to consider the concepts of *urgency* and *importance*. Urgency means, "Requiring swift or immediate action." Importance refers to "the state or fact of being of great significance or value." Every task, every email, every phone call, project, text message, rehearsal, or whatever else that comes across a project manager's desk can be considered on the two spectra of importance or urgency. Taken together, these two axes can help prioritize actions.

Visualize an x-y coordinate-system graph, where the x-axis corresponds to importance, and the y-axis to urgency, as shown later. Each task or issue that arises during a day can be assigned a position in that coordinate system corresponding to its importance and its urgency. First thing on a given Monday, for example, a manager might be faced with

- Organizing an agenda for a 9:00 A.M. production meeting
- A phone message from the costume shop manager angry about something that appeared in a rehearsal report the previous night
- A stack of contracts to edit, print, sign, and mail (before the mail pickup at 2:00 P.M.)
- A preliminary budget for next fiscal year to continue preparing for a staff/board meeting in two weeks
- A project budget for a grant proposal focused on replacing the sound system in the theatre, due to the development department on Tuesday
- An email from the set designer for the show that is in production, with a question about material choices
- An email from the lighting designer for the show that is going into tech, about changing the (already placed) gel order

A quick evaluation of each of these items, ranking each on a scale of –5 to +5 in terms of importance and urgency (where 5 is most important or urgent, and –5 is least), helps to organize tasks (figure 4.2).

They can even be plotted in an x-y graph (figure 4.3).

	Importance	Urgency
Prep production meeting agenda	–1	5
Respond to costume shop manager's message	3	0
Finish contracts	4	4
Prep next year's budget	5	–5
Finish sound system grant budget	2	2
Reply to set designer	2	3
Reply to lighting designer	0	5

Figure 4.2. To-do list with items ranked in terms of importance and urgency

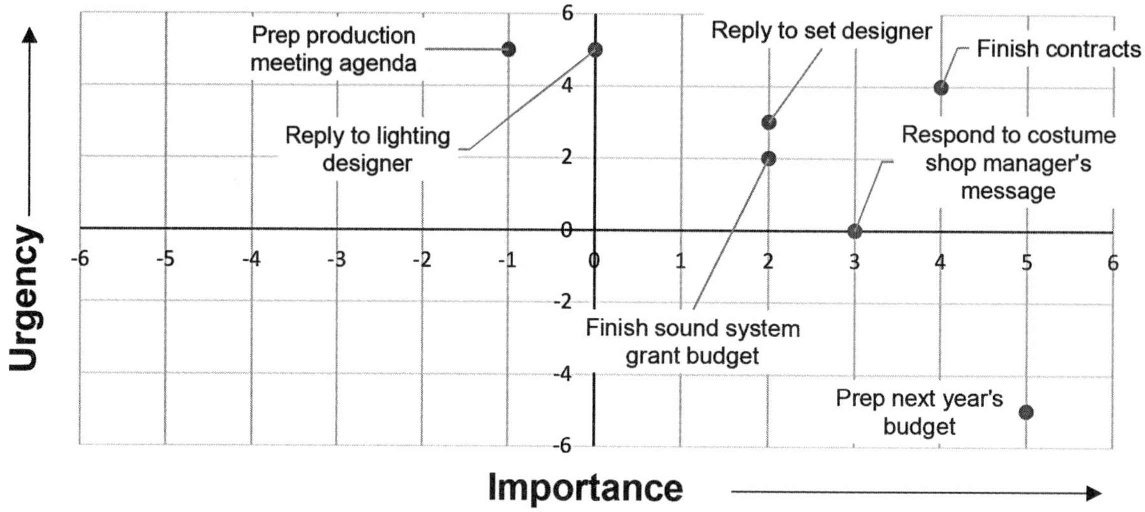

Figure 4.3. To-do list items plotted on a graph to visualize their urgency versus importance

This visualization can be used to help prioritize tasks and actions. For example, while it is somewhat urgent to put together an agenda for the production meeting happening shortly, relatively speaking it isn't considered very important. (This may be true for various reasons; for example, there may be no pressing issues to discuss at the production meeting, or the culture of the project may allow for a more relaxed approach to meeting organization.) Alternatively, because of the importance of securing designers for an upcoming project and the pressing deadline of getting contracts in the mail in the afternoon, finishing those contracts is clearly a high-priority task.

Analysis of importance and urgency can be especially helpful when considering whether and how to manage, limit, or otherwise control the flow of information coming across a project manager's desk. In spite of what conventional wisdom attempts to convince people, cognitive research has proven fairly definitively that the human brain becomes very inefficient when forced to multitask. Controlling distractions and information flow can be a successful method of ensuring focus and productivity. Many management and leadership guides suggest techniques such as turning off the ringer on one's phone or shutting off visible and audible email alerts, to reduce the possibility of phone calls or emails distracting from the work at hand.

Techniques like these, that reduce the information flow and the distraction that accompanies it, can be very effective at increasing productivity. However, live entertainment can be a fast-moving enterprise, and it is not unusual to need to be available for potentially urgent and important issues that arise unexpectedly—particularly during load-ins, technical rehearsals, and strikes and load-outs, which can be fraught with the unexpected. When expecting a phone call or an email to deal with an urgent and important issue, it may be necessary to stay "connected," as it were, even when moving on to other tasks. Weighing the need to stay connected at any given time on the scales of urgency and importance like any other task can help to make the decision to "unplug" and control some or all of the information flow on a project for a period of time.

The Apollo program featured the first computers on NASA spacecraft. During the Apollo 11 moon landing in July 1963, the computer in the lunar module signaled a 1202 program alarm. This alarm indicated that the computer was receiving more information than it could handle, and would stop doing what it was doing, reboot, and restart. In computer architecture and networking, this is called an "ACK OVERLOAD" error: the receiving computer acknowledges that data was sent, but signals that it didn't do anything with it because it received more information than it could handle. "ACK OVERLOAD" is a good metaphor for our highly connected lives.

Conflict Management

It would be an amazing world if everyone always got along. However, even with the best team members, inevitably there will be conflict, and it is the team leader's responsibility to make sure conflicts are resolved quickly and effectively. In any organization or on any project, there are going to be two types of conflicts that arise: conflicts that are about the work—the project or the organization—and conflicts that are about the people. How a leader manages each is slightly different; because many other texts discuss handling interpersonal conflicts far better than this text can, the focus here is on project- or organization-related conflicts.

Project- or Organization-Related Conflicts

Conflicts that arise primarily out of disagreements related to the work being done—functional or project-based work—can often be attributed to miscommunication. For example, consider a production meeting that devolves into a debate about whether the props master or the master electrician was supposed to manage making the tip of Prospero's walking staff glow magically. Although the argument may revolve around whether one or the other "did his job," in truth the question under discussion is, "Whose responsibility is it to make Prospero's walking staff glow?" This is a question of communication: if *who* is responsible had been communicated clearly earlier on, there would be no debate at the production meeting.

Similarly, miscommunication of scope, expectations, quality, areas of authority, and ongoing progress can all result in conflict. These conflicts can often lead to emotional outbursts and attacks. Even when someone has done something that seems blatantly inept or just plain foolish, it is unlikely in most cases that this is due to anything other than a misunderstanding of expectations. Focus, first, on the substance of the conflict and how to resolve it moving forward. What is the misunderstanding that led to the issue, and how can the issue be addressed? Determine who is the best person to make Prospero's staff glow (based on time, resources, and skills), and assign that responsibility to that person. Clearly communicating what was miscommunicated earlier should address any immediate hostility and frustration.

Once the specific issue is resolved (or there is a plan for resolution), address how the miscommunication occurred. Is this a systemic problem that needs to be addressed by reiterating organizational communication processes? Or is this an isolated incident due to either not sending or reading an email, making or taking a phone call, or some other means of communication? Was this a simple mistake or misunderstanding? Addressing the reasons for the initial miscommunication and developing a plan to ensure they won't happen again will go a long way toward alleviating any remaining frustrations.

Strategic Thinking

Leadership is about people, to be sure. But it is also about vision, about being able to see beyond the milieu of *what is* to *what can be*. Often this is referred to as strategic thinking, and while this phrase may be somewhat tired (ask anyone who has engaged in the process before how badly she wants to work on a "strategic plan" for an organization ever again), the description is accurate. Thinking strategically means to think in relation to long-term or overall aims and goals and about how to achieve them.

A good leader will balance strategic thinking against tactical thinking. (Tactical refers to actions that are carefully planned to gain a specific end.) A good example of this in live entertainment often comes up in a budget or costing meeting for a project. A given item—part of the set, a piece of lighting equipment, a costume, a tool of some kind—may be needed for the project, but is beyond its budget. Tactically, this means rethinking the scope of the project to either reallocate resources to shift the budget parameters or to change the design or expectations to make the item unnecessary. Strategic thinking, in this moment, means to consider whether this item might be used again in the future or to broaden the capabilities of the facilities for future projects, and consequently find alternate ways to fund the purchase. A project leader may even decide to strategically go over budget to acquire this item if it can be proven to be valuable enough for the future.

Strategic thinking—and nurturing a culture of strategic thinking—doesn't only contribute to the long-term growth and development of an organization. Demonstrating vision in this way, and encouraging team members to engage in forward-looking thinking and planning, can develop a sense of community and long-term contribution. Team members can become bound together through a specific shared vision beyond a single project, or even through the idea that there is a vision of the future to which they might contribute in large or small ways, regardless of what that vision might be. Strategic thinking is one of the primary ways leaders inspire people.

So what does strategic thinking entail? How do you do it? An important step in practicing strategic thinking is leaving room for it. Partly, this is following the techniques discussed above for managing time. More importantly, though, a good leader makes time for thinking strategically by not "sweating the small stuff": leaving the work of thinking about tactical issues and concerns to those to whom they've assigned responsibility for it. By trusting the members of one's team to fulfill the responsibilities they've been assigned, a leader can focus his attention on long-term, visionary, strategic thinking.

A leader isn't just a dreamer in an office, of course. As indicated earlier, every project manager must address any number of management-style tasks that take up their attention. However, by using good personal time-management techniques and trusting team members to do their own jobs, a good leader can carve out room in the workweek to think long-term.

Providing opportunities for team members to raise and discuss strategic issues is another important means of enculturating strategic thinking within a team. Regular team meetings of functional area managers (e.g., technical directors, costume shop managers) outside of project-specific production meetings are one way of doing this. Other ways might include annual retreats or postproject closing meetings (discussed in chapter 10).

Organizational Communication

Effective communication in any organization—functional or project-based, theatre or not—is important for productivity. After all, if people don't know what they need to know to get their jobs done, they can't do them very well. There is a good chance that if you're reading this you've been involved in a production when miscommunication or mixed messages or just plain lack of communication resulted in mistakes, problems, and extra work. No amount of diligence can eliminate the chance of mistakes and miscommunication, but better to eliminate as much as possible through good communication practices.

Direct Reports

An important concept in any organization is the idea of "direct reports." A direct report is an employee whose position is directly below that of someone else, and who is managed by that someone else. For example, in the case of a carpenter in a small summer-stock theatre scene shop, the staff might be comprised of a technical director, an assistant technical director (whose responsibilities in this theatre are similar to that of a scene-shop manager or shop foreman), and two carpenters. In this situation, the carpenters are direct reports of the assistant technical director, and the assistant technical director is a direct report of the technical director.

Why does this matter? Typically, while a manager may be responsible for the work of a group of people, it is possible that he is not responsible for giving direct instruction or direction to the individuals in that group. This distinction has a strong impact on the nature of communication within an organization. In most cases, the technical director will communicate direction and instruction to the assistant technical director, who will then disseminate instruction to the carpenters who are her direct reports.

The closer two positions are in an organization, the less risky it is to operate outside the typical chain of communication; for example, it might be less problematic for the technical director to communicate instruction directly to a carpenter than it would be for a production manager, director, or producer to do so. However, communication of instruction or direction that falls outside the "chain of command" can set the stage for confusion and miscommunication.

For example, consider a situation a few minutes before the start of a technical rehearsal in a venue, when the carpenters are in the space addressing last-minute issues on a moving piece of scenery. If these issues are not addressed, the scenery won't move and rehearsal will come to a screeching halt during the first scene shift. While working, the stage manager approaches a carpenter and says, "There's a couple of screw heads sticking up on the stage floor downstage, right where the actors do a lot of crawling and kneeling, and I need you to fix it before we start." The stage manager is not wrong in being concerned about this issue, nor in the fact that a carpenter should address it. However, approaching the carpenter this way poses a dilemma for the carpenter: continue working on the moving-scenery problem as directed by the technical director, or address the screw-head issue as directed by the stage manager. Doing either one and not the other will have a similar effect on the upcoming rehearsal, but the carpenter is neither in a position in which she is directly responsible for either effect on rehearsal, nor in possession of any authority to determine which effect is less desirable or how to proceed.

The carpenter in this situation has, essentially, two choices: tell the stage manager no, and risk looking like she doesn't value safety concerning screw heads as much as the stage manager; or drop what she is doing, and look like she doesn't value getting the moving scenery working. Better, instead, for the stage manager to approach the technical director and discuss the screw heads; the technical director is responsible for *both* issues, and has the authority to make decisions about how to proceed in terms of allocating labor to address both problems, or to call for a discussion of prioritizing the issues if resources cannot be reallocated to address both.

Other examples of miscommunication due to providing direction to those who are not one's direct reports might include a costume designer telling a stitcher to assemble a garment in a particular way that contradicts what a draper or first hand had intended; a director telling a painter that a paint color for one step in a multistep process is too blue; or a stage manager telling a properties master that a magazine rack on stage must look a particular way that in no way matches the aesthetic desires of the set designer. Most often, these kinds of out-of-chain communications are intended to be helpful or beneficial for all involved. It is rare that a team member would deliberately jeopardize a project by maliciously miscommunicating information. Benevolent intent, however, doesn't minimize the impact these kinds of communication might have.

One way to avoid these kinds of miscommunication is by ensuring that team members have a clear picture of the organizational reporting structure of both the organization and the project, as described in chapter 1. Additionally, develop processes and systems for regular communication of information—both planned and unexpected—and communicate these processes clearly to team members. (Some of these will be discussed in chapter 8.) Emphasize to team members the importance of communicating through proper channels and using proper systems and processes.

Decorum

Meetings

While a more detailed discussion of meetings and other communication processes comes later in chapter 8, a chapter on leading the team wouldn't be complete without some discussion of a leader's responsibility to model good etiquette and decorum in all modes of communication; in meetings, emails, phone calls, and text messages, a leader's manner of communication sets an example that team members will follow.

Many live-entertainment organizations function on a fairly casual basis; you don't see a lot of business suits in regional theatres. However, a level of professionalism is expected. Consider group meetings, for example; "official" or "formal" group meetings may take the form of staff meetings, design meetings, production meetings, costing/budget meetings, and other types of meetings. Some good rules of thumb for meetings like these follow.

INVITE ONLY THOSE NEEDED

Meetings with large groups of attendees can be unwieldy and difficult to manage. Invite only those team members who have responsibility for aspects of the organization or project under discussion. For example, a production meeting doesn't typically include the actors or the stitchers; they shouldn't attend unless a meeting deals with a topic directly related to their responsibilities.

HAVE AN AGENDA AND STICK TO IT

This doesn't have to mean "Roberts Rules of Order," where people are recognized to speak by the chair of the meeting, and motions need to be made, seconded, and voted upon. However, keep the meeting on task. Team leaders should encourage conversation when needed but also be mindful of time and suggest smaller breakout meetings when it is clear the conversation will be long or the participants limited to a small number of people.

BE TIMELY

Start and end meetings on time. If the meeting is scheduled to begin at, for example, three thirty, start no later than a few minutes after that time—before three thirty-five. It's important to wait for people to arrive, to be sure, but starting late encourages attendees to *be* late for future meetings. Additionally, respect that team members have planned their days around the anticipated ending time for meetings; if a meeting is scheduled to end at four thirty, end at that time. If conversations need to continue to resolve situations, call another meeting to do so.

DISTRIBUTE MEETING NOTES

Sharing a summary of the meeting—in particular, decisions made and actions decided upon—ensures everyone on the team has the same understanding when leaving the meeting and that team members can be held accountable for those decisions and actions in the future. Some organizations will expect formal meeting minutes or formatting of these summaries. In others, or on specific projects, a quick bulleted list may be sufficient. Whatever the organizational expectation, distribute meeting summaries and notes in a timely manner to all who attended.

BEHAVE WITH DECORUM

This should go without saying, but, in case there is any confusion, here it is anyway: behave like a professional in meetings. Be polite. Be courteous. Ask questions and listen to answers. Seek consensus, and put the needs of the project and organization before any personal agenda.

Emails

Little would get done these days without email. Near-instant written communication has become a fundamental part of how organizations and projects function. However, that near-constant connection doesn't mean that professionalism and decorum are unnecessary. Rather, the very rapidity of written communication requires circumspection and attention to etiquette to ensure productive and effective communication. No one should be unaware of the speed at which online communication can devolve into finger-pointing and name-calling; a good leader will demonstrate, model, and hold team members accountable for appropriate communication behavior.

The first—and perhaps most important—rule of email communication should be to *slow down*. The ability to communicate right away doesn't necessarily mean someone should. This is especially true when emotions run high—which happens quite a lot in theatrical environments. (After all, most live-entertainment projects are under development in short time frames with less-than-ideal resources and involve artists who are passionate about their work; this is a recipe for heated exchanges.) Take a breath before firing off an accusatory email or responding to an accusatory email that you've received. Anything that requires immediate attention, potential conflicts, or negative information should all be communicated with a phone call, not an email, anyway; take some time to gain perspective and focus on what is necessary for the project and organization, not on emotional content.

Consider who needs to be included in a conversation when sending or responding to an email. It is easy to address an email to everyone when only a handful of people are responsible for the topics under discussion; however, no one wants to be distracted by reading a message that has nothing to do with his or her work. Conversely, it's also easy to neglect to include important people on an email's recipient list, potentially marginalizing key team members and missing out on important insights and perspectives. Review your recipient list carefully before hitting "send." (This applies as well to email replies—avoid the dreaded "reply all," unless absolutely appropriate.)

Though its rapidity might suggest an email exchange is a conversation, it is not. An email exchange, or thread, is a series of written correspondences; as such, good practice is to treat each message as singular, and assume that participants in the exchange have been involved in other matters, conversations, and work between messages. This means recipients may not remember the context of responses or questions, may not have read each message in a thread, or may otherwise be out of the loop. A well-written email will account for this. Good email practice means writing well and using complete sentences; good practice includes using concrete references (no using, for example, "that means" without specifying what "that" is); good practice is quoting relevant text from previous emails in the body of a response.

Consider figure 4.4, an email reply sent by a production manager to the stage manager in response to a rehearsal report.

Notice how the reply includes text quoted from the original rehearsal report, and how the response is clear and concise, but also well written and with concrete references: "I'll have someone from the shop take a look at the table and see what we can do," as opposed to, "Someone will take a look at it," or something similarly unclear.

Phone Calls and Messages

In live-entertainment production, things can move quickly. Live-entertainment production in a generation used to instant answers and always-online access to information and communication can move even faster. The era of the phone call gave way to the email; the email is quickly giving way to the text message—it is faster and requires even less conversation and discussion than a phone call. A

"Reply-all" to rehearsal and performances reports. For subsequent messages and for messages that do not originate with reports include all relevant parties. Copy your major professor and that of anyone else on the email.

Dionne, Richard M

To:	Anna Lee Tarabini
CC:	[Reply All]
Subject:	Re: Crimes, Rehearsal Report #15, 9/8/16

Include the note to which you are responding in your response. This also means indicating to what area the note was directed. In this case, that area was "General Notes."

General Notes: The grey folding table in room 2164 has a leg that is questionably attached, it came apart during rehearsal but can be easily reinserted.

Be clear and specific. Use complete sentences. Avoid indefinite antecedents (using "this" or "that" without naming the thing to which you are referring first). State clearly any actions you plan to take.

I'll have someone from the shop take a look at the table and see what we can do.

R

--

Rich Dionne
Assistant Professor and Technical Director
Department of Theatre, Patti and Rusty Rueff School of Visual and Performing Arts
Faculty Fellow, Purdue Polytechnic Institute
Purdue University | (7658) 494-3073 | rdionne@purdue.edu

If you include the text of the original email, include it below your response. It is not necessary to include the full text of the original email, however.

From: Anna Lee Tarabini
Sent: Thursday, September 8, 2016 12:46 AM
To: [Redacted]
Subject: Crimes, Rehearsal Report #15, 9/8/16

Crimes of the Heart

Rehearsal Report #15

Thursday, September 8th

Rehearsal:	15	**Started:**	6:30pm	**Location:**	Pao 2164
Date:	9/8/16	**Ended:**	10:30pm	**Late/Absent:**	Kailey Merida (7:10 arrival)

Figure 4.4. Template for clear email communication

text message is the ultimate in send-it-and-forget-it, allowing someone to fire off a few words with his question, concern, or comment, then turn back to whatever demands his attention right now—at least until a return message comes through.

Text messaging is a genie that won't go back in the bottle; only naiveté would lead someone to shake her fist at the sky and condemn the use of text messages as unacceptable in professional practice. However, one should set expectations on the use of text messages in live production to maximize their effectiveness and to minimize the miscommunications that can come from using short messages fired off in haste as a means of sharing information.

Texting can be useful. Sometimes it can even be essential. During a performance of a musical at Purdue University not too long ago, the communications system suffered a power surge and went down. The stage manager, thinking quickly, pulled out her cell phone and began texting the remainder of her calls for the performance, calling cues to lighting, sound, and assistant stage managers (as well as communicating with house management) for nearly the entire performance, and no audience member or cast member was any the wiser. This is an extreme example, of course, and should not be taken as general approval of the use of cell phones during a performance; the use of texting is in most situations far more banal.

When are text messages appropriate? In most situations, this will depend on the organization and the project. However, these rules of thumb provide some guidance to consider when making determinations about how and when to use text messages as "official" means of communication.

- *Text messages are typically short.* That messages are short is both their advantage and their drawback. Used for rapid communication about straightforward topics, text messages (figure 4.5) can be the perfect means of communication.

  When the topic is more complex, requiring fuller explanations and/or a series of questions, typing out all that information actually takes longer than simply making a phone call. If a question, comment, or concern will require a conversation of any depth, consider an email, or—better—a phone call.
- *Text messages don't allow for real-time "full-duplex" communication.* Some messaging services (such as Apple's iMessage and Facebook's Messenger) can indicate whether a message has been viewed by the recipient, and even whether the recipient is actively typing a response. However, text messages (like walkie-talkies of old) are essentially single-duplex, asynchronous forms of communication: when one person is typing, she isn't reading responses, or even waiting for the recipient to consider and formulate a response. Conversations can quickly devolve into multiple, asynchronous threads, with questions asked and answered in and among other questions and answers. This overlapping effect often brings more confusion than clarity.
- *Text messages are limited at best in conveying body language, facial expressions, and emotional content.* Although libraries of emoji continue to expand, and text messages gain an ever-increasing vocabulary of tiny images intended to convey nonverbal meaning, the truth is that text messages cannot reliably convey much meaning beyond the words used. Consequently, they may be a poor choice for sharing information that must also convey nonverbal content. Indeed, communicating much beyond factual information via text message in a professional environment can easily create an opportunity for miscommunication and misunderstanding.

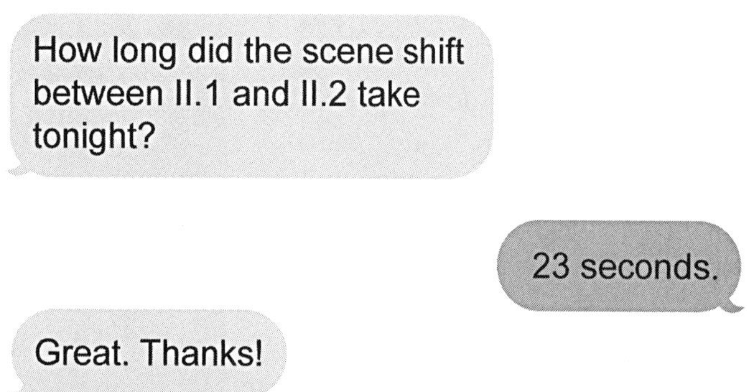

Figure 4.5. Example text messages, showing rapid, factual communication

Frankly, when considering how to communicate with someone on a team, remember that emotional, sensitive, intuitive content is best delivered face to face, while factual content can be relegated to less personal forms of communication (figure 4.6). The more a conversation can suffer from miscommunication, the more important it is to communicate in person. The less vulnerable a conversation is to miscommunication, the more suited it may be to phone calls, email, or texting.

Summing Up

Managing and Leading

Managing focuses on resources, schedules, plans, and procedures. Leading focuses on people: providing vision, establishing trust, motivating action, and demanding accountability. A good project manager will balance managing and leading her team.

Authority, Responsibility, and Accountability

Accountability refers to the willingness (and obligation) to be answerable for the specific actions, choices, and decisions one makes.

Responsibility refers to the obligation to perform tasks or take actions assigned by others.

Authority refers to the ability to assign tasks, direct resources, and make decisions related to a project.

Job Evaluations: Mentoring and Coaching

- Coaching should be FAST: frequent, actionable, specific, and timely
- Mentoring of team members should happen regularly:
  - Understanding and nurturing professional growth. Soliciting and acting on feedback from team members.
  - Recognizing when it may be necessary to let an employee go or change his or her areas of responsibility

Personal Time Management

Managing one's own time is essential for balancing the many competing demands on a project leader's time, but also for modeling good life-balance behaviors and expectations for the team. One effective technique for managing time is to consider the competing demands for one's time on two spectra: urgency and importance. Demands that are both urgent and important get attention first; demands that are neither urgent nor important get attention last.

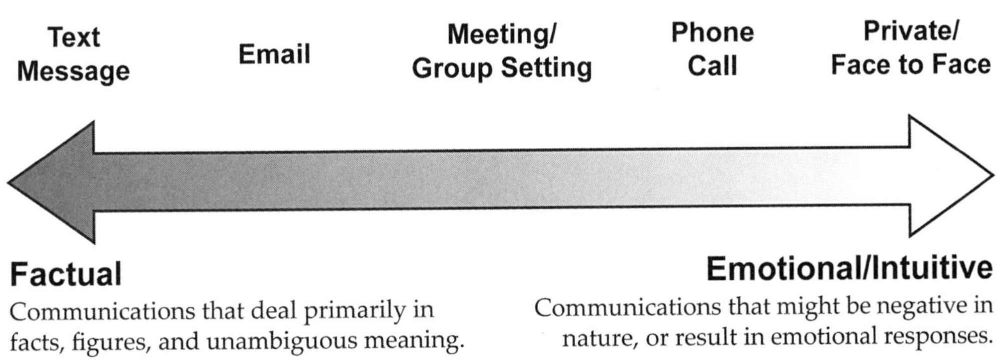

Figure 4.6. Modes of communication mapped on a spectrum based on their ability to share facts and feelings

Conflict Management

Organizational conflicts are often the result of miscommunication; resolution comes by determining the error, correcting the misunderstandings, and developing a method for avoiding similar miscommunication in the future.

Strategic Thinking

Thinking strategically means thinking in terms of long-term or overall aims and goals, and how to achieve them. A good team leader will leave room to consider the issues while managing the regular operations of an organization or project. A great team leader will develop a culture of strategic thinking, encouraging team members to think about how actions and decisions now can impact and affect long-term goals.

Organizational Communication

Direct Reports

A direct report is an employee whose position is directly below that of someone else, and who is managed by that someone else. Often, miscommunication in an organization or on a project comes from team members providing direction to someone who is not their direct report. Better to know the reporting structure of one's organization or project, and to speak to the people who have both responsibility for and authority over decisions related to the concern or question.

Decorum

MEETINGS

- Invite only those needed
- Have an agenda and stick to it
- Be timely
- Distribute meeting notes
- Behave professionally

EMAILS

- Write well and use complete sentences
- Provide and use concrete references (avoid saying "that means," for example, without including what "that" is)
- Quote relevant text from previous emails in the body of the response
- Write only to those who need to be included

PHONE CALLS AND TEXT MESSAGES

Text messages are effective for short, fact-based communication. If a communication may include emotional, nonverbal, or intuited content, don't text—call instead, or speak face to face.

PART II
Planning the Project

Planning the project is an essential task for any project to be successful. Planning comprises all of the work that begins after the project has been conceived, but before the actual work of realizing it is completed. This includes the design process, any estimating and scheduling that happens, revisions to designs, and the eventual decision to move forward with a project or to scrap it.

In the chapters that follow, we'll examine some of the more technical aspects of the planning process, specifically estimating and scheduling tools and techniques. While much of this text is focused on the highest-level project manager for a production project, these techniques are useful for technical managers at all levels. In fact, many of the examples are taken from technical direction work on a variety of projects, focused on scenery construction planning. Hopefully, these chapters will be as useful for technical managers in individual production areas as they are for project and production managers.

A live-entertainment project is a complex thing, comprised of many facets that could easily be considered projects all on their own. To imagine that a project manager will be able to generate a cost estimate for the overall production project at the same level of detail as a technical director will for the scenery aspects of the project would be to envision a project manager with far more time on her hands and far greater and broader expertise than would be realistic. In practice, a project manager will break up a project as complex as a typical live-entertainment project into subprojects and assign individual team managers to get into the details of each. In a traditional theatrical project, these teams would likely comprise scenery, costumes, lighting, and sound, among others. However, as discussed in chapter 1, a project may require a different team makeup, and a project manager should identify the appropriate leaders to organize the team around and to assign the responsibility for generating the detailed estimates, work breakdown structures, Gantt charts, and other planning and management tools for individual subprojects that will inform similar tools that represent the project as a whole.

In this part of the book, chapter 5, "Estimating," explores analogous and parametric estimating techniques and methods.

Chapter 6, "Costing: Definitive Estimates," presents steps in generating definitive costing estimates.

Chapter 7, "Scheduling and Estimating Time," examines project scheduling and understanding logical dependencies between project tasks and resource allocation.

5. **Estimating**

The ability to effectively, quickly, and accurately generate a time and cost estimate of a project is one of the most important—and, if you'll forgive the pun, most underestimated—skills a project manager can have. With it, a project has a better chance of sailing smoothly from conception to realization; without it, a project design can get bogged down in costly overruns and consequently show up at the load-in or costume tech incomplete. This inevitably leads to raised tensions, angry designers and technicians, and a production manager wringing his or her hands trying to find a way to keep everyone sane and at the same time get the show completed.

Topics covered in this chapter:

- Top-down versus bottom-up estimating
- Analogous estimates: top-down estimating
  - Advantages and disadvantages
  - Reference material
  - Application
- Parametric estimates: bottom-up estimating
  - Advantages and disadvantages
  - Reference material
  - Application

Top-Down versus Bottom-Up Estimating

What is an estimate? This seems like a straightforward question with an easy answer—but it really isn't. Types of estimates vary in accuracy, and differ in the amount of time required to complete them. Consequently, different types of estimates have different uses, which can (and should) be deployed at different phases of the project process to help guide the artistic team to a project that can be completed with the resources available. There are two diametrically opposed approaches for considering a project as you estimate it: *top-down* or *bottom-up*. Each of these approaches is dependent on the amount of time available to complete the estimate and the level of accuracy required. There are three basic *types* of estimates for a project: the *analogous* estimate, the *parametric* estimate, or the *definitive* estimate. Each of these types has distinct advantages and disadvantages, and consequently are useful tools at different points in the development of a project.

Top-Down

Early in the life cycle of a production project, relatively little will be known about the scope of the design—indeed, at the earliest stages of the process, the only thing that may be known about the project is the title of the play. Estimates created during the earliest stages of a production obviously cannot rely on lists of units for design elements, or on steps required to complete the construction of those units, as they haven't been designed yet. These estimates instead build from an understanding of the broadest scope of the production (i.e., a production requires a period box set, or an abstract unit set that can function as multiple different locations; a production requires costumes that are abstractions of animal forms, or include multiple changes for most characters).

Estimates that are generated from broad ideas, rather than detailed information specific to a project, are *top-down* estimates. The best example of a top-down estimate is an *analogous* estimate, which uses comparative data (from previous seasons, for example), and is therefore generally not very accurate. (This should be expected, given the relative lack of detail available from which to make an estimate.)

Bottom-Up

Bottom-up estimates are the extreme opposite of top-down estimates. Bottom-up estimates begin with the lowest level of detail on a project; estimates are generated for these detail elements, and then summed together into increasingly higher levels of broader inclusion, until the entire project has been estimated.

Bottom-up estimates, of course, rely on a significant level of detail to be accurate, and can only be completed when a detailed list of units and/or tasks for a design have been determined. Bottom-up estimating styles include the parametric estimate and the definitive estimate. (Definitive estimates will be covered in chapter 6.)

Analogous Estimates: Top-Down Estimating

When you're asked to quickly tell someone how much something might cost, what's the first thing you do? Perhaps you take the time to look up some material prices, or count the number of characters to estimate the size of the cast; maybe you draw some quick sketches of how something might be built or determine amounts of material you might need for costumes. But most often, if you are asked to make a quick, off-the-cuff estimate, odds are you are comparing what you see in front of you with what you've seen or done before. You want to take your significant other out to dinner and a movie, and figure it will cost about $50, unless you're getting popcorn and candy, in which case it jumps up to something like $70 (if you're paying for your date). You know this because that is about what it cost last time. This time you may order a bottle of wine, or your date may order the lobster; that will make the total more expensive than you had anticipated. That's one of the pitfalls of this kind of estimation: it cannot be very accurate, because it isn't based on the details of a project, but rather on its broad similarities to other projects.

This kind of estimate is called an *analogous* estimate: you are basing an estimate on the fact that the items being estimated have significant similarities—are analogous—to items that you already know the cost of. In this case, the costs of dinner and a movie this Friday are probably similar to the costs of dinner and a movie two weeks ago, even if the movie isn't the same and you go to a different restaurant.

In the fast-paced world of summer stocks and small to mid-size regional theatres, some form of analogous estimation is a common approach for managers to apply. This approach generally requires the least amount of time-on-task, and in these environments, shaving time off a process can be essential. By applying an analogous approach, a manager can quickly generate estimates for a project based on previous, similar projects. For example, she may look at the costume designs for a cast of twenty-five actors in Renaissance-period clothing with wealthy and lower-class garments, and based on her experience doing a similar-size and style show in the previous season, say that the project might cost $3,000 to $8,000 and take approximately six weeks to build, fit, and alter—depending on the skills of the available labor—prior to tech.

A manager may also use an analogous approach only on specific parts of a project, while relying on other, more detailed estimation tools. He might quickly look at a translucent stage drop, for example, and knowing that such a drop would need to be sewn seamless for the translucency to work, look up the cost of the last seamless-translucent drop of a similar size, and feel reasonably confident the new drop will cost about the same as the previous one.

Advantages and Disadvantages

ADVANTAGES

- Quick
- Not resource intensive
- Reasonably accurate (within 25 percent)

DISADVANTAGES

- Relies on previous experience or knowledge of previous work
- Only about 25 percent accurate

Advantages

QUICK

As noted earlier, one of the biggest advantages of the analogous estimation approach is how quick it is to use. This is primarily because it is a simple comparative process: Is there a project I have done in the past that is similar to this one? How much did it cost? How long did it take? Did I have similar available resources for that project as I do for this one?

NOT RESOURCE INTENSIVE

Because an analogous estimate relies primarily on past experience, few resources are required to complete it. A project manager could create an analogous estimate from as little material as a summary of the play and an idea of the cast size, and the setting or passage of time during the play. More information serves to refine an analogous estimate, of course, but very little information is required to generate one. A project manager can generate an analogous estimate with a calculator and her previous experience: no material lists are needed, no price charts referred to. An analogous estimate could be backed up by historical records from the previous project, but in practice (at least in theatre), these estimates can often be based on a project manager's recollections.

REASONABLY ACCURATE

"Reasonably accurate" is, of course, an unreasonably vague term. However, depending on the amount of information available, and the body of knowledge drawn from, an analogous estimate can have a margin of error of +/- 25 percent.

Disadvantages

RELIES ON PREVIOUS EXPERIENCE

The analogous approach is quick and dirty; however, it can be very dependent on a project manager's previous experience—the more (and more varied) productions she has worked on the more likely she will be to have an analogous experience to draw from. Material costs can vary wildly in different geographic areas, and the skills and speed at which team members can work can differ from venue to venue. This is one of the many reasons why accurate record keeping is an essential part of a project manager's job:

being able to go back to a previous project and see exactly how much money was spent on a unit (or entire project) and how much labor was required to complete each unit (or project) can make this analogous approach much more accurate.

TENDS TO BE INACCURATE

As quick as the analogous approach is to deploy, however, it has a downside: it has a wide margin of error. While on the one hand, we can say that an analogous estimate can be within as *little* as 25 percent of the actual cost of a project (either above or below that cost), that also means the estimate can be as *much* as 25 percent off. Twenty-five percent can be a big number: when you give an analogous estimate of $10,000 for a project, for example, you're saying the project may cost as little as $7,500 or as much as $12,500.

Reference Material

Although an analogous estimate can be completed with very little information, the more information available to a project manager completing an analogous estimate, the more that estimate will approach being within about 25 percent of the actual cost of a project. Two kinds of information are important to making an analogous estimate as accurate as possible: knowledge of the production history of a venue or theatre or geographic location, and an understanding of the scope of the production.

Production History

Having a clear record of past productions at a venue is invaluable for the purposes of analogous estimation. An accurate record of total material and labor costs for previous productions provides a baseline set of numbers from which to extrapolate new estimates. However, a simple list of numbers tallying material expenses and labor allocations is not enough information; how does one know which previous production to compare to? What is needed is some indicator of the scope of these productions.

We often get so bogged down in getting productions open, that thinking about how to pass on institutional knowledge like production histories and scope of production for previous productions can get lost in the shuffle. However, passing on this kind of information is an essential part of every project. Chapter 10 examines this important part of a project's life cycle: the close out.

One of the easiest ways to indicate scope of production is through photographs. This is demonstrated by the example page from a production history focused on scenery at Purdue University (figure 5.1); along with total scenery labor and material expenses, the record for each production includes a pair of photographs. From these photographs can be determined the size of each set, how many scene shifts might have been involved, probable material choices, level of detail, design style, and aesthetic. These photographs can be used to identify previous projects with similar attributes to the one under consideration: if the current project required a box set, the information for *The Foreigner* might be more applicable (from this example) than would that for *The Importance of Being Earnest.*

Another, potentially less accurate, method of recording scope information is to include a list of identifying attributes in a production history. These might include

***The Importance of Being Earnest*, Fall 2006**
Written by Oscar Wilde
Directed by Kristine Holtvedt
Set Designer: Stephen Barnes

Technical Director: Ben Davidson
Materials: $8,422
Labor: 5 weeks: 120 hr/wk shop; 100 hr/wk paint

***The Foreigner*, Fall, 2007**
Written by Larry Shue
Directed by Larry Sommers
Set Designer: Stephen Barnes

Technical Director: Rich Dionne
Materials: $7,656
Labor: 10 weeks 40 hr/wk shop; 40 hr/wk paint

Figure 5.1. Example production–cost history records

statements such as "unit set, non-realistic pieces; flown units; skeletal shapes formed from steel; oversize wrought-iron work," or "multiple changes, modern clothing; stylized headwear and boots; paint and dye heavy." These words leave a lot of space for interpretation, and, consequently, it may be more difficult to draw strong analogous comparisons, but lacking photographs this can be a useful method for documenting a production.

Production Scope

Having a record of the scope of previous productions is important; knowing which of those previous productions is pertinent to the production at hand is also vital to being able to draw analogous comparisons.

A statement of the scope of the production—whether in words, or with sketches, models, or full-blown plans and elevations—provides an understanding of the production under consideration for useful comparison. From this statement of scope, one can parse a production history and identify productions with a similar scope, with material and labor costs that can form the basis for an estimate of the project.

Knowing which past productions to use as referents for the purposes of comparison when generating an analogous estimate can be tricky. The best way to approach this problem is to begin by working up a list of applicable elements of the scope, style, and quality of the production under review, and then to mine production history data for projects that have similar qualities. It is unlikely that any one previous production will be *exactly* like the one under consideration; rather, looking through historical records will probably reveal anywhere from a half dozen to a dozen productions completed recently enough that the data is still applicable, and which can be compared to the current production based on many different elements.

A checklist of design parameters that typically play a major role in material and labor costs at a venue can be a useful tool in developing a pool of previous productions with which to compare the production under consideration. A typical list that might be examined for scenery includes:

- Size of venue
- Size of set
- Unit set
- Box set
- Multiple scene shifts
- Multiple wagon units
- Multiple flown units
- Complicated, nontraditional construction
- Automation or control issues
- Style (realistic, surreal, abstract, oversized, detailed)
- Complicated rigging required
- Special effects required (flying, pyro, smoke and haze)

A similar list for costumes might include the following:

- Number of characters
- Number of actors
- Number of costume changes and how quickly they happen
- Complexity of hair and makeup elements
- Period or contemporary clothing
- Realistic or stylized elements
- What is in costume stock or can be rented?
- What items need to be built or purchased?
- Nontraditional items (prosthetics, special effects) required

Having lists of parameters or questions such as those listed above when generating an analogous estimate for a project can provide context for a project manager. This context can provide insights into what previous experiences may have analogous expenses and labor requirements.

Application

When to Use an Analogous Estimate

Given the relative speed with which the analogous approach can be deployed, and given the overall lack of accuracy the analogous approach provides, knowing when to rely upon it is essential. Certainly, the analogous approach is the wrong choice for a final costing approval, as analogous estimates can vary as much as 25 percent in either direction, as indicated previously. You'll have an unhappy producer when she finds out that though she agreed to pay $4,000 for a set, she's spent $5,000, or an unhappy artistic team when they realize that the $2,500 in costumes they cut to bring the design estimate down to within the budget never had to be cut at all.

An analogous estimate is likely to be most advantageous during the initial process of budgeting a project. For standalone projects, this can be straightforward: consider the scope of the project as defined during the conception of the project, compare with analogous projects, and determine an estimate. For projects that happen as part of a venue or organization that produces multiple productions or projects within a single season, the analogous estimating process can be a little different.

Sometimes a production manager will have the opportunity to do the budget for the season knowing what shows will be in which slot, which means they're comparing each production to similar productions produced in the past. Other times, she won't know any of the shows, and must come up with averaged numbers for each slot that she will then revise later once actual productions have been determined. In either case, the production manager is taking the analogous approach of comparing the shows for the current season with previous productions to determine a ballpark estimate for material and labor costs. It can be helpful to enlist the assistance of the various functional and technical managers with greater expertise in their areas. For example, a technical director or costume supervisor who is employed by a company at the time of season budgeting may be asked to provide his or her own analogous estimates as part of the budgeting and planning process.

Many technical managers in theatre try to skip the whole "reading-the-play" part of the production process. They have a thousand other things to wrestle with, and generally someone else *has* read the play, right? In many situations technical managers may be brought on board too late to suggest changes to the amounts budgeted for each production. However, with an understanding of the story or play, they can be better prepared to offer their insight into whether staying within those budgeted amounts might be difficult, or whether doing so might require some special considerations. This is the perfect place for an analogous approach.

Parametric Estimates: Bottom-Up Estimating

If you've ever been involved with building a new home, or worked with a contractor to renovate an old home, you are probably familiar with the parametric approach to estimating. This approach uses a mathematical model to predict the cost of a project. For example, you might consider that, on average, a typical, bare, hardcover flat (standard or Hollywood style, 1 × 3 framing) costs $1 per square foot: a sheet of ¼-inch lauan costs about $15; a sixteen-foot stick of 1 × 6 primed pine costs about the same, for a total of $30 for a 4 × 8 flat. Divide $30 (the total cost) by thirty-two square feet (the total area of the flat) and we come up with about $0.94 per square foot, which we can round up to $1. We might be able to say that it will take an average carpenter a half day (a four-hour shift) to build a 4 × 8 flat, or about ten minutes per square foot of flattage.

In a *parametric estimate*, we can use these numbers (or *parameters*), to quickly estimate the total cost of a twenty-foot-tall and fifty-foot-wide wall that is nonarchitectural, has some texturized paint, and is constructed as a hardcovered unit. A thousand square feet of flattage, with a materials cost averaging $1 per square foot, will cost about $1,000, and with a labor estimate of ten person-minutes per square foot, will take about ten thousand person-minutes or 167 person-hours. (Obviously, a flat this large will require more than one person to build and move around; a *definitive* estimate that includes resource scheduling will take these kinds of issues into consideration.)

We can apply parametric estimates to costuming as well, although instead of square footage or linear feet, we might consider types of garments as parameters. A typical suit coat takes three yards of wool at $20 per yard, three yards of lining at $9 per yard, a set of hymo fronts at $15, shoulder pads at $4, and fifteen buttons at $4.50. This totals $110.50 in materials, round up to $111. Additionally, we might be able to say the patterning, construction, and finishing will take about four eight-hour workdays. In a parametric estimate, we can use these numbers (or parameters), to quickly estimate the total materials cost for a set of barbershop quartet suit coats to be about $444, and about 128 hours of labor. The choice of material will affect the labor needed—velvet or plaid fabrics take more time to cut and stitch, of course—just as would be true when considering linear footage of molding in scenic estimates.

As the mathematical model becomes more detailed, the estimate will become more accurate. For complex projects, parametric models can have any number of different modifiers with varying values to represent different aspects and variances in a production. For example, you might have a base rate of $1 per square foot for hardcovered flattage; to this you might add a modifier of between $.50 to $2 per foot based on the number of doors or windows in a unit; you might add a modifier based on the amount of trim detail and the period or style of the set. For decks, you might add modifiers for the number of changes in level. These modifiers provide ways to bring the estimate to a greater level of accuracy.

Parametric models can be quick—any spreadsheet program can turn this into an easy plug-and-chug process. The time and energy expended in the parametric approach is in generating accurate mathematical models. (This is where the accurate record keeping mentioned above can be helpful.) Using a spreadsheet program can make refining these models easy, however.

Advantages and Disadvantages

ADVANTAGES

- Relatively quick
- Reasonably accurate (within 15 to 20 percent)

DISADVANTAGES

- Requires significant effort to develop reference material based on parameters
- Accuracy dependent on accuracy of reference material

Advantages

RELATIVELY QUICK TO IMPLEMENT

There are two elements required to generate a parametric estimate for a production: a cost per unit reference number, and a number of units. The first element, cost per unit, is generally recorded somewhere in a spreadsheet or other file. The second element is determined in a costing meeting or design meeting with a set of drawings, a model, renderings, or other relevant materials representative of parts of the project under consideration. Calculating area of flattage, for example, can be completed quickly, and generating an estimate from that is as fast as multiplying that area by a parametric reference number. Similarly, calculating a parametric estimate for a costume design requires determining the number of garments (petticoats, dresses, doublets); what kind and how many pairs of footwear are needed (sandals, riding boots); how many wigs or haircuts are needed; and multiplying each of these by appropriate parametric reference numbers.

REASONABLY ACCURATE

Parametric estimates, with accurate reference information and relatively detailed information about the scope of a production, can be accurate to within 15 or 20 percent of what the total material and labor cost of a project might be. This is a significant improvement over the accuracy of an analogous estimate, which will only approach at best 25 percent accuracy.

Disadvantages

ACCURACY DEPENDENT ON AVAILABLE REFERENCE MATERIALS

Just as with an analogous estimate, the accuracy of a parametric estimate is a function of the accuracy of the reference materials. If you were to base an estimate on an average cost of $10 per square foot for a Hollywood hardcover flat when that cost is really something like $3 per square foot, or $70/ per yard for wool when the actual cost is $15/ per yard, your estimate is going to have significant error. This is compounded by the fact that if your reference materials are not based on the prices of local materials, the ability of the particular shop in which you will be building a project to perform specific techniques, the skill sets of the employees who will be completing the work, or other venue-specific variables, they are likely to be more inaccurate.

> But wait: What about pulled costumes? Or stock scenic units? The estimating process presented in chapters 5 and 6 focuses on what might be called the "dream" build: if we could create everything the designer asks for from scratch. Obviously, this is rarely possible, but starting with a fully realized estimate when creating parametric and definitive estimates avoids making any assumptions about what items should be prioritized as new builds. Subsequent conversations about what to cut, what to make from stock or pull should include the designers and directors—i.e., those with the absolute authority to make aesthetic decisions at this level. These conversations should also include producers and artistic directors—i.e., those with the authority to allocate additional funds and/or labor. In this way, we open up the possibility of finding more funds for that must-have design element and avoid wrong assumptions about which items can be pulled together from stock.

REQUIRES SIGNIFICANT EFFORT TO DEVELOP REFERENCE MATERIALS BASED ON PARAMETERS

Parametric estimates rely on more detailed resource data than analogous estimates.

As pointed out above, this resource data is heavily dependent on the realities of the venue in which the work will be completed. Consequently, generating accurate parametric resource data can be a time-consuming task. Once this data is generated, however, keeping it up to date as material costs and labor skill sets change is relatively easy, especially if the data is stored in a computerized spreadsheet.

Reference Material

Material Costs

There are two methods for developing a set of reference numbers for generating parametric estimates. The first is a bottom-up approach, determining a cost per square foot, yard, or item based on actual material prices and available labor. The second is a top-down approach, determining a cost per square foot, yard, or item based on historical material and labor data from previous projects. Both methods require some work to complete; however, the bottom-up approach has some advantages that the top-down approach does not: accurate historical data isn't required, and if prepared using a spreadsheet program, the data reflected in it can flex with changes in local material costs and changes in available labor. With either method, after the data is generated, little time is required to maintain and update the information for subsequent uses.

To create a spreadsheet of parametric data to work from, begin by listing the different kinds of work that might need to be estimated. (As comprehensive as you try to make this list, it will inevitably take many versions before it is *exhaustively* comprehensive; this is okay, as with each project you can add more categories and create more parameters, making the resource more useful for subsequent projects.) Good beginning lists for scenery and costumes might look like this:

SCENERY

- Hollywood-style hardcover flats
- Standard-style hardcover flats
- Standard-style softcover flats
- Flooring—hardboard/Masonite
- Flooring—carpet
- Flooring—ground cloth
- Flooring—linoleum
- Flooring—lauan planks
- Drop—seamed, opaque, medium-weight
- Drop—seamless, translucent, medium-weight
- Decking—platforms and legs or trusses
- Decking—plywood and trusses
- Doors or windows with trim
- Cabinets
- Escape stairs

COSTUMES

- Corsets
- Petticoats
- Character shoes
- Tights
- Riding boots
- Modern men's three-piece suits
- Collared button-down shirts
- Period pants
- Doublets
- Hats (top hats, tricorns, bowlers)
- Vests
- Floor-length skirts
- Belts
- Various fabrics by the yard
- Various trims by the yard

Each of these categories can be assigned a per-square-foot, per-linear-foot, or per unit material and labor cost. For costumes, a category may be assigned a purchase price, rental price, or material cost. Labor cost will vary depending on whether the item is purchased or built new. This is often done by determining how much it would cost and how long it would take to create the smallest version of each kind of unit—for example, you might consider how much a 4 × 8 standard-style hardcover flat might cost, and how long it will take to assemble and paint—determining the area of that unit, and dividing the overall cost by the area.

Once you have completed this basic list, you can begin adding additional information for various parameters of construction: Does adding architectural trim increase the cost by a couple of dollars per square foot? Does adding a multilayer paint treatment increase labor requirements by 8 or 10 hours? Does adding lace to every petticoat ruffle increase the materials cost by $2 per yard? Does choosing velvet for the doublet increase the labor by 10 to 12 hours? These parameters can be refined and added to as new situations arise.

It is important to remember that the point of a parametric estimate (figure 5.2) is to be more accurate than an analogous estimate, but not as accurate as a definitive estimate. Consequently, there will be error: your parameters will be *averaged* costs—some architectural molding will cost more than others, some paint treatments will take less time than others. This is okay—you just need to be sure everyone involved in the project understands the degree to which there may be error in these numbers.

> There are two ways to consider labor costs in a parametric (and, later, a definitive) estimate. Labor can be considered in terms of time (person-hours, or how much work can be completed by one employee in one regular work hour) or in terms of cost (how much does it cost to pay an employee to complete a task). In either case, having a sense of the total amount of labor required to complete a task is the purpose of the parametric estimate. This can then be compared with the total amount of labor available (either in terms of person-hours or payroll funds) to determine the viability of a project.

Application

When to Use a Parametric Estimate

There are three primary times during the production process when deploying a parametric estimate is most effective: at a preliminary design presentation, when the direction a production is heading may be clear but specific design details may not be; at the beginning of the construction process, when determining what method of construction might be most cost-effective; whenever changes are introduced to the production, and a rapid assessment of the impact of a change is required. The use of a parametric estimate at each of these stages in a production is examined below.

PRELIMINARY DESIGN MEETINGS

By the preliminary design milestone, the production team should have a clear idea of the direction in which the design is headed; designers will probably have a well-defined ground plan and an idea of the broad strokes of the scenic units for scenery, and renderings with some samples of fabric swatches for costumes, for example. This is also a time when the design team would benefit from valuable feedback about the feasibility of the direction in which a design is headed, and about potential bottlenecks in terms of

4x8 Hollywood Flat (Hardcover, Raw, 32 sqft)

1 @ 4x8x1/4" Lauan	$15.00	$15.00
1 @ 1x6x16 Primed Pine	20.00	20.00
	Total Materials	$35.00
	Price per sq foot	**1.09**

4x8 Standard Flat (Hardcover, Raw, 32 sqft)

1 @ 4x8x1/4" Lauan	$15.00	$15.00
1 @ 1x6x16 Primed Pine	20.00	20.00
1 @ 4x8x1/4" BC Ply (cornerblocks and straps)	25.00	25.00
	Total Materials	$60.00
	Price per sq foot	**1.88**

4x8 Standard Flat (Softcover, Raw, 32 sqft)

1 @ 1x6x16 Primed Pine	$20.00	$20.00
1 @ 4x8x1/4" BC Ply (cornerblocks and straps)	25.00	25.00
3 @ 60" MW Muslin (per yard)	4.35	13.05
	Total Materials	$58.05
	Price per sq foot	**$1.81**

Flooring (Hardboard/Masonite, Raw, 32 sqft)

1 @ 4x8x1/4 Hardboard/Masonite	$15.00	$15.00
	Total Materials	$15.00
	Price per sq foot	**0.47**

Flooring (Groundcloth, Raw, 30 sqft)

1 @ 120" HW Muslin (per yard)	$7.25	$7.25
	Total Materials	$7.25
	Price per sq foot	**0.24**

Flooring (Linoleum, Raw, 9 sqft)

1 @ Vinyl/Linoleum Flooring (per sq yard)	$6.00	$6.00
	Total Materials	$6.00
	Price per sq foot	**0.67**

Flooring (Lauan, Raw, 32 sqft)

1 @ 4x8x1/4" Lauan	$15.00	$15.00
	Total Materials	$15.00
	Price per sq foot	**0.41**

Figure 5.2. Example of a scenic parametric estimate reference worksheet

time or materials. Unfortunately, by this point in the process there is generally not enough detail available to make the effort required for a definitive estimate worthwhile, in part because what details are available are likely to evolve as the design continues to develop.

Because a parametric estimate not only doesn't depend on specific details, but can also be generated relatively quickly (perhaps even while the design presentation is happening), it can be a highly effective tool at this stage of the process. As pointed out above, with a robust set of modeling parameters, this estimate can be relatively accurate, within 10 to 20 percent. Ideally, a parametric estimate provides the team a clear-enough picture of labor and material costs for the project to make adjustments to ensure the project falls within budget once the design process is completed. (Occasionally, adjustments to materials and construction techniques can be enough to bring a project in line with the budget, but typically a parametric estimate that exceeds the budget indicates a need to reduce the scope of the project.)

DETERMINING A BUILD METHOD

Some project elements can be completed by using different construction methods; for example, a balcony unit might be built using traditional joist-and-stringer construction, using platforms (framed with 2 × 4s) on legs, or using stressed-skin panels. A period woman's dress might be created using a corset to achieve the silhouette under a built bodice, or by building only a boned bodice. The cording on the bodice might be finished by hand or by machine. With more complicated construction projects, completing a comprehensive, definitive estimate of each construction approach can be time consuming and an inefficient use of time. Enter the parametric estimate.

By generating a parametric estimate for each construction approach on a project, a technical manager can quickly determine which approach might be more expensive but less time consuming, more labor intensive but less costly, or any other combination of material and labor costs. These quick-and-dirty estimates can then be used to provide a framework for a conversation about priorities within an overall production with the designer and director.

MID-PROCESS CHANGES

As project managers facing a firm deadline—opening night doesn't change because the set construction is behind—we all want to believe things shouldn't change in a design. But the truth is, the production process is usually—and should be—one in which new discoveries are made, and changes in a design are inevitable. Parametric estimates can provide a means for discussing changes to a design within a framework of reasonably accurate estimates of labor and material costs. (Changes like these are discussed in more detail in chapter 9.)

Sometimes, parametric estimates of proposed changes will bear out those sinking-belly feelings that a change might be the straw that breaks the camel's back. Conversely, a parametric estimate may demonstrate that with some minor changes in the build schedule, a change to the design can be implemented easily. In either case, deploying a parametric estimate in response to changes to a design provides an effective framework for discussing any changes in a way that emphasizes hard data about materials and resources rather than emotional responses to changing expectations.

Summing Up

Top–Down versus Bottom–Up Estimating

There are two basic approaches to estimating: the top-down or the bottom-up estimate. *Top-down* estimates proceed from a general idea of the project; estimates are made without specific, detailed information, and are therefore relatively inaccurate. *Bottom-up* estimates begin using detailed information about how the project will be completed, and are generally much more accurate than top-down estimates.

Analogous Estimating

How to Generate an Analogous Estimate

Analogous estimates are generated by comparing a current project with the labor and materials required for similar previous projects (or similar elements from multiple previous projects).

Advantages and Disadvantages

Analogous estimates can be very quick to generate. However, they have the potential to be very subjective (as they tend to rely on past experience) and they can vary by 25 percent or more from the actual material and labor costs of a project.

Reference Materials Required

Analogous estimates are most effective when there is a comprehensive reference of previous productions at a given venue that details material and labor costs for a project manager to draw from.

Application of Analogous Estimates

Because of these limitations, analogous estimates are best deployed when little detail is known about a project.

Parametric Estimating

How to Generate a Parametric Estimate

Parametric estimates are generated using averaged cost-per-measurement or cost-per-item numbers (usually cost-per-yard, cost-per-square-foot, cost-per-linear-foot, or cost-per-unit/piece). Generate a parametric estimate by determining the amount of the type of parameter present in a project and multiply that amount by the cost indicated. The sum of the estimated parametric costs is the total estimated cost of the project.

Advantages and Disadvantages of a Parametric Estimate

Parametric estimates can be relatively quick to generate, and only vary from actual costs by about 15 to 20 percent. However, their accuracy is a function of how accurate and comprehensive the resources they are drawn from are.

Reference Materials Required

Parametric estimates are most effective when based on comprehensive charts with multiple parameters to choose from.

Application

Parametric estimates are best deployed when some—not all—of the detailed information is available, or when swiftness is required, including at preliminary design presentations, when choosing among multiple construction methods, or when changes in the project are requested.

6. Costing: Definitive Estimates

At some point in the development of a project, people will want to know definitively how much the project that has been dreamt up will cost, and how long it will take to realize. This is usually the point in the process when a project is either given a green light, or sent back to the drawing board because it cannot be realized with available resources. This is a make-or-break moment in the evolution of any project. A green light here means a commitment to see a project through; miscalculations in the cost of the project—material or labor costs—will mean cost and schedule overruns down the road. This is as true for a theatrical project as it is for any other kind of project.

The costing meeting—sometimes called the budget meeting or final design meeting—is generally where this make-or-break moment falls in many theatrical projects. At a costing meeting, technical managers from different production areas will present comprehensive lists of the material and labor costs of the design elements that comprise the production project and compare those to the available resources—how long the build is, how much money has been allocated to each element, and what kind of stock resources can be drawn upon. (For some production projects, these estimates are provided from all the different production areas at the same time; on other projects, these meetings are staggered due to the interdependencies between production and design areas—lighting design materials are often heavily dependent on a finalized set, for example. Whether presented simultaneously or in a staggered fashion, the concept is the same.) Because this meeting often determines whether the project moves forward, the success of the project depends on the accuracy of this information, and significant mistakes here can mean dramatic problems later. Hence the importance of the *definitive estimate.*

Definitive estimates are not estimates in the truest sense of the word; instead of being well-educated guesses of the materials required to complete a project, they reflect a considered and detailed plan for the completion of the project, down to the construction techniques and materials required for each element of each unit. Developing a definitive estimate requires a significant amount of time-on-task, as well as an extensive amount of reference material to draw upon. In this chapter, we'll examine the different resources required as well as the process used to complete a comprehensive definitive estimate.

Topics covered in this chapter:

- Task lists
- Work-breakdown structure
- Definitive estimate

Task Lists

A definitive estimate requires an outline of the tasks and/or operations required to complete a project. Ideally, this *task list* will be comprehensive and extremely

A definitive estimate focuses on resources and materials, but often not on labor. With a parametric or analogous estimate, a tallying of the number of person hours required to complete a project is sufficient information given the level of detail and accuracy expected at the point in the process those types of estimating methods are used. However, at a costing meeting, a more definitive idea of the labor required and the allocation of labor resources is necessary; a tally of person hours is insufficient to indicate whether and how different aspects of the project can be completed on time and how labor must be allocated in order to achieve deadlines. This scheduling information and how to generate it will be covered in more detail in chapter 7.

detailed, communicating every material and labor cost in a project. For a scenic design, for example, we often can find a preliminary task list in the form of a *unit list* in the set design drawings, and many scenic costing meetings present cost estimates organized around the unit list. This is often because scenic units are understood and visualized by nontechnical participants in the meeting much more easily than the component tasks and processes that go into completing units. Figure 6.1 includes a unit list (with cost estimates) for a production of *The 39 Steps* at the Weston Playhouse Theatre Company.

When considering a costume design, this preliminary list often takes the form of a dressing list (figure 6.2). From the dressing list, a pull/rent/build/buy chart is generated. The development of cost estimates for each item (piece) relate to the choice of acquisition. Commercial theatre venues employing independent costume houses and large regional theatre costume shops rely on definitive estimates during their bidding and planning processes.

Work-Breakdown Structure

A work-breakdown structure is a project management tool to assist in visualizing, scheduling, tracking, and organizing the completion of a project. It is essentially a comprehensive list of the "things" (a deliberately vague term) required to bring a project to 100 percent completion. These "things" may be information, tasks, subtasks, products, or other elements that when taken together describe the entire scope of a project. Each "thing" might also be broken down into further discrete elements, which together describe the entire scope of the "parent" element. We continue this process of describing every element in increasingly specific chunks, until we have a series of elements that can no longer be subdivided.

For example, consider a bicycle. We might break a bicycle up into component parts that together make up the whole: frame, wheels, crankset, brake system, and integration. ("Integration" is not a physical thing, but represents the work required to make the individual elements work together.) We might break "frame" up into further elements: frame, handlebars, seat post, and fork.

The lowest elements (or *terminal elements*) in a work-breakdown structure—those elements that can no longer be subdivided—are often referred to as "work packages," and represent those tasks, materials, and processes that can be estimated in terms of cost, resource

39 Steps

General Information

Show Name:	39 Steps	
Theatre Name:	Weston Playhouse	
Estimate by:	Rich Dionne	
Material Budget:	$ 2,400.00	
Contingency:	10%	added to each unit
Shop Time:	0	
Time Contingency:	1.65	added to each unit

Show Budget Breakdown

Show Budget		$	3,000.00
Royalty			
Paint	15%	$	450.00
Welding		$	-
Hardware/Load In	5%	$	150.00
Dumpster		$	-
	0%	$	-
Subtotal		$	600.00
Material Budget		$	2,400.00

Shop Time Available

Date	Labor	Hrs	Wks of Build	Total
Monday	0	0	0	0
Tuesday	0	0	0	0
Wednesday	0	0	0	0
Thursday	0	0	0	0
Friday	0	0	0	0
		Total:		

Page	Unit	Cost Estimate	Time Estimate
1	Upstage Wall	415.18	0
2	Masking Walls	632.98	0
3	Roll Drops		0
4	Folding Screen	159.84	0
5	Inn Sign	47.61	0
6	Shellach Wall	124.56	0
7	Edinburgh and Vote Signs	289.95	0
8	Curtain Unit	73.92	0
9	Bridge Unit	109.74	0
10	Stile	39.55	0
11	Apron Plug	277.05	0
12	Trap Plug	316.22	0
13	Door Units	113.78	0
14	Train Unit	109.16	0
15	15		0
16	16		0
17	17		0
18	18		0
19	19		0
20	20		0
	Total:	2,709.54	
	Budgeted Amount:	2,400.00	
	(Surplus) Deficit:	309.54	

Figure 6.1. Unit list (with cost estimates) for *The 39 Steps*

The Crucible **Dressing List**

Character	Costume Piece
John Proctor	Tights/Long Socks Period Shirt Brown Knickers Coat/Doublet Collar and Cuffs Gun holster Knee High boots Jacket with Tie in Sleeves Distressed Period Shirt Distressed knickers Hat?
Reverend Parris	Tights Period Shirt 2 pc. Coat/Sleeves 2 pc. Knicker Collar and Cuffs Heeled Shoes Hat Cape
Reverend John Hale	Tights Period Shirt 3 pc. Knickers 3 pc.Waist coat 3 pc.Coat with cuffs Cravat Buckle shoes Hat
John Putnam	Tights Period Shirt 2 pc. Knickers 2 pc. Coat Lace Collar and Cuffs Hat Buckle Shoes
Deputy Governor Danforth	Black Tights Brown Cord Knickers Period Shirt Coat Black Judges robe White Cravat Judges Wig Black buckle shoes
Judge Hathorne	Tights Period Shirt Knickers Waiscoat Robe Hat Buckle Shoes
Giles Corey	Tights Baggy Knickers Period Shirt Simple Vest w/ tie Hat? Shoes

Figure 6.2. Dressing list for a production of *The Crucible*

requirements, and time required. Terminal elements, then, are those tasks, materials, or processes that can be *scheduled*—they require a specific set of resources, take a known (or reasonably estimated) duration, and cost a known (or reasonably estimated) amount of money to complete.

Most of those who manage technical projects in theatre do some of this already—often as part of the costing process, for example, when breaking a set design up into "units" (e.g., walls, platforms, and flown flats), or a light plot into hang charts for different positions, or a costume design into types or classes of characters to begin to understand the units/items (e.g., leads, ensemble, party looks, women's wear, men's wear, hats, masks, and shoes). However, without specifically generating a work-breakdown structure and thinking in detail about the ways in which the project, and each unit, and each part of each unit, and each component of each part (or each costume rendering, each part of each rendering, and each component of each part) can be broken down into more specific and detailed elements, we miss the opportunity to fully understand how a set or costume design will work its way through the shop.

In theory, creating a work-breakdown structure is straightforward: simply list the steps involved in completing the project. However, in practice generating a work-breakdown structure relies on a handful of important and not necessarily intuitive tenets.

- *The work-breakdown structure must include 100 percent of the work required to complete the project.* It is easy to remember you have to build the flat, paint the floor, buy the fabric, or make a mock-up. It is sometimes easy to forget, however, that you have to get stock flats from storage, pull the correct-sized petticoats from storage, inventory the shoes in stock to be prepared for the first fitting, or rent a truck (to get stock flats from storage and return them after strike). It is also easy to forget that all the management work—estimating, scheduling, drafting, and the like—is part of the project. To be useful, a work-breakdown structure must include all the work that makes up the project, from drafting to estimating, to patterning and cutting, to fittings, to applying trim, and touching up paint scuffs on the floor prior to opening. (See more on this in the section "'Software' or 'Planning' Tasks" below.)
- *The work-breakdown structure need not be sequential.* A work-breakdown structure represents the work that needs to be done to complete a project, but does not represent how or when that work will be completed.
- *The work-breakdown structure need not be symmetrical.* Some branches of a work-breakdown structure will be more complicated than others, requiring multiple levels before being broken down to the smallest packages. For example, a complex, detailed, architectural wall may have more levels than a simple projection surface; an Elizabethan dress with farthingale understructure, large mutton sleeve, and neck ruff will have more levels than a 1920s flapper dress.
- *Parent, or higher level, packages or nodes should represent the*

total of all the packages or nodes immediately below them. Work-breakdown structures function a little like outlines: each level is a component of the level above it, and entirely encompasses all the levels below it.
- *Each branch must end in a package that represents the smallest level of detail required on the project (sometimes called a "deliverable").*

Consider the example below for the unit list of *The 39 Steps*. The topmost level consists of five parent nodes, which represent the entirety of the project: (a) planning and prep work; (b) static wall units; (c) units that are pushed on from the wings; (d) units that are flown and/or tracked on stage; and (e) decking or plug units for the stage floor. Each of these parent nodes is broken down into smaller packages; these child nodes comprise the entirety of each parent node. For example, the "push-on units" node is broken down into the following nodes: (a) the "folding screen"; (b) the "Shellach Wall"; (c) the "Edinburgh" and "Vote" signs; (d) the "bridge unit"; (e) "fence-stile" unit; (f) "door" units; and (g) "train" unit. In figure 6.3, the "folding-screen" node is shown broken down into its component child nodes.

Level of Detail

One of the key questions to ask about a work-breakdown structure (or a task/unit list), is how far do you break the project down? How small a task is small enough? Unfortunately, there's no easy answer to this question; the work represented by the lowest nodes in each branch must be small enough to be easily estimable and schedulable, but not so small that these managerial tasks become overwhelming, impractical, and unproductive. It is easy, for example, to break the task "build a flat" into increasingly smaller nodes until you get to tasks like "get screws," "drill pilot holes," "staple joints." It is unlikely that at the technical manager level you'll be scheduling the timing and order of these tasks in the build of the flat; rather, you'll likely want to deal with larger-scale issues like "cut framing," "attach facing," and "paint," or "pattern mock-ups," "first fittings," "polish shoes."

One good rule of thumb is to consider the smallest unit of time you'll consider scheduling or that you are responsible for managing: Is this an hour, a day, a week, a month? (Quarter- to half-day, or two- or four-hour increments tend to work well.) Nodes within the work-breakdown structure should not be broken down into tasks that take less time to complete than the length of this smallest unit. For example, if you plan to break your schedule up into week-long increments, a package that takes a day to complete is too small.

> When thinking about the level of detail in a work-breakdown structure the scalability of this management tool becomes clear. For example, a technical director might break down tasks to the level of a day or half-day increments, as indicated here. However, a production manager in charge of planning the whole project may think in terms of weeks, not days. Both are acceptable choices; they simply reflect the different scale of detail each level of management of the project is responsible for.

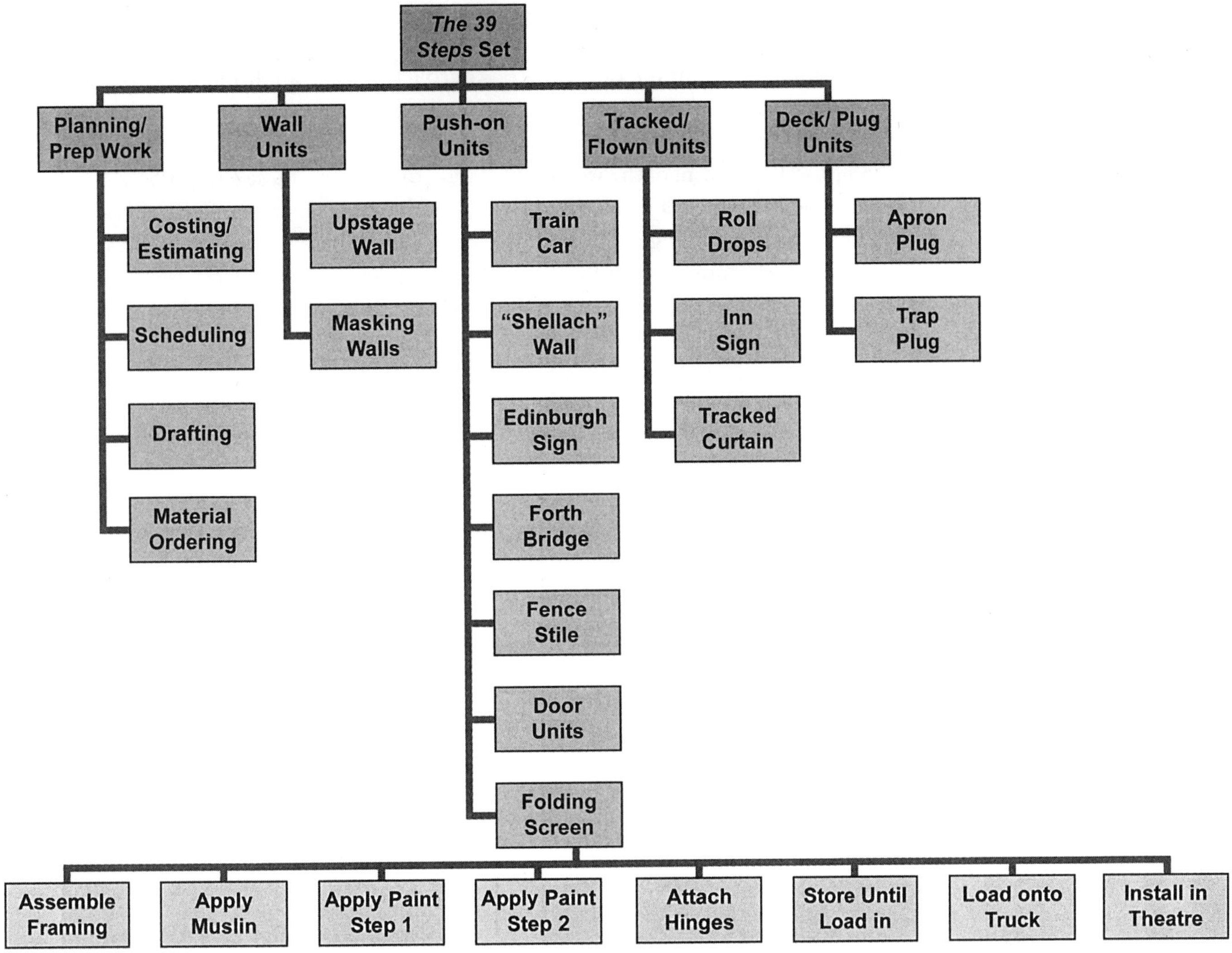

Figure 6.3. Example of a work-breakdown structure for a scenic design for *The 39 Steps*. Due to space, this figure shows only the lowest level of nodes for the "folding screen" node.

"Software" or "Planning" Tasks

When creating a work-breakdown structure, the physical tasks required to complete a project are easy to remember and identify; you can't build a flat without assembling the framing or assemble a costume without stitching the sleeves in, for example, so it is unlikely the "assemble framing" or "stitch fabric" packages will be forgotten on your breakdown. We might consider these tasks *hardware* tasks—they require equipment, materials, and other physical "hardware" to complete.

Every project also includes *software* tasks. Software, obviously, refers to computer applications, and includes all those tasks that require software applications to complete. These might include generating schedules or cost estimates, writing inspection manuals, preshow or postshow checklists, load-in plans, strike plans, and the like. But software tasks might also, less obviously, include planning steps that don't necessarily require software but aren't really hardware: calling vendors for material quotes, placing material orders, and attending scheduled or impromptu production or design meetings.

No work-breakdown structure can be said to comprise 100 percent of the work required to complete a project if software tasks are not represented along with hardware tasks. Unfortunately, software tasks often fly under the radar screen of most technical managers. Remembering to consider and include these tasks in the work-breakdown structure can make subsequent estimating and scheduling tasks (examples of software tasks, incidentally) significantly easier and more accurate.

Forgotten Tasks (Contingency)

Of course, no project would be complete without all the myriad things that were forgotten by those involved. How many times have you worked on a scenic build where a technical director said he had forgotten to confirm that the shop had enough shackles to rig a unit, or a set designer said she didn't remember until during the first read through that the sink on stage had to actually work for that one minor scene in act 2? Contingencies are ways to deal with these elements.

Additional costs due to forgotten elements or unforeseen circumstances can't simply be billed to the client/producer. They usually can't easily be subsumed by the team members the way contractors might on a more traditional industrial project. Consequently, it is important in the definitive estimate of any project to include a contingency line item. This line represents funds not currently allocated, but that are available should things go sideways. Typically, a solid contingency amount will comprise about 10 to 15 percent of the total expenses of a project.

> In contrast to contingencies, which are helpful for managing the unexpected on a project, padding is often applied to cost (and labor) estimates to account for efficiency and for quality of materials. For example, a delivery of 2 × 4 lumber may include sticks that are too warped to be useful, or some portion of fabric from a bolt may be discolored or stretched in ways that make it unusable. Adding padding—inflating the cost estimate for each material by 1 or 2 percent, or by rounding the amount of materials required slightly higher—allows the cost estimate to account for these situations. Of course, padding must be done carefully and with integrity; a design element that requires only four 2 × 4s shouldn't result in an estimate padded to ten 2 × 4s, or a costume that requires two yards of chiffon shouldn't be estimated at five. Adding an extra stick or a yard, in each of these examples, would be sufficient.

Definitive Estimate

Compared to the analogous and parametric estimation approaches discussed in the previous chapter, the definitive estimate is significantly more time consuming. In a definitive, bottom-up approach, each project is broken into constituent units, and each unit is separated into component work packages (remember those work-breakdown structures?); these packages—the smallest deliverable chunk of each unit (think items, not processes—nouns, not verbs: "constructed framing," "applied facing," "base paint," "completed mock-up," and "fitted fabric costume") are assigned specific cost and labor estimates. Work-package estimates are totaled to generate unit estimates; unit estimates are totaled to arrive at total-project estimates. Given the specificity of the bottom-up approach, these estimates can generally be relied upon to be time consuming, but also incredibly accurate—provided the initial work-package estimates are accurate.

Tasks, packages, and nodes are all terms that refer to specific parts of different management and planning tools that are sometimes used interchangeably. Technically speaking, a task, a package, and a node are not all the same thing, but for our purposes the differences aren't especially significant. Each term can be used to refer to the smallest element of a work-breakdown structure, as discussed in this chapter, or in critical path analyses, precedence diagrams, and Gantt charts, as discussed in chapter 7.

Advantages and Disadvantages

Advantage of Accuracy

Just as a parametric estimate is more accurate than an analogous estimate—due to the increased level of detail involved—a definitive estimate is significantly more accurate than either an analogous or parametric estimate. A properly prepared definitive estimate can land to within 5 to 15 percent of the actual cost of a project.

Disadvantages

ACCURACY DEPENDENT ON LEVEL OF DETAIL

As was the case with parametric estimates, the accuracy of a definitive estimate is directly proportional to the level of detail of the estimate. This makes the work-breakdown structure an essential element of the definitive estimate; the more detailed the breakdown, the more likely it is that the cost projections that a technical manager assigns to each package and unit will be hard or fixed. The less detailed the breakdown, the more likely those cost projections become (educated) guesses.

REQUIRES SIGNIFICANT AMOUNTS OF TIME

Achieving the level of detail expected in a definitive estimate can be time consuming—indeed, it should be time consuming: the information provided in a definitive estimate should represent as comprehensive a look at the costs of a project as is possible before the project is under way. Generating a work-breakdown structure takes a lot of time; assigning specific costs for all the materials required for each package takes even more. However, comprehensive completion of the definitive estimate usually saves significant time later in the process.

REQUIRES FULLY FLESHED-OUT DESIGN

A definitive estimate is only as accurate as the definition of the scope of the project provided to the technical manager. Lack of detail or ambiguities of detail in designer drawings, costume renderings, light plots, or models produce gaps in the picture that the work-breakdown structure provides, and, consequently, hamper the accuracy of the definitive estimate.

Elevations for the walls of a period box set may have only a vague suggestion of a crown molding and chair rail. A technical manager may indicate in the estimate that these details will have only minimal cost—believing them to be either painted or built from shapes already in the shop—but when, in the rehearsal process, she finds that those trim details will instead be made of six-dollar-per-foot custom-fabricated molding, the technical director's estimate becomes completely inaccurate. Similarly, based on costume renderings that feature squiggly lines around the hem of a wrist ruffle, a costume shop manager has provided an estimate for wide lace fabric. In conversation, however, she discovers that the fabric is chiffon with an applied lace edging. The estimate is now inaccurate, appropriate materials still need to be acquired, and labor needs will increase.

Reference Material

Construction Methods

One of the most important resources for generating the definitive estimate, once the work-breakdown structure has been completed, is an understanding of the construction methods and materials used for each and every deliverable or work package in the work-breakdown structure. This will usually come in the form of construction drawings, renderings, costume patterns, or other artifacts, or, at the very least, in relatively detailed sketches. Unfortunately, for the project manager, these details don't often come from the designers or the director on a live-entertainment project. Rather, members of the team responsible for the technical areas realizing the designs need to come up with both the estimates and the materials that inform those estimates. A technical director has to not only estimate the cost of construction of the set, but also generate the plans for determining how the set is constructed. The draper and the costume-shop manager must coordinate in determining how the costumes will be made as well as how much it will cost to make them.

> Why do all the work of drafting the construction of an entire show when you haven't even determined that you can produce the show? On the face of it, this certainly seems like a waste of time, especially when there are competing pressures—in, say, a regional or summer-theatre venue—to complete any number of other projects. Conversely, however, how definitive can one be in stating how much material is required to complete a work package until one has determined how much material is required? The more detailed knowledge a project manager has of the construction materials and techniques that will be applied toward each work package, the more detailed the estimate of those packages will be.

Current Material Costs

Material costs, depending on the time of year and the area of the country in which you are working, can vary wildly from month to month—or even week to week. Having an up-to-date list of current material costs from your regular suppliers—as well as from those vendors you turn to less often—is an invaluable resource when generating a definitive estimate. Plywood costs can swing by as much as ten dollars per sheet from winter to summer months, for example; after Hurricane Katrina devastated the Gulf Coast, plywood prices soared as demand for ever-dwindling supplies increased during attempts to rebuild.

A quick and easy way to generate a material-cost reference sheet is to send out a "request for pricing" or "request for quote" sheet, listing all the materials you expect to use during a given production, season, or time frame (figure 6.4). Vendors will usually send a list of prices back within the same day. Once you have received replies, you can collate the information and determine who has the best prices for which materials.

Keeping all this information in a spreadsheet is also incredibly useful, as it can be referred to quickly and easily. *Dynamic* spreadsheets are even more useful—by simply indicating units of material, the spreadsheet "looks up" the price and tallies the cost. Dynamic spreadsheets

Weston Playhouse
703 Main Street
Weston, VT 05161

Request for Pricing
May 25, 2010

Contact
Rich Dionne

Vendor
RK Miles
Manchester Center, VT

Materials:

Dimensional Lumber
1x4x8', D Spruce
1x4x10', D Spruce
1x4x12', D Spruce
1x4x16', D Spruce
1x6x8', D Spruce
1x6x10', D Spruce
1x6x12', D Spruce
1x6x16', D Spruce
1x10x8', D Spruce
1x10x10', D Spruce
1x10x12', D Spruce
1x10x16', D Spruce
1x12x8', D Spruce
1x12x10', D Spruce
1x12x12', D Spruce
1x12x16', D Spruce
1x4x8', #2 Pine
1x4x10', #2 Pine
1x4x12', #2 Pine
1x4x16', #2 Pine
1x6x8', #2 Pine
1x6x10', #2 Pine
1x6x12', #2 Pine
1x6x16', #2 Pine
1x10x8', #2 Pine
1x10x10', #2 Pine
1x10x12', #2 Pine
1x10x16', #2 Pine
1x12x8', #2 Pine
1x12x10', #2 Pine
1x12x12', #2 Pine
1x12x16', #2 Pine
2x4x8', #2 Pine
2x4x10', #2 Pine
2x4x12', #2 Pine
2x4x16', #2 Pine
2x6x8', #2 Pine
2x6x10' #2 Pine
2x6x12', #2 Pine
2x6x16', #2 Pine
2x8x8', #2 Pine
2x8x10', #2 Pine
2x8x12', #2 Pine
2x8x16', #2 Pine
2x10x8', #2 Pine
2x10x10', #2 Pine
2x10x12', #2 Pine
2x10x16', #2 Pine
2x12x8', #2 Pine
2x12x10', #2 Pine
2x12x12', #2 Pine
2x12x16', #2 Pine
Sheet Goods (4'x8', unless otherwise noted)
1/4" AC Ply
1/2" AC Ply
3/4" AC Ply
1/4" BC Ply
1/2" BC Ply
3/4" BC Ply
1/4" CDX Ply
1/2" CDX Ply
3/4" CDS Ply
1/4" MDF
1/2" MDF
3/4" MDF
1/4" OSB
7/16" OSB
1/2" OSB
3/4" OSB
1/8" Tempered Hardboard (Masonite)
1/4" Tempered Hardboard (Masonite)
1/8" Non-Tempered Hardboard (Masonite)
1/4" Non-Tempered Hardboard (Masonite)
1/8" Lauan
1/4" Lauan
1/4" "Brickenite" or "Z-Brick"

Notes

Please indicate delivery charges, if any.
Please fax back to Rich Dionne

Figure 6.4. Request for lumber-pricing template

include cells and formulae that reference other cells and data in other parts of the spreadsheet. Generating a dynamic spreadsheet that includes a table of material-pricing information, individual-unit sheets, and referential equations can be time consuming. But the time saved in future estimate generating often makes the investment worthwhile (unless a colleague has one he is willing to share).

Method

Completing a definitive estimate is a straightforward process: for each package in the work-breakdown structure, determine how it will be constructed or whether it will be pulled from stock, purchased, or rented. From that information, determine what materials will be required, and how much of each material will need to be purchased (and how much can come from stock, or be borrowed or rented). It is good practice to add padding to these numbers to accommodate the occasional lower-quality piece of material. Using the materials cost reference information described above, it is relatively easy to determine total materials costs from the amount of materials required for each package.

Once each package has been totaled, these totals can be added together to determine the total cost for the project. A contingency of between 10 and 15 percent should be added to either each unit or to the total for the project. (Be sure the contingency figures are clearly labeled and represented in all documentation.) This final number represents the total, definitive estimate for the project.

Sample Formats

One of the primary purposes of the definitive cost estimate is to communicate information to the rest of the production team and the producer. Because different people understand information in different ways, having a variety of presentation formats and methods for the data contained in a definitive estimate is always very useful.

Figures 6.5 and 6.6 are examples of fairly bare-bones definitive-estimate cover sheets for a scenic and a costume build. These sheets summarize the pertinent information about the production, categorized by units, characters, items, or pieces. (Definitive estimates for multiple individual work packages, in most cases, are summed to generate these costs.)

One of the advantages of the unit/dressing breakdown is to demonstrate which aesthetic elements of the play cost the most money. This can be useful in that it allows the team to determine whether the amount of money spent on a unit is worth the impact that unit has on the overall production design. Typically, cover sheets like these are accompanied by multiple pages detailing the materials required for each unit.

Figure 6.7 is another definitive cost-estimate cover sheet; this cover sheet, however, presents some of the data in visual ways that may be more accessible to some members of the team. (It is fair to say that some people can be easily overwhelmed looking at figures on a page.) In this example, the relative cost of each unit compared to the whole is presented using a colored pie chart, making it easy to see how much of the total budget has been allocated to each unit. (This estimate cover sheet also includes a useful area for tallying up-to-date actual costs, which can be helpful during production meetings.)

The best-prepared definitive estimates do more than simply present an estimate

Damn Yankees

General Information

Show Name:	Damn Yankees	
Theatre Name:	Weston Playhouse	
Estimate by:	Rich Dionne	
Material Budget:	$ 4,000.00	
Contingency:	10%	added to each unit
Shop Time:	0	
Time Contingency:	1.65	added to each unit

Show Budget Breakdown

Show Budget		$	5,000.00
Royalty			
Paint	15%	$	750.00
Welding		$	-
Hardware/Load In	5%	$	250.00
Dumpster		$	-
	0%	$	-
	Subtotal	$	1,000.00
	Material Budget	$	4,000.00

Shop Time Available

Date	Labor	Hrs	Wks of Build	Total
Monday	0	0	0	0
Tuesday	0	0	0	0
Wednesday	0	0	0	0
Thursday	0	0	0	0
Friday	0	0	0	0
			Total:	

Page	Unit	Cost Estimate	Time Estimate
1	Floor and Apron	81.38	0
2	False Proscenium	455.52	0
3	Portal One	243.58	0
4	Portal Two	243.58	0
5	Grey Masking	247.10	0
6	Meg's House	850.60	0
7	Locker Room-Dugout		0
8	Roving Stands	193.05	0
9	Orchestra Platform	424.86	0
10	Applegates		0
11	Welch's Signs	45.44	0
12	Billboard	253.83	0
13	Pennants	231.58	0
14	Escapes		0
15	Traveler		0
16	16		0
17	17		0
18	18		0
19	19		0
20	20		0
	Total:	3,270.52	
	Budgeted Amount:	4,000.00	
	(Surplus) Deficit:	(729.48)	

Figure 6.5. Cover sheet from estimate for *Damn Yankees*

The Statesman Designer: Judy

Costume Estimate Cover Page

Actor	Character	Act/Scene/ Costume	Cost Estimate
Mandy	Melody	1.2	$910.00
		2.1	$250.00
		2.2	$300.00
		3.1	$315.00
		3.2	$450.00
		Subtotal	$2,225.00
Rob	Statesman		$1,125.00
		Subtotal	$1,125.00
Matthew	Police Officer		$375.00
	Davey		$1,355.00
		Subtotal	$1,730.00
John	Phil	1.1	$815.00
		1.2	$815.00
		2.2	$650.00
		3.1 (repeat 1.1)	$0.00
		3.2	$820.00
		Subtotal	$3,100.00
Benjamin	Justin	1	$700.00
		2.1 (repeat 1)	$0.00
		2.2 (remove tie from 2.1)	$0.00
		3	$505.00
		Subtotal	$1,205.00
		Total	**$8,260.00**

Figure 6.6. Cover sheet from a costume estimate. Names have been altered to honor confidentiality agreements.

of the cost of the production: they help guide a conversation about those costs by highlighting areas of interest or concern. This is important when a definitive estimate exceeds the funds budgeted for the project. It is generally not helpful to simply be informed that the show is not affordable. It is better, instead, to be shown how and why a show is not affordable, in a manner that highlights possible paths to reconciling the situation.

What makes the *Beauty Queen* budget presented in figure 6.7 so appealing is that it is immediately clear how much each unit costs. Had the scenic design been significantly over budget, however, it

The Beauty Queen of Leenane

Preliminary Cost Estimate

David Cermak – Technical Director | Current as of: 11/4/11

Central "Island"	Expected Costs	Actual Costs
Trusses	$517.17	
Main Deck	$632.75	
Upstage of Wall Deck	$118.24	
Facing	$29.68	
Total:	$1,297.84	

Wall	Expected Costs	Actual Costs
Flats	$558.79	
Window	$62.13	
Door	$93.31	
Steel Door Frame	$27.50	
Total:	$741.73	

Cabinets/Counters	Expected Costs	Actual Costs
Cabinets	$77.62	
Counters	$42.04	
Plumbing	$84.69	
Total:	$204.35	

Escape Bridge	Expected Costs	Actual Costs
Trusses	$52.77	
Carpet	$19.27	
Total:	$72.04	

Trap Unit	Expected Costs	Actual Costs
Staircases	$101.17	
Railings	$46.90	
Total:	$148.07	

Paint	Expected Costs	Actual Costs
Paint	$450.00	
Show Deck Paint	$260.90	
Texture Elements	$50.00	
Total:	$760.90	

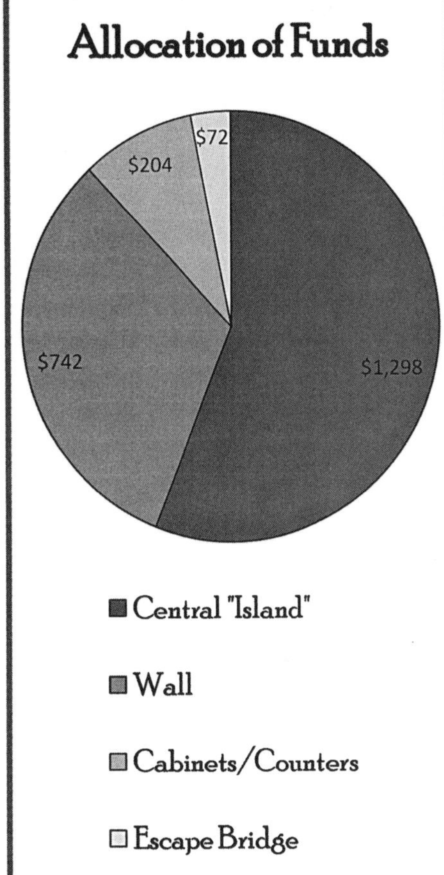

Budget Summary:	
Construction Materials	$3,224.92
Dumpster	$150.00
Show Deck	$300.00

Show Total	$3,674.92
Allowable Budget	$3,500.00
Difference	-$174.92

Figure 6.7. Cover sheet from scenic estimate for *The Beauty Queen of Leenane*

might have been useful to see the "central island" portion of the graph broken up even further (since it is where the majority of funds are allocated). The "central island" refers to the raised playing area center stage on which the set sat; knowing how much of this number went toward framing of supports, platforms, the carved foam treatment the designer specified, and facing, would have enabled the team to immediately see possible options such as changing the carved treatment, reducing or increasing the height of the deck to be able to use stock supports, or changing the shape of the deck to be able to use stock decking materials.

This becomes the fundamental challenge of the definitive estimate: determining the places where specific decisions have caused the cost of the project to increase or decrease dramatically, and presenting the estimate in such a way that the ramifications of those decisions are clear to everyone working on the project.

The estimate in figure 6.8 for *Blithe Spirit* organizes costing information in a slightly different way. The *Blithe Spirit* set was a box set, and the technical director used a pie chart to indicate how much money was allocated for rough construction materials, how much for paint and scenic art, how much for molding and trim, how much for doors and windows, and how much for the automation effects that comprised the ghost effects called for in the script. This was a clever presentation of information, as it was unlikely a wall might be cut from the box set, but the amount of money allocated to paint and finish details like trim and molding might have been easy places to address cost overruns, as might also have been true of the ghost effects.

Figure 6.9 shows a detail page from the *Blithe Spirit* estimate. From this page, one can see clearly what specific materials and costs comprise the totals represented on the cover page. Figure 6.10, similarly, is a detail page from a costume design for a production of *The Statesman* (name changed to respect confidentiality agreements).

> The *Beauty Queen* and *Blithe Spirit* cover sheets include tracking information for actual expenses. However, the *Blithe Spirit* sheet also includes a visual comparison of actual expenses to estimated expenses in the form of a bar chart in the lower right. This tracking information can be especially useful for producers, directors, or production managers who might want an at-a-glance understanding of the state of actual expenses for the project. Tracking expenses during the project life cycle will be discussed in more detail in chapter 8.

Application

A definitive estimate is aptly named: it is a *definitive* prediction of the cost of a project, based on information that is as detailed as possible. Consequently, it can only be undertaken effectively when there is significant detail available; typically, in the theatre production process, this is after the design of the set has been finalized. The definitive estimate, because of this timing, can form a natural boundary between the project-definition and project-planning phases. Indeed, it often represents the first step in actively planning the execution of the set project.

Proper timing of the definitive estimate is essential. Too early, and there's not

Blithe Spirit 1/30/2012

Purdue University - Nancy T. Hansen Theatre

Scenery and Paints

Units	Estimated	Actual
Wall A	$0.00	
Wall B	$58.70	
Wall C	$152.50	
Wall D	$30.50	
Wall E	$61.00	
Wall F	$0.00	
Wall G	$129.20	
Wall H	$0.00	
Wall J	$61.00	
Wall K	$150.20	
Wall L	$140.85	
Wall M	$0.00	
Wall N	$61.00	
Wall P	$0.00	
Wall Q	$61.00	
Wall R	$0.00	
Wall S	$0.00	
Wall Supports	$56.55	
Total	$962.50	$962.50

Molding/Panels	Estimated	Actual
Panelling	$318.77	
Crown Molding	$175.67	
Chair Rail	$35.88	
Picture Rail	$59.94	
Total	$590.26	$590.26

Doors & Windows	Estimated	Actual
French Doors	$39.55	
Jambs/Casings	$309.66	
Window	$16.76	
Hardware	$212.00	
Total	$577.97	$577.97

Miscellaneous	Estimated	Actual
Bushes	$38.48	
Deck	$168.48	
Delivery	$25.00	
Total	$231.96	$231.96

Automation	Estimated	Actual
Misc. Materials	$250.00	
Total	$250.00	$250.00

Paint	Estimated	Actual
Paint	$800.00	
Total	$800.00	$800.00

Contingency	Estimated	Actual
10% Contingency	$316.27	
Total	$316.27	$316.27

Total Expenses	Estimated	Actual
	$3,728.96	$3,728.96

Actual Cost Breakdown

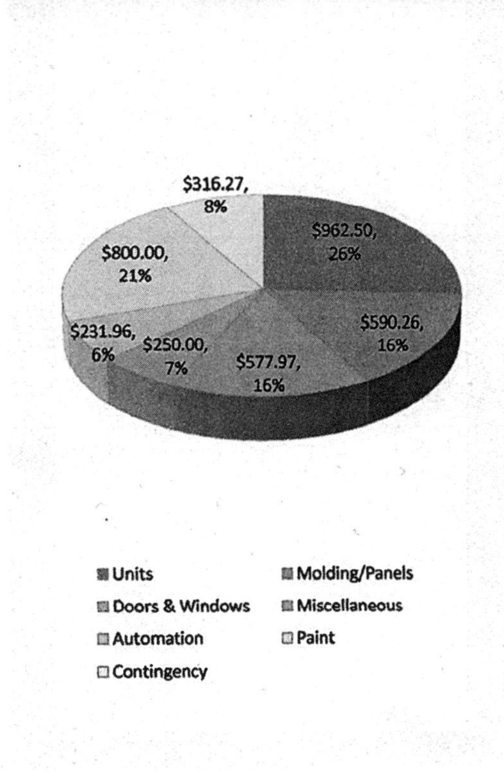

Estimated vs. Actual

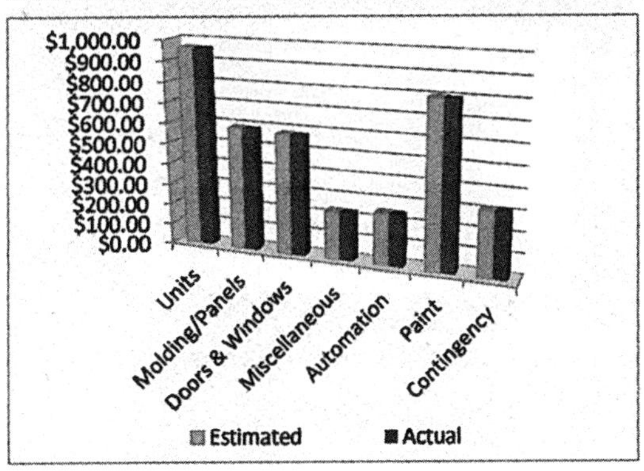

Spring 2012
TD: Jeremy Jenkins

Figure 6.8. Cover sheet for the scenic cost estimate for *Blithe Spirit*

Scenic Unit	Product Name	Unit	Price	Qty.	Quote Date	Vendor	Material Cost
Wall A	Stock Flat	4'x14'	$ -	1		Stock	$ -
Wall B	1x6x16	16' stick	$ 18.85	1	1/25/2012	Von Tobel	$ 18.85
	1/4" Lauan	sht	$ 11.65	1	1/24/2012	Menards	$ 11.65
	10' Muslin	yds	$ 7.05	4		Stock	$ 28.20
Wall C	1x6x16	16' stick	$ 18.85	5	1/25/2012	Von Tobel	$ 94.25
	1/4" Lauan	sht	$ 11.65	5	1/24/2012	Menards	$ 58.25
	10' Muslin	yds	$ -	1.5		Stock	$ -
Wall D	1x6x16	16' stick	$ 18.85	1	1/25/2012	Von Tobel	$ 18.85
	1/4" Lauan	sht	$ 11.65	1	1/24/2012	Menards	$ 11.65
	10' Muslin	yds	$ -	1.5		Stock	$ -
Wall E	1x6x16	16' stick	$ 18.85	2	1/25/2012	Von Tobel	$ 37.70
	1/4" Lauan	sht	$ 11.65	2	1/24/2012	Menards	$ 23.30
	10' Muslin	yds	$ -	1		Stock	$ -
Wall F	Stock Flat	2.5'x14'	$ -	1		Stock	$ -
	10' Muslin	yds	$ -	0.5		Stock	$ -
Wall G	1x6x16	16' stick	$ 18.85	5	1/25/2012	Von Tobel	$ 94.25
	1/4" Lauan	sht	$ 11.65	3	1/24/2012	Menards	$ 34.95
	10' Muslin	yds	$ -	4		Stock	$ -
Wall H	Stock Flat	2.5'x14'	$ -	1		Stock	$ -
	10' Muslin	yds	$ -	0.5		Stock	$ -
Wall J	1x6x16	16' stick	$ 18.85	2	1/25/2012	Von Tobel	$ 37.70
	1/4" Lauan	sht	$ 11.65	2	1/24/2012	Menards	$ 23.30
	10' Muslin	yds	$ -	1		Stock	$ -

Spring 2012
TD: Jeremy Jenkins

Figure 6.9. Detail scenic cost sheets for *Blithe Spirit*

enough information to be as definitive as possible; too late, and there may not be time to make changes necessary to the scope of the project definition and still complete the project. A carefully planned production calendar will take this balance into account, scheduling "budget meetings" or "costing meetings" at such a time that there is ample opportunity to both complete the design process and make necessary changes before the build of the project is put at risk.

Summing Up

Task Lists

Task lists (or unit lists) form the backbone of any definitive estimate; they are comprehensive lists of the units, structures,

The Statesman Designer: Judy

PIECE LIST

Mandy

Act	Character	Add/Remove	Costume Piece Description	Notes	Cost	total
1.2	*Melody*		girdle		2 @$50	$100
			bra: 60s style		2 @$100	$200
			dress: greyish-blue tint w boxpleat, a-line	belted		$300
			jacket: matching jacket like a 2pc suit	double breasted		$200
			shoes: dark-coloured, plain	avoid ankle strap	$100	$100
			earrings: simple			$10
			wig			
2.1	*Melody*		wig			
			blouse: button-down, puffed sleeves			$100
			skirt: a-line, brownish pattern			$100
			scarf: silk, greenish blue, yellow			$50
2.2	*Melody*		dress: purple plaid shirt dress	belted		$300
3.1	*Melody*		dress: sea-green, pleated, belted			$200
			campaign button			$15
			cream shoe			$100
3.2	*Melody*		dress: coral pencil dress, yoked			$300
			gloves: crème			$20
			shoes: crème		repeat from 3.1	
			necklace: pearls			$30
			hat: white to go with gloves			$100
					Total	**$2,225**

Figure 6.10. Detail cost sheet from a costume estimate. Names have been altered to honor confidentiality agreements.

and tasks that need to be completed for the project to be fulfilled.

Work-Breakdown Structures

Work-breakdown structures are detailed versions of task or unit lists.

Work-breakdown structures break a project into the smallest units (called work packages) that can be easily estimated.

Work-breakdown structures must represent 100 percent of the work required to complete a project, including physical, mental, design, and other *software* work.

Work-breakdown structures need not be sequential, nor need they be symmetrical. Some branches will be longer than others.

Work-breakdown structures should break the project down into packages that are no smaller than the smallest unit of time scheduling; for example, if a build is scheduled in half-day chunks, a work-breakdown structure should break the project up into chunks that take about a half day (or longer) to complete.

Generating a Definitive Estimate

Definitive estimates should be based on the packages determined by the work-breakdown structure.

Definitive estimates are usually accurate to within 5 or 10 percent of the actual cost of a project.

Definitive estimates, because of the level of detail, are time consuming to complete.

The accuracy of a definitive estimate is dependent on the level of detail of the design materials being estimated and on the level of detail of the estimate itself.

To generate a definitive estimate, you need:

- A detailed, completed design
- A detailed understanding of the construction techniques used for each package
- A detailed list of the materials required for each package
- An up-to-date listing of materials costs, including freight costs

Definitive estimates should be presented in a manner that presents an overall picture of the costs of the project, highlights pertinent information, and suggests avenues of discussion for handling over-budget projects. This might include graphs, charts, and other visual aids.

7. Scheduling and Estimating Time

Any effective plan for a project must consider both the cost of materials and the amount of time the project will take to complete. While some industries may be able to stall project deliveries (due to poor planning or unexpected delays), the delivery date for a live-entertainment project usually cannot change. As the saying goes, "The show must go on," and the inviolability of opening night is a deeply entrenched value. Consequently, knowing whether a project can be completed before opening night, and planning how, are two essential aspects of the planning process for any live-entertainment project.

While few technical directors, production managers, directors, set designers, producers, or artistic directors have any trouble understanding how to compute the cost of materials for a given design, understanding and quantifying the *time* it will take to complete a project is a lot harder. We develop tools in our everyday lives to handle estimating costs. Just going to the grocery store teaches us to come up with a rough idea of how much we're putting in the cart so we don't show up at the register and find out we don't have enough money. But methods for planning and estimating time are a little more elusive.

We intuitively recognize that complex factors contribute to the difficulty in estimating how much time a project might take to complete.

- Different people work at different speeds.
- Some projects might be completed more quickly with more people doing them.
- Some projects might take more time to complete with more people doing them.
- How much space we have in which to work might make a project take longer.
- Having the right materials or equipment impacts project speed.
- The completion of one part of the project is dependent on the completion of another part.

These are just a few of the many factors that contribute to the time a project takes. Because many of us have not had to wrestle with these kinds of considerations in our daily lives, we may never have had to develop intuitive methods for quantifying time.

Some people—experienced technical directors, costume shop managers, production managers, and others with many shows under their belts—have developed, over time, an awareness of the many complexities that impact the scheduling of a project and determining how long a project will take to complete. These calendar magicians can often look at a project and accurately predict which elements will be completed quickly, which will take more time, and when the entire project might be completed. The rest of us, however, will need some tools to help us out.

Theatre has never been shy about emulating the best techniques, methods, equipment, and materials from other industries. And neither should theatre practitioners be shy about borrowing the best in the realm of project planning. Major historic undertakings (such as the Manhattan Project, the Polaris nuclear submarine project, and the Mercury-Gemini-Apollo space missions) have given rise to tools managers of live-entertainment projects can use to help quantify, visualize, and, most importantly, understand how time and available resources (including labor) impact the schedule of a project (and the time required to complete that project). These tools include the work-breakdown structure, the program evaluation and review technique (PERT), precedence diagrams, the critical-path method, and the Gantt chart.

Topics covered in this chapter:

- Estimating time and PERT
  - Efficiency and productive time
- Precedence diagrams
  - Nodes and work packages
  - Arrows and dependencies
  - Creating a precedence diagram
- Critical path
  - Early/late start/finish
  - Slack
  - Critical path
- Gantt chart
  - Milestones
  - Labor and resources
  - Resource- and time-limited scheduling
  - Duration, work, and units
  - Software tools

Estimating Time and PERT

The concept of a work-breakdown structure was explored in some detail in chapter 6. To review, a work-breakdown structure is a comprehensive chart detailing 100 percent of the work required to complete a given project. Like an outline, successively lower levels of a work-breakdown structure break a project into increasingly smaller and more-detailed nodes representing the work needed to complete the project. At the lowest level, the nodes represent work that can be scheduled and estimated, to which labor and resources can be assigned.

A work-breakdown structure provides a blueprint for the work required to complete a project, but that information has relatively little usefulness without an understanding of how long that work will take. Determining the amount of time required to complete any task or node is, in some ways, a subjective, or at least highly variable, process. I may take two hours to complete a task you can complete in one, or you may take two days to complete a task I can do in one. Further, estimating the time required for a task I've never done before is exceptionally challenging—I have no frame of reference to start from. To make matters even more complicated, the resources available to complete a task have an impact on how long each work package or node can take to complete.

One technique that can make estimating time less arbitrary is accurate time tracking during the completion of a project. Well-maintained records about how long work packages or nodes on projects took to complete (and the resources required to complete them) can be incredibly helpful references for determining the length of time required for analogous tasks on current or future projects. (Progress tracking will be covered in more detail in chapter 8, and archiving and maintaining project records will be covered in chapter 10.) As with analogous cost estimates, analogous time estimates are not terribly accurate, but can be a useful starting point.

Parametric estimates, discussed in chapter 5, are more accurate than analogous estimates, and can also be used to develop estimates of duration for work packages or nodes for which good parametric information exists. For example, we might know that, on average, painting faux-finish treatments on flats takes approximately one minute per square foot per step of treatment. If I have a thousand square feet of wall to paint using a treatment that takes three steps to complete, I can estimate that completing each step will take a thousand minutes, or about fifteen hours to complete.

Definitive time estimates—like definitive cost estimates—break down each package into component steps that can be easily estimated individually and added together to determine the total time required for a task. For example, consider the time required to assemble the framing for a 4-foot × 8-foot flat. It may take five minutes to get a 1 × 6 from the lumber rack and rip it to two 1 × 3 boards. It may take another ten minutes to make all the crosscuts in each piece of 1 × 3, and another ten minutes to gather all of the pieces together and lay them out on the work table. Another five minutes may be required to measure and mark the locations of the toggles. Once all this is done, it may take another five minutes to glue and staple each corner, and a final two minutes to put the assembled frame out of the way to make room for the next task. In all, this work package can be estimated to take a total of thirty-seven minutes to complete.

Definitive time estimates like the one detailed above are incredibly tedious to complete. And, unlike definitive cost estimates, they can prove wildly inaccurate, as they depend on the specific experiences of the person doing the estimating. (As pointed out above, I may take ten minutes to do something you can complete in five.) And, typically, there isn't a plethora of parametric information available for many of the kinds of tasks a manager in theatre may need to estimate. Consequently, time estimates are often completed using an analogous approach.

To account for the inherent inaccuracies in an analogous approach to estimating time for work packages, an approach like that used in the PERT process can be used. The PERT method was developed in the 1950s for the US Navy Special Projects Office to manage the Polaris nuclear submarine project. It is a method for determining the duration of work nodes and packages in a work-breakdown structure. In the PERT process, four different estimates are generated for the duration of each activity or node:

- Pessimistic time (p): the maximum possible time required to accomplish an activity assuming everything goes wrong (excluding major catastrophes).
- Optimistic time (o): the minimum possible time required to accomplish an activity assuming everything proceeds better than normally expected.

- Most likely time (m): the best estimate of the time required to accomplish an activity assuming everything proceeds as normal.
- Expected time (e): the best estimate of the time required to accomplish an activity, assuming things don't always proceed as planned—that they sometimes go better, and sometimes go worse.

By considering the relationship among a pessimistic estimate of time, an optimistic estimate of time, and a "realistic" estimate, we can develop an average "expected" time estimate. The relationship among these four different estimates is described using the equation

$$e = \frac{(o + 4m + p)}{6}$$

In other words, the expected time to complete a task is the average of the optimistic, pessimistic, and most likely time estimates, with the most likely time estimate weighted four times greater than the optimistic and pessimistic times.

Consider, for example, a typical scenic flat, fourteen feet tall and ten feet wide, with a lauan cover and Hollywood-style framing. One might imagine that framing and skinning this flat might comprise a single work node, and that we could imagine this work taking about three hours to complete ($m = 3$). However, if things didn't go well—the lumber was warped, the lauan wasn't square, glue bottles were empty, and so on—this could take as long as five hours ($p = 5$). If things go very well, it might take as few as two ($o = 2$). Using these three estimates, we can calculate that the expected time required to complete this task would be 3.16 hours (about three hours and ten minutes). This expected time (e) is the duration of the task.

$$e = \frac{(2 + 4{\times}3 + 5)}{6} = 3.16 \text{ hours}$$

Efficiency and Productive Time

Each team member's skill level impacts how long he or she will take to complete a task. So does his or her efficiency. Efficiency can be defined as the amount of useful work completed compared to the amount of effort expended. In practice, efficiency relates to things like taking two trips to carry lumber when someone could have taken one, or marking a board on the wrong side and then remarking it, for example; these actions make a task take longer than it ideally needs to. (It is worth pointing out that while some employees may be more efficient than others, no one is 100 percent efficient.) A good rule of thumb for an average shop is to assume that your team members are about 80 percent efficient.

Further, on any given day, team members don't work for every hour; they take breaks (often mandated by state law and/or labor agreements), and they spend time getting the work space prepared at the beginning of the day and cleaning up at the end of the day. Any estimate of the time required to complete a task should take into consideration that these nonproject tasks take time as well, and therefore take time away from each work package.

Finally, as with cost estimates, some contingency should be planned for the unexpected—saw blades break, needles need to be replaced in sewing machines, for example. Unexpected events also take time from the work done on specific work packages or nodes. To account for this, some small contingency should be added to any time estimate; a typical contingency for time is about 10 percent.

The impact of efficiency, breaks, nonproject tasks, and contingency can be calculated using the following equation for determining a productivity multiplier.

$$h_{actual} = \frac{h_{worked}}{(h_{worked} - h_{unproductive}) \times \eta} \times c$$

Where:

h_{actual} = the actual length of time a task will take

h_{worked} = the hours worked per day/shift

$h_{unproductive}$ = hours worked without producing (e.g., breaks, cleanup)

η = average efficiency of team members (usually 0.80)

c = contingency for time estimates (usually 1.10, or an additional 10 percent)

Consider, for example, a typical eight-hour workday, with a mandated fifteen-minute break mid-morning and mid-afternoon, in a shop that typically sets aside about thirty minutes for cleanup at the end of each work day. (Team members also take a lunch break, but that is unpaid and not included in the eight-hour workday.) Because of these breaks, for every eight hours worked (h_{worked}), team members work one unproductive hour ($h_{unproductive}$; fifteen minutes in mid-morning, fifteen minutes in mid-afternoon, and thirty minutes at end of day). Given this, we can see that for every hour we estimate for a task, we should consider the task to actually take 1.57 hours.

$$h_{actual} = \frac{8}{(8 - 1.0) \times 0.8} \times 1.10 = 1.57 \text{ hours}$$

This equation can be used when determining pessimistic, optimistic, and most-likely time for use in PERT-weighted time estimates as described above. For example, if I envision the most-likely time for a work package to be 3 hours, and I have calculated a productivity multiplier of 1.57, I would use 4.71 hours (3 × 1.57) as the most likely time for my PERT calculations.

Because the concepts presented here and in the rest of the chapter are best illustrated using concrete examples, we'll refer throughout this chapter to the same example project while examining the application of these processes. The project "getting ready for work in the morning" is a good, easy-to-understand example of a project that will allow us to explore the concepts presented here. Figure 7.1 presents a work-breakdown structure for this project.

The lowest level nodes of the "getting ready for work" project comprise the following list:

- Brush teeth
- Shampoo (while showering)
- Wash (while showering)
- Iron shirt
- Put on clothes
- Put on tie
- Cook toast
- Pour cereal and milk
- Eat
- Clean dishes
- Warm up car
- Drive to work

Using the equations examined above, we can generate time estimates, as shown in figure 7.2, for each of these nodes. In this case, efficiency and the ratio of hours worked to productive hours are relatively inconsequential (we can safely assume that our imaginary person getting ready for work—let's

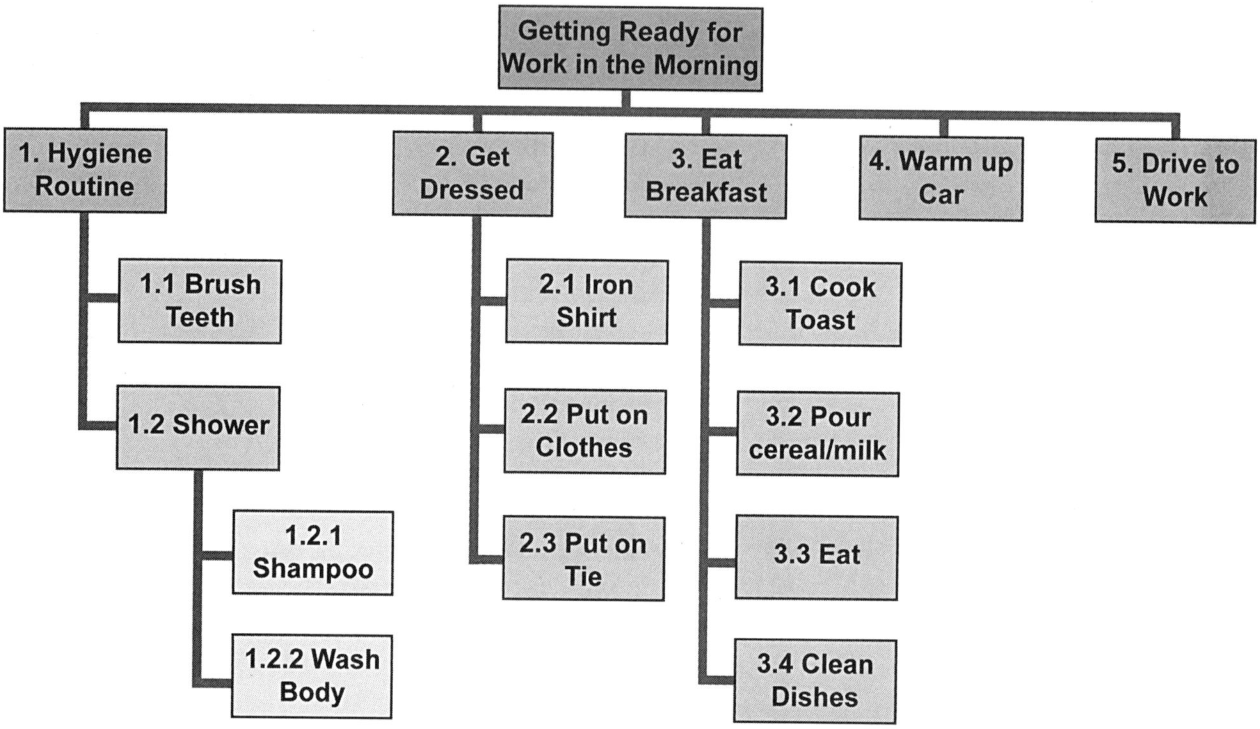

Figure 7.1. Work-breakdown structure for the project "getting ready for work in the morning"

Work Package	Pessimistic Time	Optimistic Time	Most Likely Time	Expected Time
Brush teeth	5 minutes	1 minutes	2 minutes	2.57 minutes
Shampoo (while showering)	7 minutes	3 minutes	5 minutes	5.5 minutes
Wash (while showering)	7 minutes	3 minutes	5 minutes	5.5 minutes
Iron shirt	7 minutes	3 minutes	5 minutes	5.5 minutes
Put on clothes	7 minutes	3 minutes	5 minutes	5.5 minutes
Put on tie	7 minutes	3 minutes	5 minutes	5.5 minutes
Cook toast	5 minutes	1 minutes	3 minutes	3.3 minutes
Pour cereal and milk	3 minutes	.5 minutes	1 minutes	1.38 minutes
Eat	20 minutes	12 minutes	15 minutes	16.87 minutes
Clean dishes	5 minutes	1 minutes	3 minutes	3.3 minutes
Warm up car	13 minutes	9 minutes	10 minutes	11.37 minutes
Drive to work	20 minutes	12 minutes	15 minutes	16.87 minutes

Figure 7.2. Time estimates for "getting ready for work in the morning"

call her Jane—isn't sitting around taking a break while getting ready, and is generally pretty efficient at this point in her life in the typical "getting ready" tasks). We can consider adding a small contingency—say, 10 percent—to any estimate we make to account for unexpected issues (such as spilling milk, dropping the shampoo bottle, or other things). Consequently, we should multiply our time estimates by 1.1.

> But wait: Doesn't the amount of time a task, work package, or node takes to complete depend on how many people are doing it (as well as how many other resources are used to complete it)? Absolutely—having two people work on a task instead of one can often ensure that task is completed more quickly; having two welding setups going at once can definitely hasten a metal fabrication project. However, what we are concerned with when we look at time estimates for projects is the time it would take if we completed a task as efficiently as possible—meaning with the most efficient allocation of resources. Later, when scheduling and resource allocation are completed, the impacts of whether enough resources are available can be accounted for. (Resource allocation and scheduling are discussed later in this chapter.) Doing so places the agreed-upon scope of the project as the most important constraint for completion of the project, not labor availability.

Precedence Diagrams

Once we have determined the length of time each work package in a project will take to complete, it would appear that simply adding the total time estimates for each work package will tell us how long the total project will take to complete. Unfortunately, planning and scheduling the work packages in a project is not that simple. Knowing how long each work package will take to complete doesn't tell us anything about when we can begin any of these elements, if any can be completed simultaneously, or what impact completion of any one element has on the rest of the project. A precedence diagram, however, takes this information and describes the relationship between each element by indicating dependences: which elements require the completion of other elements before they themselves can be started or completed, and which elements are required for the completion of other elements.

Precedence diagrams are one example of a variety of project-planning methods collectively known as network analysis. Network analysis methods are generally grouped under two umbrella categories: *activity-on-arrow* and *activity-on-node* networks; precedence diagrams are an example of the latter. In activity-on-arrow networks, arrows represent the work nodes and packages, and circular containers start, end, and duration times (figure 7.3) for each node. In activity-on-node networks, arrows represent dependencies, and rectangular boxes contain start, end, duration, and float times (figure 7.4).

Both activity-on-arrow and activity-on-node approaches have validity, but activity-on-node networks (like precedent diagrams) are more widely used as their visual representation closely resembles

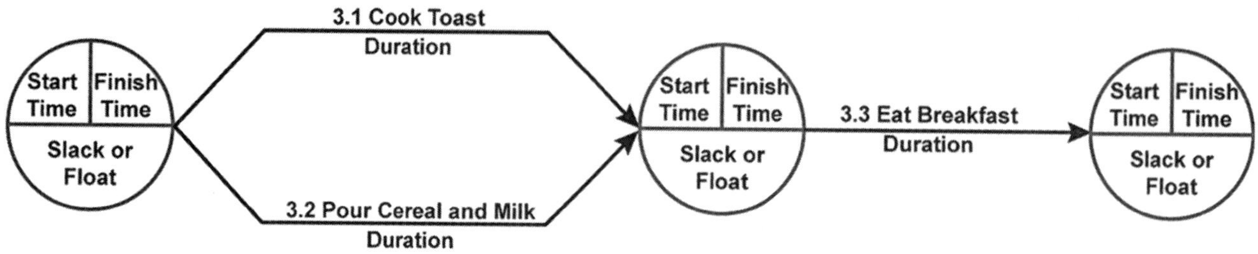

Figure 7.3. Activity-on-arrow network

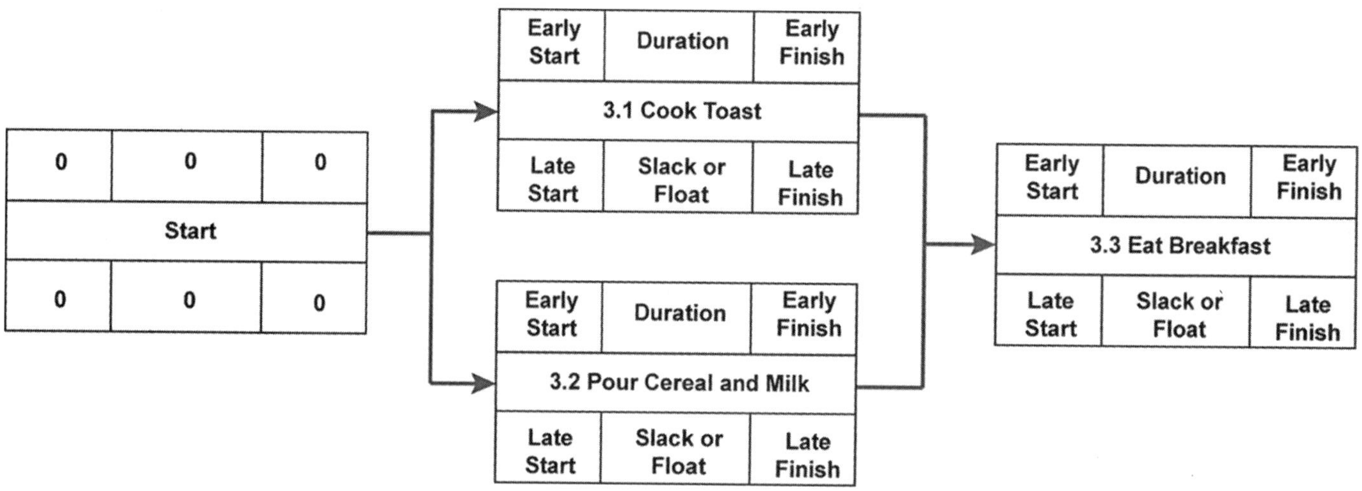

Figure 7.4. Activity-on-node network

Precedence diagrams, by definition, are comprehensive examinations of the work involved to complete a project, and the relationships between different chunks of the total project. Consequently, they can be big projects in and of themselves, taking a lot of time and effort to complete. It is tempting to ask, given how time consuming they can be to create, how often one will actually do it? Live-entertainment projects can often be fast and furious, and in that kind of environment, creating a comprehensive precedence diagram may seem daunting—if not impossible. Truthfully, not every manager will be able to take that kind of time.

However, precedence diagrams represent a *way of thinking* about scheduling a project. Learning to think about a project in terms of precedence and critical path gives a project manager a huge advantage when considering the build of even a quick-turnaround production project. Internalizing this mode of thinking is best done by applying the practice fully whenever time allows.

Given the complexity of precedence diagrams—and the understanding of a project in terms of work packages and their relationships—the next few sections of the text walk through the process of creating a precedence diagram step by step. You'll understand the material best by following along, pencil and paper in hand.

that of flowcharts, making them somewhat more accessible to those less experienced with network analysis. Additionally, critical paths (discussed later in this chapter) are easier to see and understand on activity-on-node diagrams than on activity-on-arrow diagrams. This makes precedent diagrams a good choice for managing projects in live entertainment, where many involved in the project will likely have little experience or background in network analysis.

A precedence diagram is made up of two main components: nodes and arrows. Nodes represent work packages—the lowest-level elements in a work-breakdown structure. Arrows represent *dependency relationships* between nodes: what nodes can't be started until others are completed, for example. When completed, a precedence diagram provides a visual representation of all the dependencies among nodes, and how those dependencies impact the scheduling of each node. When based on a work-breakdown structure—which, by definition, represents 100 percent of the work needed to complete a project—a precedence diagram will also represent 100 percent of the work required as well as the time required to complete the project based on the dependency relationships among nodes.

Nodes and Work Packages

Before creating the precedence diagram, for each node in the work-breakdown structure a list of *predecessor* and *successor* nodes should be compiled; predecessor nodes are nodes that must be completed before a certain other node can be completed, and successor nodes are nodes that are dependent on the completion of a certain other node for their completion. Just to keep things complicated, nodes can have multiple predecessor or successor nodes. (The dependencies between nodes can, of course, be other than the "finish-to-start" dependencies defined here; types of dependencies and their impact on the precedence diagram will be described in more detail later in this chapter.)

Consider our example project of Jane getting ready for work in the morning. To generate a precedence diagram for this project, we'll need to consider sequencing of the work packages in our work-breakdown structure. We do this by identifying predecessor and successor nodes. For example, the node "brush teeth," although listed first in our work-breakdown structure, probably doesn't happen until after the node "eat"; "eat" is a predecessor for "brush teeth," and "brush teeth" is a successor to "eat."

If we develop a list of predecessors and successors for each node in the work-breakdown structure, we might come up with a revision of the list that looks something like figure 7.5.

The list refers to each node by a unique number. Often, in precedence diagrams, unique numbers are assigned to nodes to make them easier to read. Next to the name of each node is the estimated length of time each task will take (from figure 7.2 above). Having identified all the dependencies among nodes in the work-breakdown structure, we can move on to defining the nature of those dependencies, then to building the precedence diagram.

Arrows and Dependencies

While the nodes in a precedence diagram represent the individual tasks and work packages determined in a work-breakdown structure, arrows

ID	Name	Duration	Predecessors	Successors
1.1	Brush teeth	2.57 minutes	3.3	5
1.2.1	Shampoo	5.5 minutes		1.2.2
1.2.2	Wash	5.5 minutes	1.2.1	2.2
2.1	Iron shirt	5.5 minutes		2.2
2.2	Put on clothes	5.5 minutes	1.2.2, 2.1	2.3, 4
2.3	Put on tie	5.5 minutes	2.2	5
3.1	Cook toast	3.3 minutes		3.3
3.2	Pour cereal and milk	1.38 minute		3.3
3.3	Eat	16.87 minutes	3.1, 3.2	1.1, 3.4
3.4	Clean dishes	3.3 minutes	3.3	5
4	Warm up car	11.37 minutes	2.2	5
5	Drive to work	16.87 minutes	1.1, 2.3, 3.3, 4	

Figure 7.5. Predecessor/successor chart for "getting ready for work in the morning"

represent the dependency relationships between these nodes. Dependency relationships between nodes can be described in one of four ways: finish-to-start, start-to-start, finish-to-finish, and start-to-finish. The types of dependencies are described in more detail below.

Finish-to-Start

The most common dependency is finish-to-start, which reflects the fact that a predecessor node must finish before a successor node can start. Occasionally, a finish-to-start dependency may also include a required time lag—to allow for paint to dry, for example. (Sometimes, this time is included in the duration of the predecessor task, in which case it is not listed again as lag in the dependency.) This lag is typically reflected in a precedence diagram by being written just above the arrow representing the dependency.

Start-to-Start

Start-to-start dependencies describe when a successor node can begin at some time after a predecessor node begins, and need not wait until that predecessor finishes. For example, cabling and circuiting lighting fixtures during a light hang can begin once the first light has been hung; it need not be delayed until all the lights have been hung. Often, a start-to-start will include a specific lag time as part of the dependency. As above (and as will be the case with other dependency lag times), this time is indicated above the dependency arrow.

Finish-to-Finish

A finish-to-finish relationship describes when a successor node cannot finish until after the completion of a successor node. This might describe the relationship between applying texture to create a brick-like surface to flats, and painting that texture an appropriate color. The painting work cannot be finished until the texture application has been completed. As with start-to-start dependencies, there may be a delay or a lag between the two finish times included as part of the dependency.

Start-to-Finish

A start-to-finish relationship is probably the least common relationship between work nodes, and describes when a successor node cannot be finished until a certain time after a predecessor node begins. Consider, for example, a situation during a load-in in which practical lighting units need to be installed into the ceiling of a box set, where the circuiting of those fixtures is included in the installation work node. If the installation of the fixtures must start before the ceiling is rigged and locked in place, but can only be circuited once the ceiling unit is in place, this would result in a start-to-finish relationship between the predecessor node (installing the lighting fixtures) and the successor node (rigging the ceiling).

Most work node dependencies are finish-to-start. The other three dependencies are rarely the most logical expression of a relationship between one work node and another. However, they can be useful when considering ways to shorten the overall duration of a project, because they can allow for overlapping of dependent nodes in ways that finish-to-start dependencies cannot. Therefore, in practice it makes the most sense to begin by considering all dependencies to be finish-to-start relationships unless a strong logical relationship suggests otherwise, and to reserve the ability to adjust some dependencies to start-to-start, finish-to-finish, or start-to-finish as needed later when examining the overall duration of the project.

When we consider Jane's getting ready for work project, it's clear that all of the dependencies are finish-to-start: Jane can't put on clothes until after she's completed ironing her shirt and washing in the shower, for example. There are two possible exceptions to this. We could, conceivably, start driving to work before the car has finished warming up, and we could begin eating cereal before the toast has cooked, or eating toast before the milk has been poured on the cereal. However, in our example, these start-to-start relationships don't improve the sequencing of our project significantly, so we can consider them as finish-to-start dependencies for clarity and simplicity.

Creating a Precedence Diagram

Once we've identified each node in our diagram, considered the duration of each node, and determined dependencies, we can begin to generate the actual precedence diagram. Every precedence diagram

<table>
<tr><td>Early Start</td><td>Duration</td><td>Early Finish</td></tr>
<tr><td colspan="3">Work Node ID and Description</td></tr>
<tr><td>Late Start</td><td>Slack or Float</td><td>Late Finish</td></tr>
</table>

Figure 7.6. Precedence diagram node

begins with a "start" node, at the left side of the diagram, and ends with a "finish" node, at the right side. These nodes have no duration and no actual work assigned to them. (These nodes can often correspond to major project milestones, discussed later in this chapter.)

Each node on a precedence diagram should be represented by a similar box symbol, as in figure 7.6. This symbol contains space for the name of the work node and/or unique identification number, the duration of the activity, and five additional pieces of information that the diagram itself will help determine: early start, late start, early finish, late finish, and slack (or float). When initially generating a precedence diagram, these will be left blank. Later in this chapter, when discussing the critical path, this information will be derived from the precedence diagram and the dependencies between nodes.

Next, beginning just to the right of the "start" node, place the nodes for all activities that have no predecessors, and connect these to the "start" node (figure 7.7). After placing these nodes, place successor nodes to these first nodes in the diagram, connected with arrows to their predecessor nodes. Continue in this fashion, working left to right, until you have placed nodes that have no successor nodes; connect these nodes to the "finish" node at the right side of the chart.

Figure 7.7 shows a precedence diagram for our example project, "getting ready for work in the morning." Notice how this visual representation of dependencies

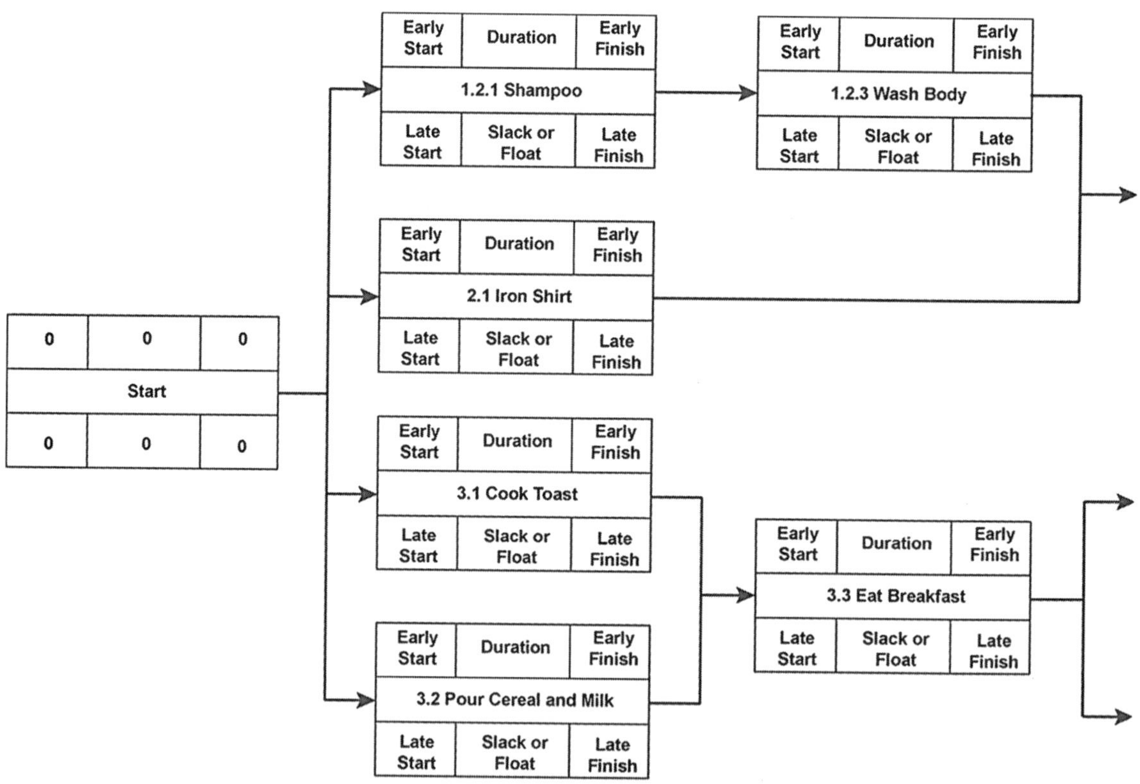

Figure 7.7. First-pass precedence diagram for "getting ready for work in the morning," showing the relationships between predecessor and successor nodes

demonstrates the logical connections between them without relying on the allocation of labor or other resources. For example, without allocating the resources, cleaning dishes, brushing teeth, and putting on clothes can all happen simultaneously. Obviously, when it comes to resource availability, that's not going to be at all possible.

There are two schools of thought on handling the allocation of resources in precedence diagrams. One approach is to assign labor and other resources now, and use that information to change the relationships of predecessors and successors (for example, changing the relationship between ironing a shirt and shampooing hair to reflect that one has to happen after the other because of labor availability). This approach assumes that labor resources are a constraint that cannot change. A precedence diagram generated in this way presents a clear picture of the amount of time a project will take to complete given the resources of the project.

The other approach to the relationship between resource allocation and precedence diagrams is to assume labor (and other resources) may not be constrained. In this approach, labor and other resources are allocated later in the process. A precedence diagram generated without allocating resources first presents a clear picture of the order and importance of nodes in the project to deliver the desired scope in the desired amount of time. This can then be used to determine what resources are needed for each node based on

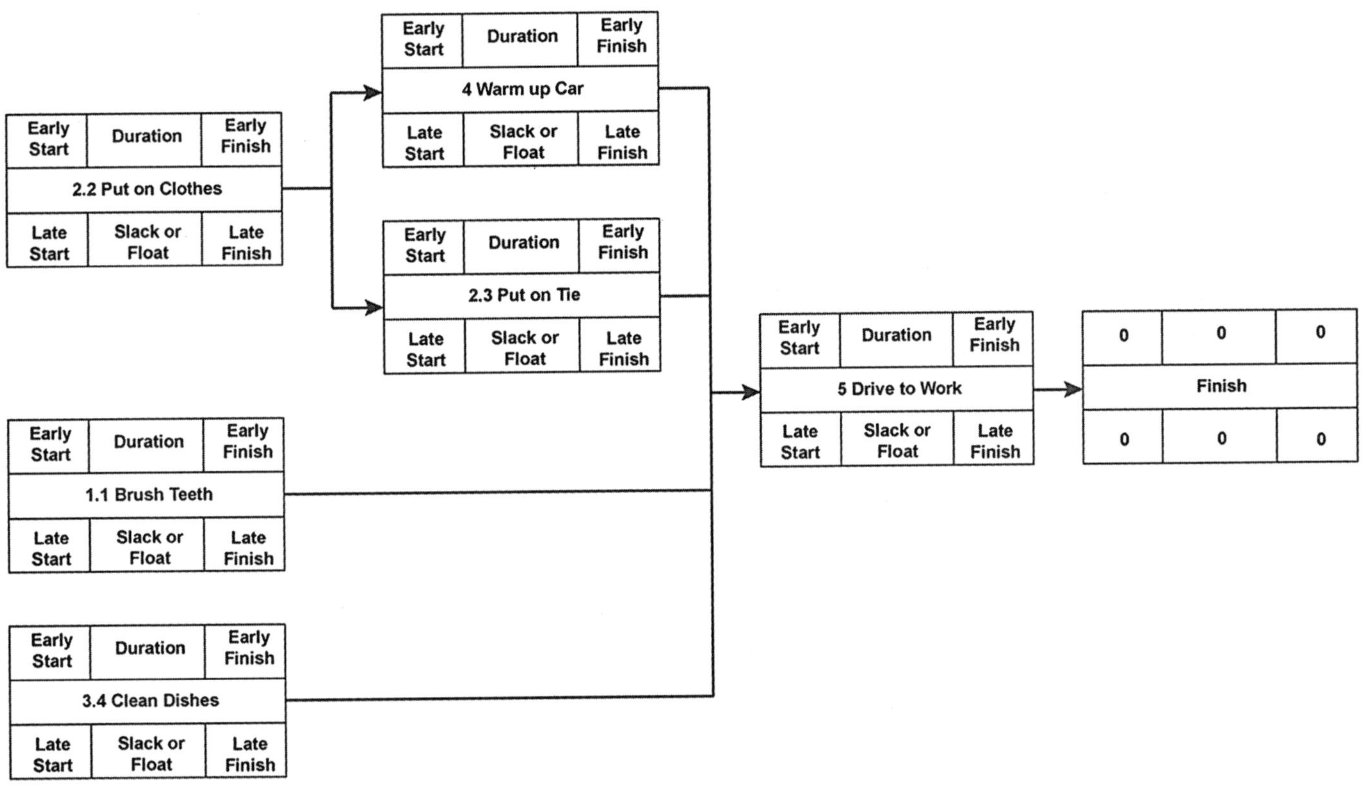

the relationships of successor and predecessor nodes (and, often, whether additional labor or other resources will need to be found to complete the project).

The first approach to labor and resource allocation assumes labor as a constraint, the second assumes scope and precedence as constraints. We will follow the second approach in this text. By demonstrating the requirements of a project based on the scope as presented by the design and artistic team, precedence diagrams that do not assume constrained labor (even if labor may, indeed, be limited and unable to change) are more transparent about the needs of the project from the perspective of the artists involved. Seeing the scope of the project in this way can help to identify areas of the project that can be slimmed down or otherwise have their scope reduced.

With the relationships between nodes visually laid out in the precedence diagram, the next step is to determine the order of priorities for these nodes and tasks. This process is commonly referred to as determining the critical path. The critical path is the sequence of dependent nodes whose completion—in order—determines the overall duration of the project. Determining the critical path relies on the "early start/early finish" and "late start/late finish" boxes we put in the precedence diagram chart nodes, and is discussed below. The critical path reveals which nodes should be allocated resources first, and how many additional resources might be needed to complete the project on time given the scope and expectations of quality defined at the start of the project.

> One of the major advantages of the precedence diagram is the way it emphasizes the relationships among work packages visually, making it easy to see the way progress in some parts of a project will impact other parts. One of the drawbacks, however, is how little a precedence diagram resembles a calendar. This can make it hard for those unfamiliar with precedence diagrams to connect the information they reveal to day-to-day or week-to-week schedules. For this reason, many turn to Gantt charts, discussed later in this chapter. Gantt charts look more like calendars, but dependency relationships can be harder to communicate clearly.
>
> Both precedence diagrams and Gantt charts can be unwieldy to generate and update, especially for larger projects. However, software tools—like Microsoft Project, and online tools like Gantter, Creately, and LucidChart—can make the process easier to work through.

Critical Path

The critical path of any project is the sequence of dependent nodes whose completion determines the overall length of the project. Using the dependencies between nodes as guides, we can determine the earliest and latest each node can begin, and use that information to identify those nodes that simply must start on time in order for the project to complete on time. These nodes and the dependencies between them define the critical path of a project, and the first step in finding the critical path is determining the *early* and *late start* and *early* and *late finish* of each node.

Early/Late Start/Finish

The precedence diagram node described earlier included a space to indicate the estimated duration of a task, as well as spaces for four additional pieces of information: "early start," "early finish," "late start," and "late finish." These five pieces, combined with the relational information the precedence diagram provides, can provide a good measure of when work nodes happen in our schedule relative to the start of the project.

For example, after building the precedence diagram for Jane's getting ready for work project, we can consider when is the earliest each of these elements can start, and—based on that start time—when is the earliest each can be completed. We do this by working forward through the chart, beginning with a start of 0 minutes. (Other precedence diagrams will use different units, such as quarter, half, or full days, as discussed previously; this example is best served by using minutes.)

Because each dependency on the diagram has been defined as finish-to-start, the "early start" time for each node cannot be any sooner than the latest "early finish" time of all predecessor nodes. For example, since the node "clean dishes," is preceded by the node "eat," the earliest start time for "clean dishes" would be the same time as the earliest completion time for the node "eat." Figure 7.8 shows the precedence chart with early start and early finish times added.

The dependencies among nodes has a direct impact on how the time analysis of each node is carried forward through the diagram. Consider, for example, the first time a single node has more than one predecessor node, node "3.3 eat." Each predecessor node has an early finish time of 5.5 minutes; consequently, the early start time for "3.3 eat" is 5.5 minutes. However, the node "2.2 put on clothes" has two predecessor nodes whose early finish times are different. In this situation, because the dependencies between nodes have been defined as finish-to-start, the earliest start time for "2.2 put on clothes" must be the *later* of the early finish times of its two predecessor nodes, 11 minutes, as it can't start before both of its predecessor nodes have been completed.

Different dependency relationships will impact the carrying forward of the time analysis in different ways. Imagine that we had previously determined that node "1.2.2 wash body" had a start-to-start relationship with the predecessor "1.2.1 shampoo," with a lag of one minute. In this situation, while the early finish time of the node "1.2.1 shampoo" would be 5.5 minutes, the early start time for node "1.2.2 wash body" would be one minute, because it could start one minute after the node "1.2.1 shampoo" starts.

After progressing forward through the diagram, we proceed *backward* from the final early finish time, 44.37 minutes; the late finish for each node will be based on the late start of all successor nodes, as shown in figure 7.9.

Similar to when progressing forward through the precedence chart, predecessor nodes with two or more successors have a late finish time equal to the earliest late start of the successor nodes. For some nodes, the early start and late start times are the same, while for others they are not. Nodes that do not have the same times for early start and late start are considered to have some amount of "slack" or "float."

Slack

Slack or float time represents the amount by which a node can be delayed (figure 7.10). Total slack (or float) refers to the amount of time a node can be delayed without causing a change in the project deadline. (It is total slack that is represented in the precedence diagram in figure 7.10.)

$$\text{Total Slack} = \text{Late Finish} - \text{Early Start} - \text{Duration}$$

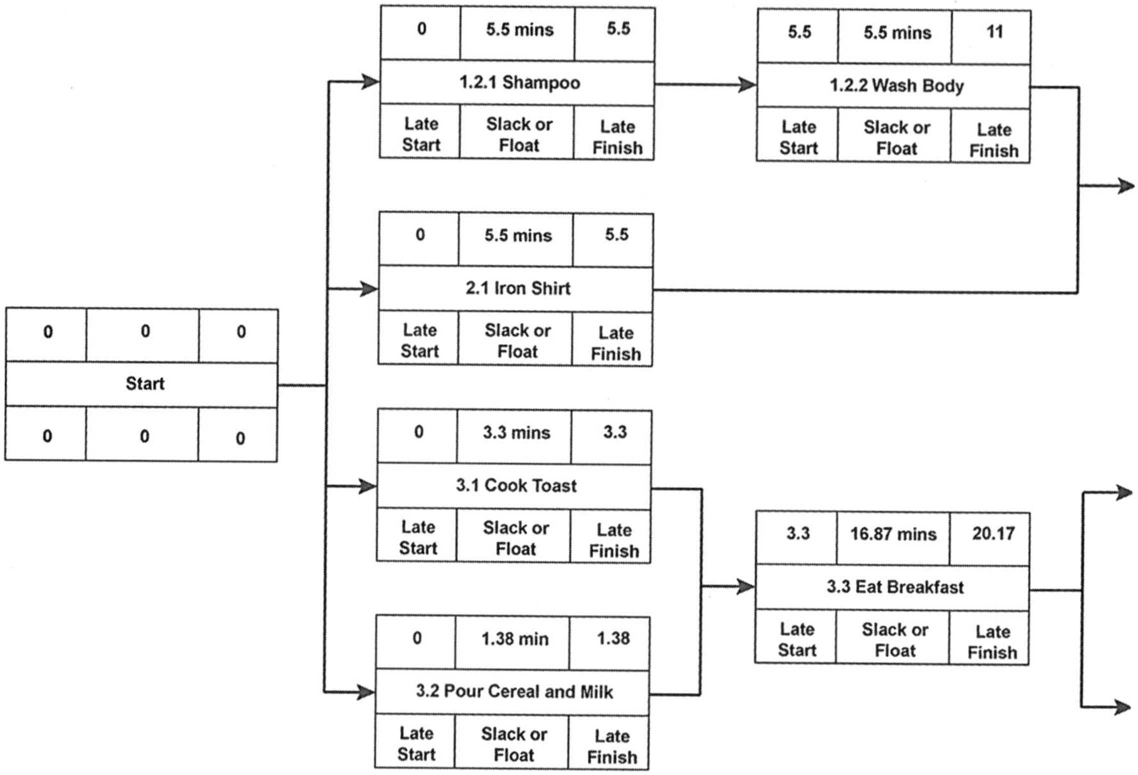

Figure 7.8. Precedence diagram for "getting ready for work in the morning," with early start and early finish times

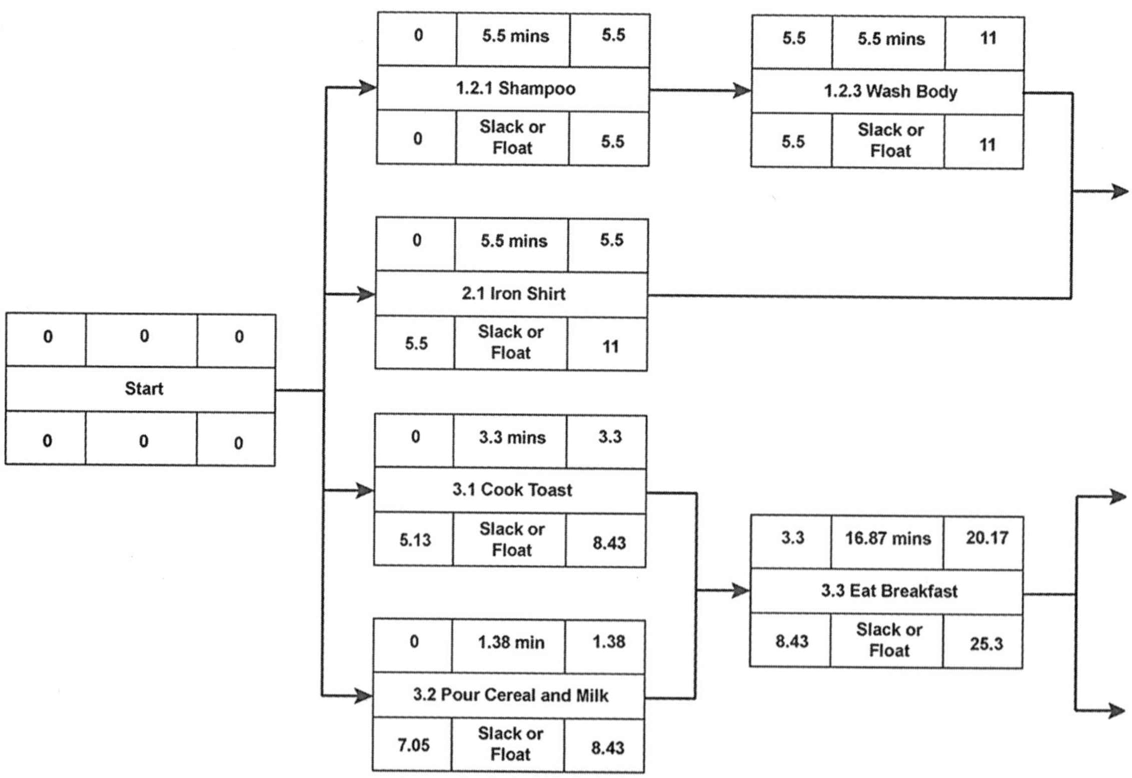

Figure 7.9. Precedence diagram for "getting ready for work in the morning," with late start and late finish times

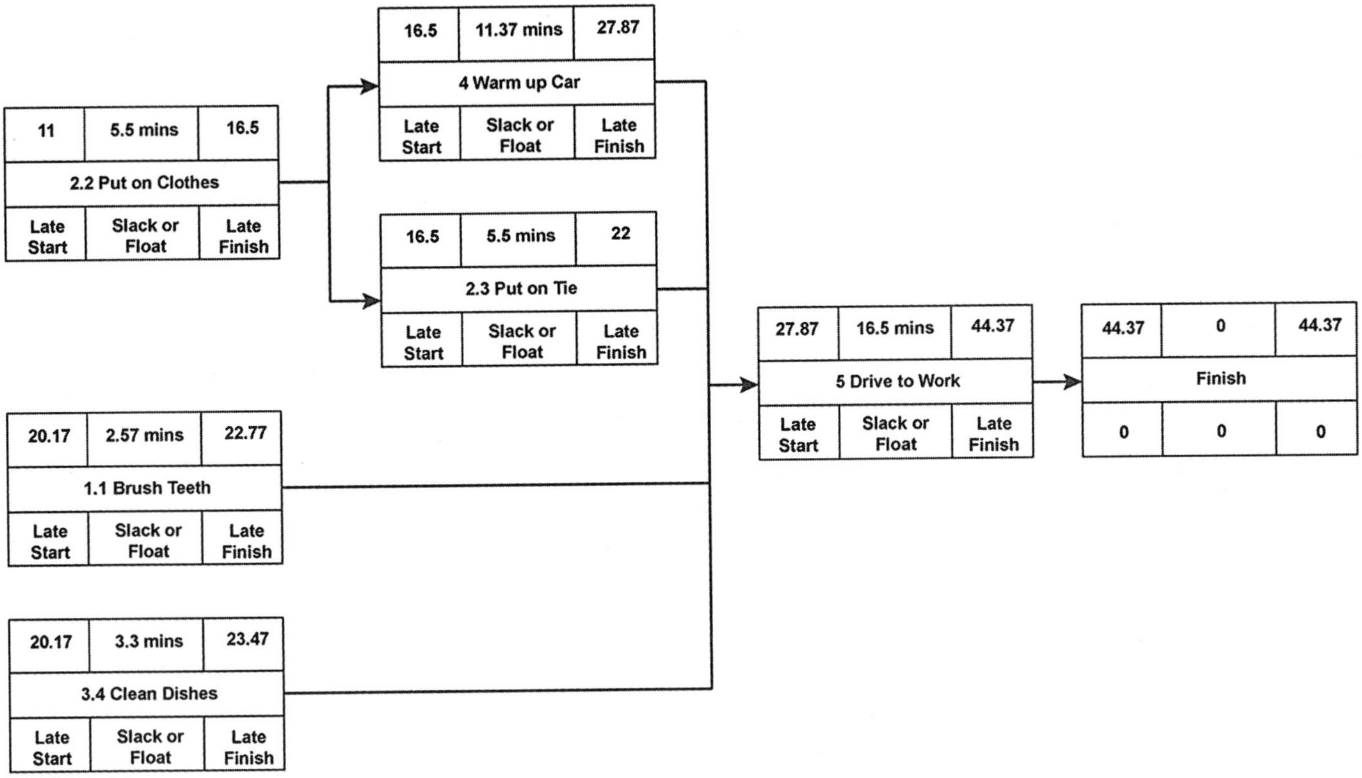
16.5
11.37 mins
27.87
4 Warm up Car
Late Start
Slack or Float
Late Finish
11
5.5 mins
16.5
2.2 Put on Clothes
Late Start
Slack or Float
Late Finish
16.5
5.5 mins
22
2.3 Put on Tie
Late Start
Slack or Float
Late Finish
27.87
16.5 mins
44.37
5 Drive to Work
Late Start
Slack or Float
Late Finish
44.37
0
44.37
Finish
0
0
0
20.17
2.57 mins
22.77
1.1 Brush Teeth
Late Start
Slack or Float
Late Finish
20.17
3.3 mins
23.47
3.4 Clean Dishes
Late Start
Slack or Float
Late Finish

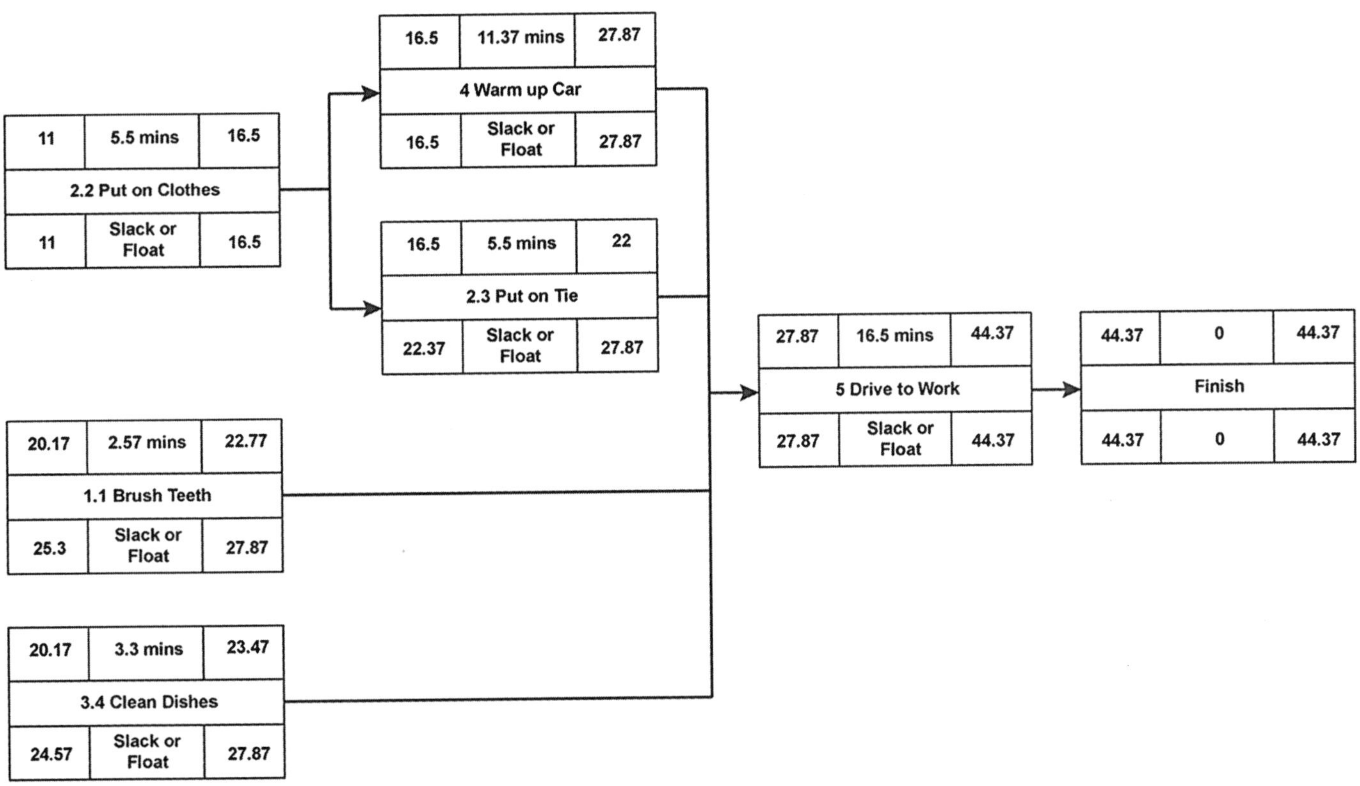
16.5
11.37 mins
27.87
4 Warm up Car
16.5
Slack or Float
27.87
11
5.5 mins
16.5
2.2 Put on Clothes
11
Slack or Float
16.5
16.5
5.5 mins
22
2.3 Put on Tie
22.37
Slack or Float
27.87
27.87
16.5 mins
44.37
5 Drive to Work
27.87
Slack or Float
44.37
44.37
0
44.37
Finish
44.37
0
44.37
20.17
2.57 mins
22.77
1.1 Brush Teeth
25.3
Slack or Float
27.87
20.17
3.3 mins
23.47
3.4 Clean Dishes
24.57
Slack or Float
27.87

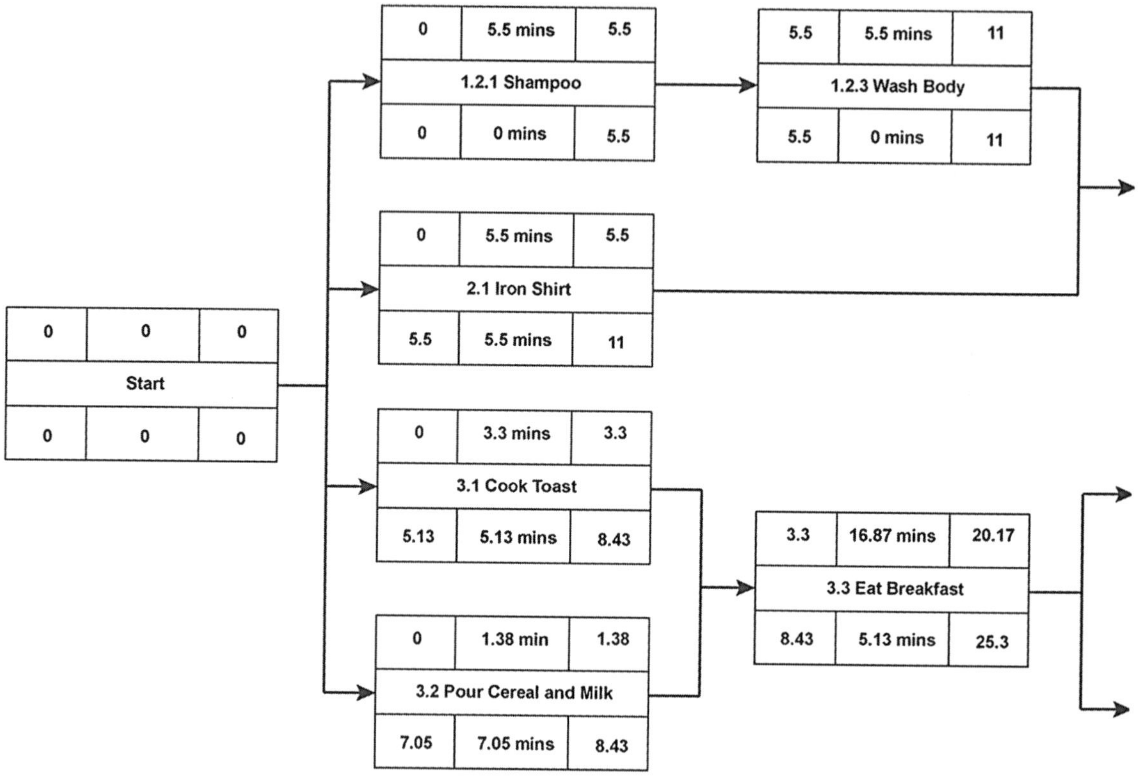

Figure 7.10. Precedence diagram for "getting ready for work in the morning," with slack times

The total slack for node "3.2 pour cereal and milk" is equal to the late finish time of the node (8.43 minutes), less the early start time (0) and the duration (1.38 minutes), or 7.05 minutes. This means the duration of this task can extend to take 7.05 minutes, or that the start of this node can be delayed by 7.05 minutes.

Free slack (or free float) refers to the amount of time a node can be delayed and still permit all successor nodes to begin at their earliest possible times. Free slack is equal to the earliest start of any successor nodes less the early finish of the node in question.

Free Slack = Early Start
(successor) – Early Finish

The early finish for node "3.2 pour cereal and milk" is 1.38 minutes, and the early start for the successor node, "3.3 eat" is 3.3 minutes. Based on this, the free slack available for this node is 1.92 minutes. Node "3.2 pour cereal and milk" has a free slack of 1.92 minutes, and a total slack of 7.05 minutes. If it is delayed by 1.92 minutes, its successor node, "3.3 eat" can still begin at its earliest time, but if it is delayed longer, "3.3 eat" must begin later than its early start time.

Independent slack refers to a node's ability to be shifted earlier or later without impacting either predecessor or successor nodes. In other words, a node has independent slack if there is any slack available when predecessor nodes end as late as possible and successor nodes begin as early as possible. This would allow for a node to be scheduled earlier or later (within the range of the independent slack) and not impact the nodes either before or after it.

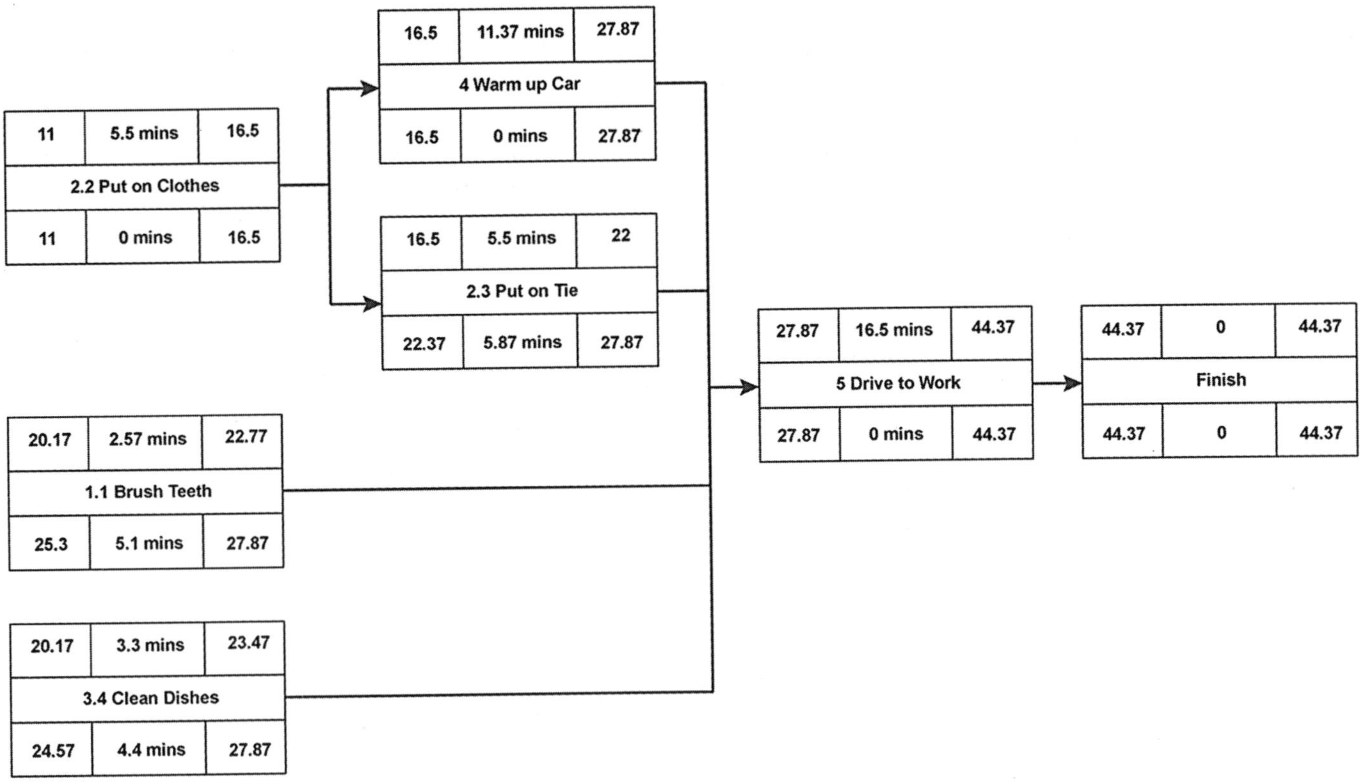

Independent Slack = Early Start (successor) – Late Start – Duration

Consider the node "3.4 clean dishes." It has a late start of 20.17 minutes and a duration of 3.3 minutes; the earliest start of its successor node is 27.87 minutes. Independent slack is equal to the earliest start of all successor nodes (27.87 minutes), less the late start of the node under consideration (23.47 minutes) and its duration (3.3 minutes): this node has an independent slack time of 0 minutes. This tells us that if all predecessor nodes are delayed to their latest possible finish times, this node must start immediately for it to be possible for successive nodes to start at their earliest times. (In this example, there are no nodes with any independent slack time.)

Identifying nodes with free and independent slack can help in identifying possible scheduling bottlenecks and those nodes that can make up for flexes in scheduling and resource allocation. If previous nodes complete as early as possible, nodes with free slack have room to begin later and still allow for successor nodes to begin as early as possible. If previous nodes begin running to their late finish times, nodes with independent slack can be shifted in time to make up for this and still allow successor nodes to begin at their earliest times.

Critical Path

In every project, there will be a sequence of nodes in the precedence diagram that have no total slack time. The longest sequence of nodes that has zero total slack is referred to as the "critical path." These nodes, from start to finish, represent the shortest amount of time that the project can take to complete. In our "getting ready for work" example, the critical path is indicated with heavier lines in figure 7.11.

Nodes that don't lie on the critical path have a total slack time greater than zero; this means that the start time for each of these nodes can be delayed by as much as the total slack time. In our example, Jane can wait a little more than five minutes before brushing her teeth and about four and a half minutes before ironing her shirt without altering the total duration of the project.

The critical path—and knowledge of slack times—is incredibly important when considering the scheduling of tasks, the allocation of labor and resources, and the overall duration of a project. For example, we know that Jane can complete the entire project of waking up in the morning (provided the correct number of resources is available to complete some tasks concurrently) in about forty-four minutes. We also know that Jane can't delay beginning work on any of the critical-path parts of the project, or the total duration of 44.37 minutes will increase. We also know where we can shift nodes forward or backward in time, by how much we can shift them, and what impact any such shifts will have on the total duration of the project.

Gantt Chart

A work-breakdown structure helps visualize the scope of work by breaking

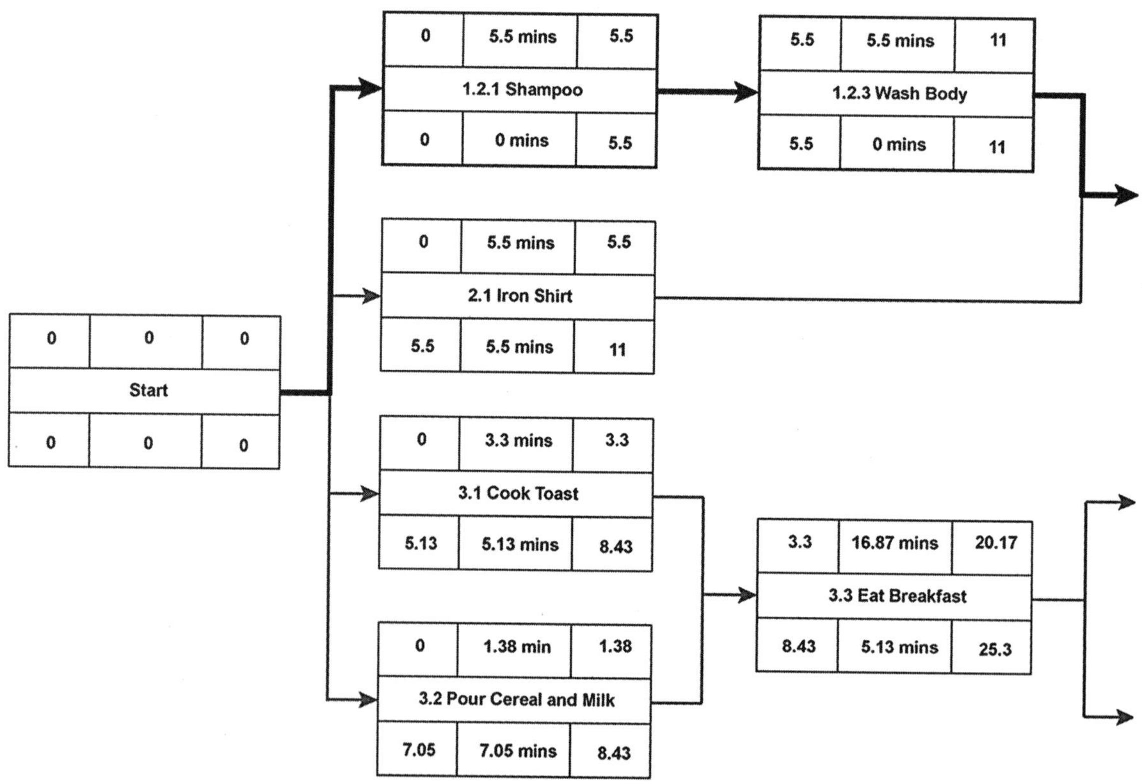

Figure 7.11. Precedence diagram for "getting ready for work in the morning," with critical path

the entire project into chunks that can be effectively estimated and scheduled. A precedence diagram builds on that information and shows the logical relationships between tasks (dependencies), including which tasks need to be completed before others can be tackled. From that information, we can get an idea of how long the project will take to complete, and see the critical path of the project: the longest sequence of project tasks (or *nodes*) that has no available slack time and that must be completed in sequence to achieve the desired scope of the project. This critical path determines the overall duration of the project.

However, none of this work has been done in a direct relationship to a calendar, nor does it reflect the availability of resources to be applied to the project. These are two vital aspects of a project that determine the schedule of the project, and are the next step in planning: allocating resources and scheduling tasks. This step can be completed directly on a precedence diagram. However, because some people like to see scheduling information in a familiar format, some managers do this work using the aid of a bar or Gantt chart. Bar or Gantt charts visually represent the duration of work involved in a project in a way that resembles a calendar. This allows for a better overall picture of the timing and scheduling of the project from the detailed information gathered for each individual node in the project. Because of this, Gantt charts are often far easier for other team members to read than precedence diagrams or even work-breakdown structures.

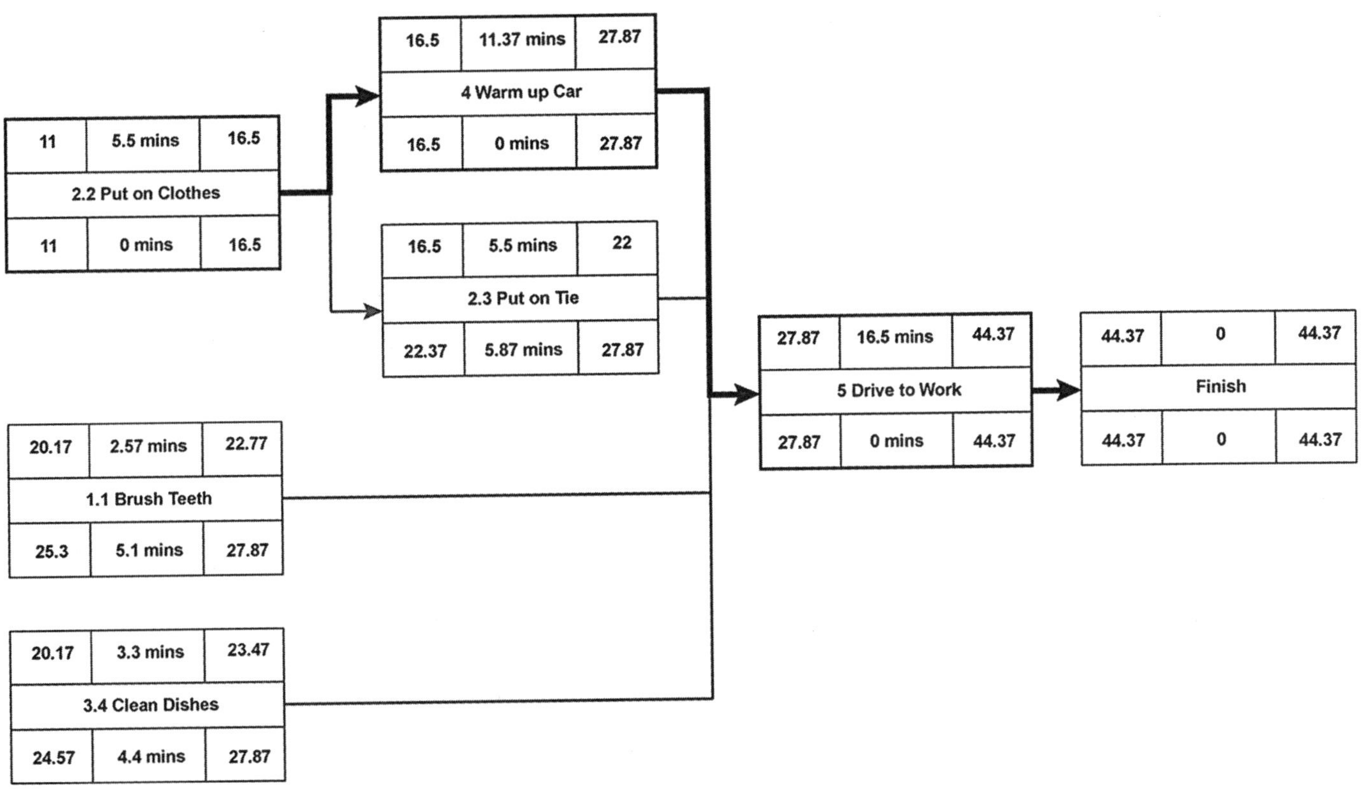

In the sample Gantt chart (figure 7.12), each row represents a different node from the work-breakdown structure for the "getting ready for work" project. The columns represent time and the colored bars visually demonstrate the duration of each node on the calendar. The dark lines and arrows connecting some of the nodes (for example, connecting the nodes "1.2.2 wash" and "2.2 put on clothes") indicate the dependencies we identified previously. Some Gantt charts might also represent the critical path of the project by displaying those tasks on the critical path in a different color (though this example does not).

In this example, there are two rows that don't correspond to nodes from our precedence diagram and which have only a black diamond in the calendar. These rows represent project milestones—in this case, the alarm clock going off to start

It is important to note that the colored bars don't represent what days/times a shop is "working on" a particular node, but rather the duration of time a node takes to complete. For example, I might know that a particular node will take four days to complete. If that node—based on the precedence diagram and the scheduling of other nodes—is intended to start on Monday, I would fill in Monday through Thursday on the Gantt chart for that node. However, if I knew that Wednesday the shop would have be attending a mandatory all-day safety training, I'd fill in Monday through Friday on the Gantt chart; the nonproject training task has caused the duration of the task to lengthen by one day (although the effort put into the task hasn't changed).

ID	Description	Duration	Predecessors	Successors
0	Wake Up Alarm			
1.2.1	Shampoo	5.5 min		1.2.2
1.2.2	Wash	5.5 min	1.2.1	2.2
2.1	Iron Shirt	5.5 min		2.2
2.2	Put on clothes	5.5 min	1.2.2, 2.1	2.3, 4
2.3	Put on tie	5.5 min	2.2	5
4	Warm up Car	11.37 min	2.2	5
3.1	Cook toast	3.3 min		3.3
3.2	Pour cereal and milk	1.38 min		3.3
3.3	Eat	16.87 min	3.1, 3.2	1.1, 3.4
1.1	Brush teeth	2.57 min	3.3	5
3.4	Clean dishes	3.3 min	3.3	5
5	Drive to Work	16.87 min	1.1, 2.3, 3.4, 4	
0	Work Shift Begins			

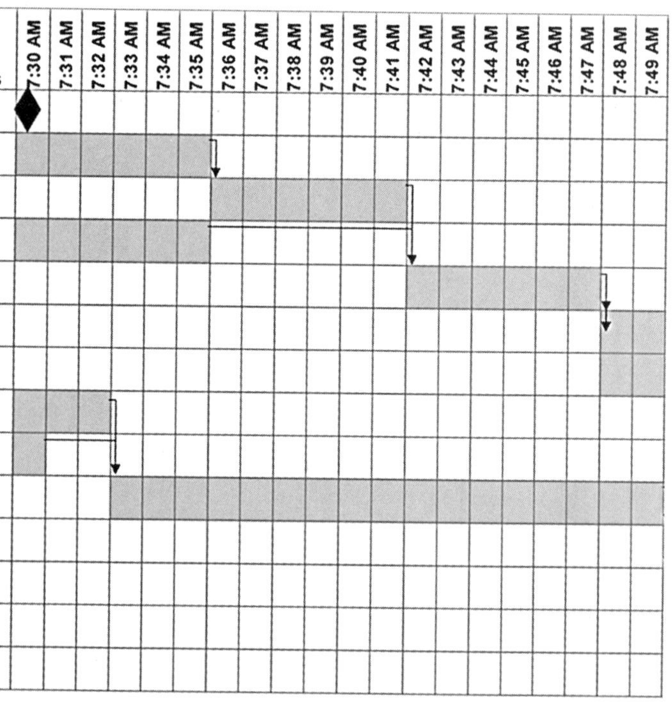

Figure 7.12. Gantt chart for "getting ready for work in the morning." Note that times have been rounded to the nearest minute for clarity.

the day, and the time we must start work. Note, also, that in this example the timescale is represented in minutes horizontally along the chart. Typically—as has been pointed out earlier in this chapter—we would probably think about scheduling a live-entertainment project in terms of quarter-, half, or full days, and our Gantt chart scale would reflect that.

Milestones

In ancient Rome, road builders erected stone obelisks to mark the ends of miles traveled along the road from the center of the Roman Empire. The word "milestone" has become a term used to indicate major waypoints or markers along the timeline of an ongoing project. Obvious milestones include the beginning and end of a project, but other milestones appear in projects as well; they are typically moments along the timeline of a project at which certain parts of the project need to be completed for work to progress.

In a live-entertainment project, many obvious milestones stand out. These include opening night, of course, but also preliminary and final design deadlines, light hang, the beginning of load-in, and the beginning of technical rehearsals, for example. These traditional milestones in a live-entertainment project represent relatively fixed moments in the project's life cycle, around which the rest of the schedule must flex or pivot.

Milestones are typically represented in Gantt charts as solid diamonds. In precedence diagrams for larger projects, milestones can often be identified by the convergence of nodes and dependencies. These are places in a project when work on some parts of the project must come

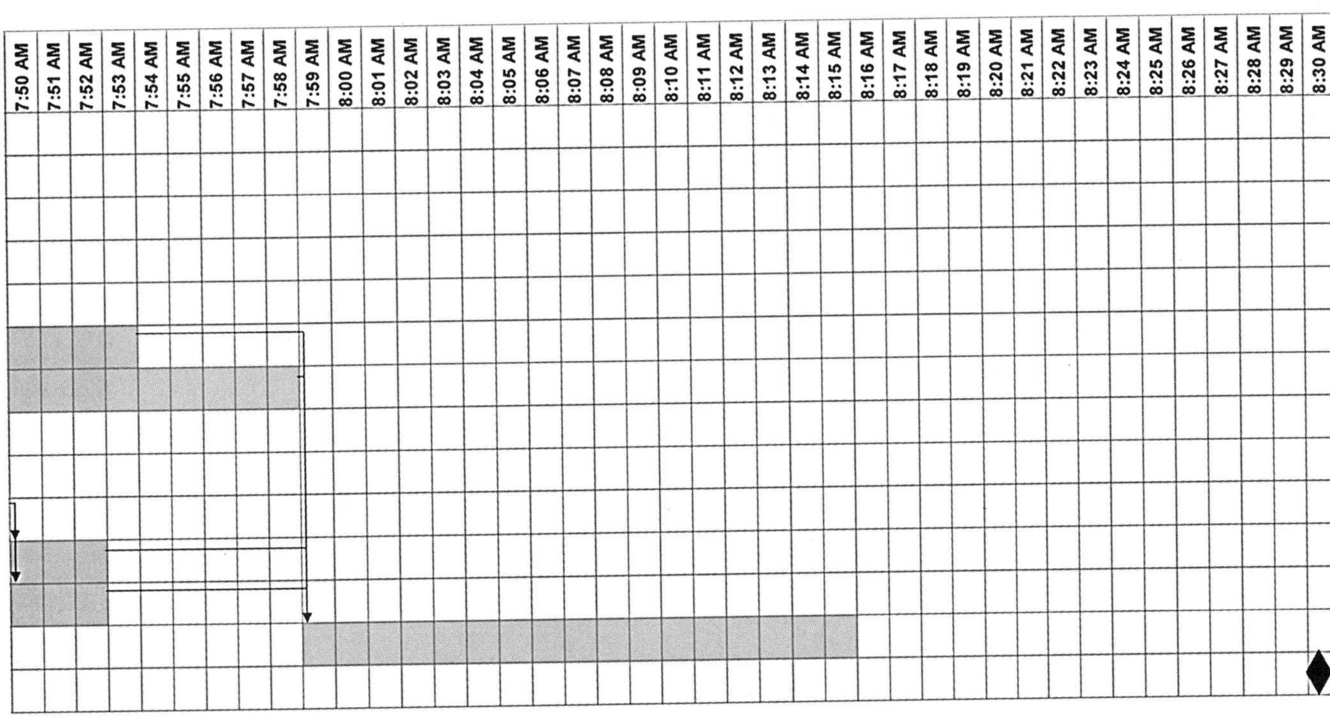

together to completion before additional work can continue.

Labor and Resources

In the example Gantt chart (see figure 7.12), it appears that Jane's getting ready for work project is in fantastic shape; according to this schedule, she does not need to be at work until 8:30, and she will arrive at about 8:15, in plenty of time to settle in for the day. Unfortunately, as was pointed out earlier in this chapter, this isn't accurate, as we have not allocated any available resources to the tasks in this project. Assigning resources will likely have a significant impact on when different tasks can be completed, and therefore on the overall schedule of the project.

Let's assume, for now, that Jane is single and lives alone. This means that only one person is available to be assigned as a resource to any of the tasks in our Gantt chart (figure 7.13). What happens when we begin assigning this resource to tasks? Obviously, in many cases, she can't complete more than one task at a time. (It would be a nearly impossible—and, frankly, dangerous—feat to iron a shirt while shampooing her hair, for example.)

Once we've assigned Jane to each individual task, the schedule looks a little less promising, assuming—except in the case of letting the car warm up, which doesn't require her attention for more than a minute, say—that Jane can't be assigned to more than one task a time. Consequently, the schedule expands beyond the "work shift begins" milestone by twelve minutes. In other words, she'll be late for work.

Now imagine that Jane has a roommate or some other person available to assist with some of these tasks. Let's call her roommate Sara. With either Sara or Jane available to be assigned to tasks in our schedule, we can make changes to our schedule that should allow us to complete the project on time (figure 7.14).

ID	Description	Duration	Predecessors	Successors	7:30 AM	7:31 AM	7:32 AM	7:33 AM	7:34 AM	7:35 AM	7:36 AM	7:37 AM	7:38 AM	7:39 AM	7:40 AM	7:41 AM	7:42 AM	7:43 AM	7:44 AM	7:45 AM	7:46 AM	7:47 AM	7:48 AM	7:49 AM	7:50 AM	7:51 AM	7:52 AM	7:53 AM
0	Wake Up Alarm																											
1.2.1	Shampoo	5.5 min		1.2.2																								
1.2.2	Wash	5.5 min	1.2.1	2.2																								
2.1	Iron Shirt	5.5 min		2.2																								
2.2	Put on clothes	5.5 min	1.2.2, 2.1	2.3, 4																								
2.3	Put on tie	5.5 min	2.2	5																								
4	Warm up Car	11.37 min	2.2	5																								
3.1	Cook toast	3.3 min		3.3																								
3.2	Pour cereal and milk	1.38 min		3.3																								
3.3	Eat	16.87 min	3.1, 3.2	1.1, 3.4																								
1.1	Brush teeth	2.57 min	3.3	5																								
3.4	Clean dishes	3.3 min	3.3	5																								
5	Drive to Work	16.87 min	1.1, 2.3, 3.4, 4																									
0	Work Shift Begins																											

Figure 7.13. Resource allocation in the Gantt chart for "getting ready for work in the morning"

By assigning Sara to even a handful of different tasks (2.1 iron shirt, 3.1 cook toast, and 3.4 clean dishes), we ensure that Jane can get out the door in enough time to arrive at work just after 8:30. Notice that although we assigned Jane and Sara each to the tasks 1.1 brush teeth and 3.4 clean dishes, allowing them to happen concurrently, this didn't really impact the overall length of the project. This is because neither of these tasks was on the critical path of the project.

Ideally, when allocating labor and resources to a project, the focus should be first on those tasks that fall on the critical path. As we've seen, these tasks must be completed on time for the project to complete on time, so assigning labor and resources to these tasks first only makes sense. Once labor and resources have been assigned to critical path tasks, we can assign them to the other, noncritical path tasks of the project. These tasks have some amount of free or independent slack, so we can have some flexibility in assigning start and finish times based on the availability of labor and resources, provided we don't extend beyond the available slack for each task.

Resource- and Time-Limited Scheduling

When we realized that Jane couldn't accomplish all the tasks required for getting ready for work before our deadline, we first turned to adding more labor to solve our problem. This is an example of time-limited scheduling. When thinking about resource allocation, project managers typically consider two overall approaches: resource-limited scheduling, and time-limited scheduling. The basic principles of each are clearly expressed in their names: resource-limited scheduling results in a plan that never exceeds available resources, and often results in a project completion date that is later than the earliest finish time indicated by the precedence diagram. Conversely,

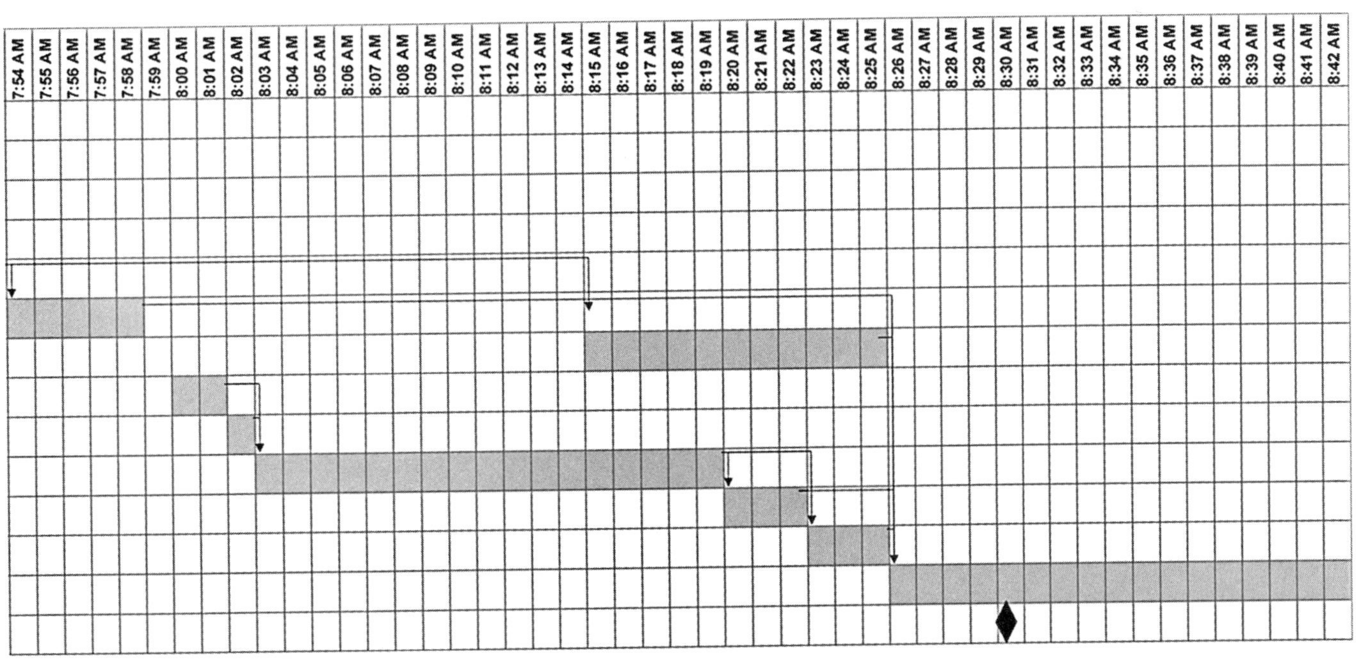

ID	Description	Duration	Predecessors	Successors
0	Wake Up Alarm			
1.2.1	Shampoo	5.5 min		1.2.2
1.2.2	Wash	5.5 min	1.2.1	2.2
2.1	Iron Shirt	5.5 min		2.2
2.2	Put on clothes	5.5 min	1.2.2, 2.1	2.3, 4
2.3	Put on tie	5.5 min	2.2	5
4	Warm up Car	11.37 min	2.2	5
3.1	Cook toast	3.3 min		3.3
3.2	Pour cereal and milk	1.38 min		3.3
3.3	Eat	16.87 min	3.1, 3.2	1.1, 3.4
1.1	Brush teeth	2.57 min	3.3	5
3.4	Clean dishes	3.3 min	3.3	5
5	Drive to Work	16.87 min	1.1, 2.3, 3.4, 4	
0	Work Shift Begins			

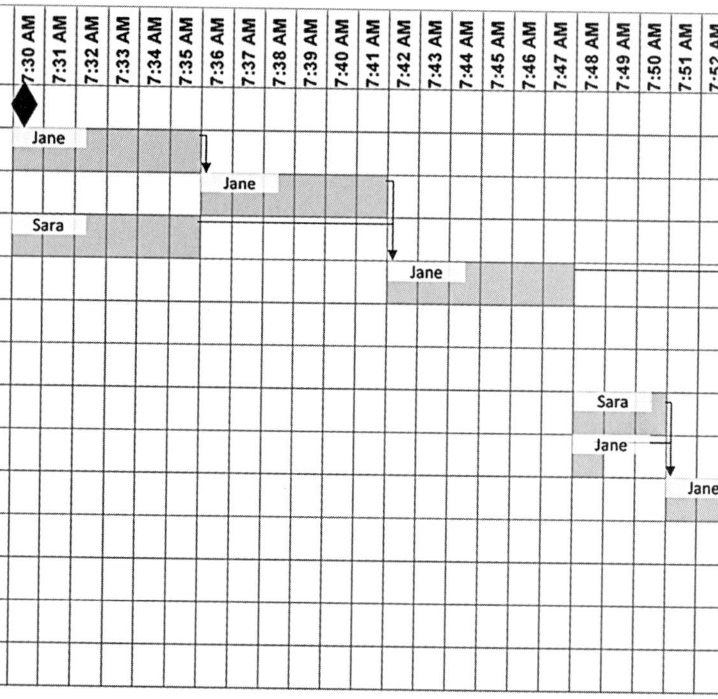

Figure 7.14. Resource allocation for "getting ready for work in the morning," after resources have been added to the project

time-limited scheduling places a priority on time, ensuring project completion by a specific date—usually this is the earliest finish time indicated in the precedence diagram, but can be some later date. Typically, a time-limited approach results in having to allocate more resources than might be available or otherwise acceptable.

It should be obvious to anyone experienced with live-entertainment projects that resource allocation for many projects by either time-limited or resource-limited approaches will present a conundrum: opening night doesn't move, so time-limited scheduling seems like an obvious requirement for resource allocation. However, most live-entertainment projects have a limited or fixed budget; consequently, it will be difficult to allocate extra resources, suggesting a resource-limited scheduling approach.

These two approaches will always be in conflict—time-limited scheduling requires being willing to accept overages in resources, and resource-limited scheduling requires being willing to accept a later delivery date.

When scheduling a live-entertainment project, it is often best to begin with a time-limited scheduling approach. It is sometimes possible to bring in additional over-hire labor, or to shift labor from one functional group to a different project area to accommodate the need for additional labor. By starting with a time-limited approach, those tasks that will require more labor to complete to meet the opening-night deadline can be more readily identified. As we saw in the example above, it became clear that to meet our final-delivery milestone (i.e., getting to work on time), adding more resources was necessary.

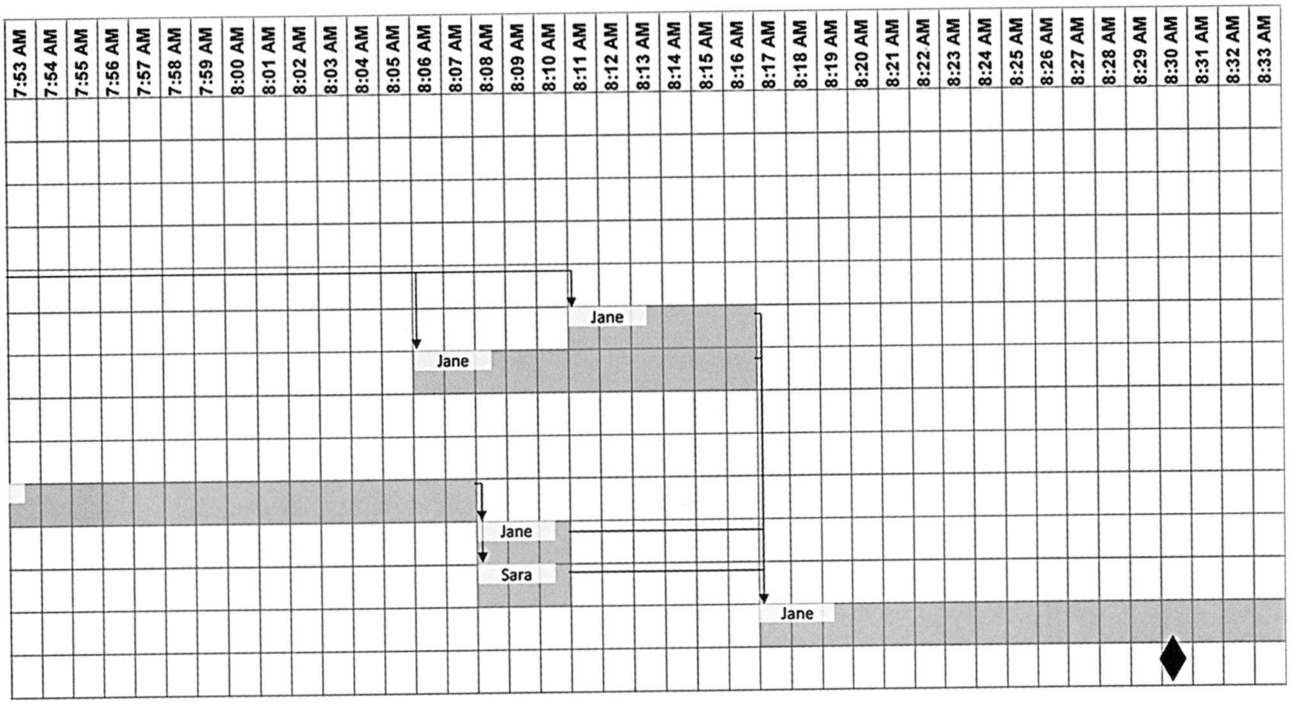

While some projects can withstand a later delivery to achieve the desired scope of the project—especially if the amount of labor and other resources is fixed—and some projects can afford to add additional labor or other resources to achieve the same goals if deadlines must be met, neither is typically the case with live-entertainment projects. As a result, managers for live-entertainment projects must look back to the iron triangle: If a project exceeds the available time, can the parameters of the project be adjusted in such a way that increasing costs can reduce the time required? Or can the scope be reduced to the same effect? This usually entails a conversation among the director, producer, and the appropriate designers and technical-area managers. This reflects a divergence from typical waterfall-management approaches as discussed in chapter 1. Time and resource constraints are dictating a revision of the project scope, and the team must go back to an earlier step in the process to redefine expectations of scope and/or quality to remain within the constraints of time and resources.

Duration, Work, and Units

For tasks on projects, the concepts of task duration, work, and number of resources are interrelated. When we first considered duration earlier in this chapter, we obliquely referred to this by indicating that when we thought about duration, we were referring to the length of time it would take to complete a task with the most efficient allocation of labor. When we unpack this idea, we recognize, for example, that a flat might take one person three hours to complete, while it might take two people only two hours to complete. In this example, adding more people (i.e., units) reduced the duration of the task (from three hours to two hours), because the amount of work required to complete the task stayed constant. (In some situations, adding a second person to the task means paying for four hours of labor instead of three, which has an additional impact on these considerations.)

The relationship between duration, work, and units impacts the scheduling process in different ways for different tasks. For some tasks, adding more units doesn't change the duration at all; for example, adding more people to a meeting scheduled to run for one hour won't make the meeting get finished any sooner—the *duration* of this task is fixed. For other tasks, adding people to the task reduces the duration of the task because the amount of work to be done can be divided among the added workers and the *work* of the task is fixed. Finally, for some tasks, it may be necessary to adjust the duration of the task because the amount of work required to complete it changes, but the number of people assigned remains the same; in this situation—consider, for example, a paint treatment on a wall that turns out to be more detailed than expected—the work required has changed, but the number of *units* assigned to the work remains fixed.

Knowing whether a task has a fixed duration, fixed work, or fixed units informs choices about resource allocation—it makes no sense to add resources to a task whose duration is fixed when trying to reduce the overall duration of a project, for example. It does make sense to add more resources to a task whose work is fixed, however, as this would reduce the duration of that task (and, potentially, of the whole project).

Software Tools

Precedence diagrams and Gantt charts are complex tools. Generating them by hand can be time consuming, and once a project is under way, tracking progress on a hand-drawn precedence diagram or Gantt chart is usually unwieldy enough to be impractical. Fortunately, many software tools are available to make this task far more manageable.

One of the most prevalent software tools on the market for project planning is Microsoft Project. Like many higher-end software products, it can be expensive for some organizations and individuals, but it offers a comprehensive suite of tools for project managers to use in scheduling and resource allocation. Other software packages exist as well, however, including cloud-based applications like Gantter, Smartsheet, and Gantt Cloud, all of which are worth checking out.

Summing Up

Precedence Diagrams

Precedence diagrams represent the relationships among work nodes and tasks in a project, demonstrating which tasks are dependent on others for completion. These relationships (dependencies) are based on logical factors (i.e., you can't paint a wall until the wall is built), not on common scheduling practices or resource availability. Tasks will have other tasks that must follow them (successor tasks), and which they must follow (predecessor tasks).

Nodes and Work Packages

Work packages or tasks are represented in a precedence diagram by nodes, which indicate activities to be completed. Nodes in the diagram typically include the name of the task, an identification number, the time required to complete the node, and space for other information including slack or float time, and start and finish times.

Arrows and Dependencies

Arrows between nodes on a precedence diagram indicate dependency relationships between nodes. Typically, nodes have a finish-to-start dependency, which indicates that a successor (following) task cannot be started until a predecessor (earlier) task has been finished. Other dependency relationships include start-to-start, finish-to-finish, and start-to-finish, although these are far more rare.

Creating a Precedence Diagram

Precedence diagrams are generally read from left to right, with a start node on the left and a finish node on the right. Immediately to the right of the start node are nodes that have no predecessors; to the right of these are the nodes that are their immediate successors, and so on until reaching the end of the project. All the nodes on the chart are connected with arrows representing dependency relationships.

Critical Path

The critical path represents the sequence of nodes and logical dependencies whose duration is the longest and for which there is no slack or float time.

Early/Late Start/Finish

Each node will have an earliest time at which it can start and finish, and a latest time at which it can start and finish based on the duration of the project. These are determined by making a forward pass and a backward pass through the project and calculating times based on the duration of each node.

Slack

The early and late start and finish times for each node are used to determine slack (or float) for each node.

- Total slack is defined as the late finish time minus the early start time and the duration of a node.
- Free slack is defined as the earliest time a node can complete (the earliest start of successor nodes) minus the early finish of the node.
- Independent slack is defined as the earliest time a node can complete (the earliest start of successor nodes) minus the latest the node can start and the duration of the node.

Nodes without slack identify the critical path; nodes with slack can be shifted in time to accommodate resource and labor-scheduling priorities or to account for schedule slippage in earlier nodes.

Gantt Chart

Gantt charts (or bar charts) provide a visual representation of the total work required to complete a project based on a calendar timeline. Gantt charts demonstrate the impact of time and resources on a project in conjunction with dependency relationships.

Milestones

Milestones in a Gantt chart represent key moments in a project's life cycle at which significant deliverables are due. They are often represented in precedence diagrams as nodes in which all predecessors converge.

Labor and Resources

Labor and resources are allocated to tasks beginning with those tasks that fall on the critical path. Resources are then allocated to other tasks as available; in order to accommodate resource availability, the start, end, and duration of tasks may need to be shifted. For those nodes that do not fall on the critical path, doing so within the constraints of available slack should have no impact on the overall duration of the project. Adjusting start, end, and duration times beyond available slack for these nodes, and adjusting start, end, and duration times for any tasks on the critical path, will change the duration of the project as a whole.

Duration, Work, and Units

Knowing whether a task has a fixed duration, fixed work, or fixed units informs choices about resource allocation. Tasks with fixed work will change in duration when the number of resources allocated to it changes. Tasks with a fixed duration will not change duration no matter how many resources are added to it.

PART III

Executing and Managing the Project

After all the work that goes into planning a project, it can be a relief to finally start executing the plan—to start rehearsals, begin constructing scenery and costumes, hang lights, build sound cues, and just "get started." Certainly, for some production projects, the hardest part is conceiving, planning, and adjusting their scope to fit available time and resources. On such projects, a technical manager's job can be easy from here on out.

Most projects are not that easy, however, and most managers are not that lucky. For any number of reasons, the execution of a project rarely plays out exactly as planned. A technical manager needs to track progress and make decisions about when and how to intervene when a project begins to deviate from the expected course. Live-entertainment projects differ from many industrial projects in that their scope often changes during the project's life cycle as rehearsals progress. A manager needs to be prepared to assess these changes to determine whether and how the plan can be adjusted to accommodate them.

Chapter 8, "Tracking and Reporting Progress," presents methods of tracking projects in terms of quality, time, and cost and discusses methods of reporting progress to the rest of the project team.

Chapter 9, "Variance and Control," examines how to recognize when a project is straying from the plan and discusses management strategies for this predicament. Methods for managing inevitable changes to the scope of the production, as the project evolves over the course of its life cycle, are also discussed.

8. Tracking and Reporting Progress

While the bulk of project planning happens *before* the project begins, a significant task, once the project gets under way, is keeping track of progress and reporting it to the rest of the team. A manager can track progress both quantitatively and qualitatively, and the tools and techniques that have been developed in the project management world for this can be applied to live-entertainment projects. The production meeting has evolved as one of the primary methods of fulfilling the role of reporting progress to the team.

Topics covered in this chapter:

- Qualitative tracking
  - Shop meetings (weekly progress review)
  - "Shop-walks" (inspection reviews)
- Quantitative tracking
  - Expense tracking
  - Progress tracking
- Reporting
  - Rehearsal reports
  - Production meetings
    - Progress reports
    - Expense reports
    - Questions and concerns
    - Production meeting reports
  - Milestone reviews
  - Performance reports

Qualitative Tracking

Qualitative tracking methods are means of getting a "feel" for progress. This might include such intangibles as team members' confidence in their ability to meet deadlines, their satisfaction with the quality of the work completed, or whether team members anticipate obstacles, challenges, or difficulties in the future. Qualitative tracking is not measurable; consequently, there is no comprehensive checklist of things to look for. Rather, qualitative assessment of progress is best achieved by establishing a culture of communication and observation that allows a team leader to have "his thumb on the pulse" of the project. One important way to lay the foundation for that culture is to be available and observant, through regular meetings and walk-throughs, while work is ongoing.

Shop Meeting (Weekly Progress Review)

A regular weekly meeting with each functional/project working area does two things. First, it provides an opportunity for leaders in each shop to raise concerns or questions that don't necessarily involve the entire team (or other functional/project groups within the team). Second, it provides an opportunity for a manager to hear each project/functional area leader's assessment of his or her own progress. This meeting should include a quantitative component—an update on current expenses and current progress against the planned calendar, particularly if there are pertinent or immediate concerns—but the primary focus in these meetings should be on the "sense" of things. Other meetings—like production meetings—provide feedback on expense and progress tracking. Shop meetings are an opportunity to get a feel for less quantitative aspects of the project: how teams feel about progress, communication, understanding of scope, and the like.

Keep track of concerns or questions brought up each week, and follow up on those concerns in subsequent meetings. For example, if the prop master expresses concern about the prop artisan's ability to carve detail into the jewelry box that is the centerpiece of a scene in *Love's Labour's Lost* during a weekly meeting, ask about progress on the jewelry box in the next few meetings. Following up in this way allows a manager to maintain a sense of progress, while also demonstrating (to the prop master, for example), that he is aware of the concerns that have been raised.

In addition to following up on expressed concerns, ask questions that narrow the breadth of concerns to the facets of resources, time, or scope. Is the concern that the carved detail on the jewelry box is beyond the capability of the props artisan? Or that it is beyond the capability of the props artisan given the time she can devote to it? Is the concern that the material of the jewelry box is not appropriate for the carving—is it too hard, too soft, or prone to splitting? Is the detail too fine for the tools available, or to be able to be completed in the time available? Asking these questions can help frame solutions, can help determine when to bring these concerns to the rest of the team, and provides a context within which to frame them when doing so. Framing the concerns this way can also make it easier to determine what assistance can be provided directly by the project manager without going to the rest of the team to redefine the scope and quality expectations of a specific aspect of the project.

"Shop-Walk" (Inspection Review)

In addition to a weekly progress review with the leaders of each functional/project work area on the team, a project manager should take time to walk through shops and working areas. These "spot checks," or inspection reviews, provide an opportunity to observe progress first-hand, without the filter presented by functional/project area leaders. While these drop-in kinds of reviews can provide insight into time and resource expenditures, they are more effective as a means of measuring (or at least examining) quality and scope.

For example, consider a walk through a scene shop during the build of the set that calls for some flats to have the appearance of bricks and mortar. This walk through can reveal the effectiveness of the specific brick-texture technique decided upon earlier in the project. In this example, in consultation with the scenic artist and the set designer, the technical director opted to build Hollywood-style flat frames out of wood, and to cover those frames with one-half-inch MDF sheets that had mortar lines routed into them on a CNC router. During the walk-through, the project manager can observe the MDF sheets as they are attached to the flat frames. She notices that the routed mortar grooves are very sharp, without the rounded, worn edges that are typical of bricks, and asks about it. The technical director answers that the scenic art team plans to hit the edges with a sander or rasp to soften them up; doing so by hand—rather than using a round-over bit in the router to create a rounded edge—creates a more irregular texture, more like what would be seen on a real brick wall.

Interactions like this one provide insight into ongoing progress and how each functional/project area is attempting to fulfill expectations of the scope of the project, as well as how each is managing quality control. These interactions also provide a manager with first-hand knowledge of progress based on her own observations. This knowledge provides a foundation for any decision making that may need to happen in the future, whether related to resource allocation, time estimates and delivery deadlines, or scope.

Quantitative Tracking

Quality and scope can be difficult to quantify, but gauging progress on both is necessary for keeping a project on track. Labor and resource expenditures and schedule fulfillment, however, are more quantitative and far more easily measured. These must also be monitored during the project life cycle. Time and cost—like quality and scope—must remain within the parameters set during the design definition phase of the project. Knowing where the project stands in terms of time and cost at any given moment allows a manager to predict whether the project is staying within those parameters, or whether changes need to be made to ensure it does.

Expense Tracking

Expense tracking is, quite simply, the process of recording each expense related to a project. In the simplest of examples, this may comprise a simple ledger of expenses, not unlike a checkbook ledger (figure 8.1). More complex examples can comprise multiple-page spreadsheets with cross-referenced cells and formulae providing relevant subtotals and percentages.

The first step in tracking expenses for a project is to determine the expected level of reporting; this will determine the organization of expense data including how it is presented, how it is totaled, and how it is analyzed. For example, a summer-stock theatre may present a season of nine productions, and have budget lines in physical production for scenery, props, lighting, costumes, and sound for each, along with a seasonal expense line in each of those areas. This would represent fifty individual budget lines that need to be tracked and monitored throughout the season in physical production expenses. (This, of course, assumes that labor is fixed and that other expenses, such as rent, utilities, and freight/portage, for example, are tracked separately or not tracked at all.)

For this fictional nine-show summer-stock season, a manager would likely want to be able to see up-to-date expense information in each area for each show. To make this possible, expenses should be recorded separately for each of these individual budget lines. Expenses might be entered into separate worksheets for each budget line in a spreadsheet program. We might then create an additional summary worksheet that references the worksheets for each budget line, providing subtotal summaries of each for quick review. The example in figure 8.2 shows a similar setup for the scenic expenses of a summer at Berkshire Theatre Festival.

Each individual worksheet contains detailed information about each expense.

- The date the purchase was made
- Tracking information for the purchase (such as a purchase order number, a petty cash report number, and a check number)
- The vendor
- A description of the purchase
- The amount of the purchase

Expense Tracking Worksheet			
Theatre:	Berkshire Theatre Festival	Production:	Coastal Disturbances
Date:	1-Mar-17	By:	Richard M. Dionne
Budget:	$ 3,000.00	Page:	2

Date	Number	Vendor	Description	Amount	Balance
6/7/2008	2569	Home Depot	Play Sand	$ 7.26	$ 2,992.74
6/12/2006	2625	Greenberg and Sons	Lumber	$ 728.35	$ 2,264.39
6/10/2006	2624	Dresser Hull	Lumber	$ 235.95	$ 2,028.44
6/9/2006	2622	Dresser Hull	Lumber	$ 253.75	$ 1,774.69
6/13/2006	2627	Home Depot	Pipe, Hardware	$ 83.77	$ 1,690.92
6/14/2006	2626	BMI Supply	Muslin, Fittings, Voile	$ 953.58	$ 737.34
6/20/2006	2630	Dresser Hull	Lumber	$ 124.74	$ 612.60
6/21/2006	2631	Dresser Hull	Lumber	$ 62.82	$ 549.78
6/19/2006	2629	Dresser Hull	Lumber	$ 231.41	$ 318.37
6/23/2006	2785	Freadman Steel	Steel (Sandbox)	$ 250.00	$ 68.37
6/29/2006	2789	Greenberg and Sons	Foamboard	$ 176.80	$ (108.43)
6/29/2006	2791	Carr Hardware	Super 77 Adhesive	$ 47.96	$ (156.39)
7/5/2006	2194	Harvest Moon Hydro	Mylar	$ 62.00	$ (218.39)
10-Jul	2909	Home Depot	Sand	$ 65.40	$ (283.79)
6/28/2006	2900	Home Depot	Sand	$ 98.10	$ (381.89)
7/4/2006	2899	Home Depot	Sand	$ 98.10	$ (479.99)
6/29/2006	2788	Limelight	Webbing	$ 24.00	$ (503.99)
7/6/2006	2903	Dresser Hull	Lauan	$ 207.75	$ (711.74)
6/3/2006	PC3	Carr Hardware	Liquid Nails	$ 13.93	$ (725.67)
			Total Expenses as of 3/1/2017	$	3,725.67
			Ending Balance as of 3/1/2017	$	(725.67)

Figure 8.1. Expense-tracking ledger

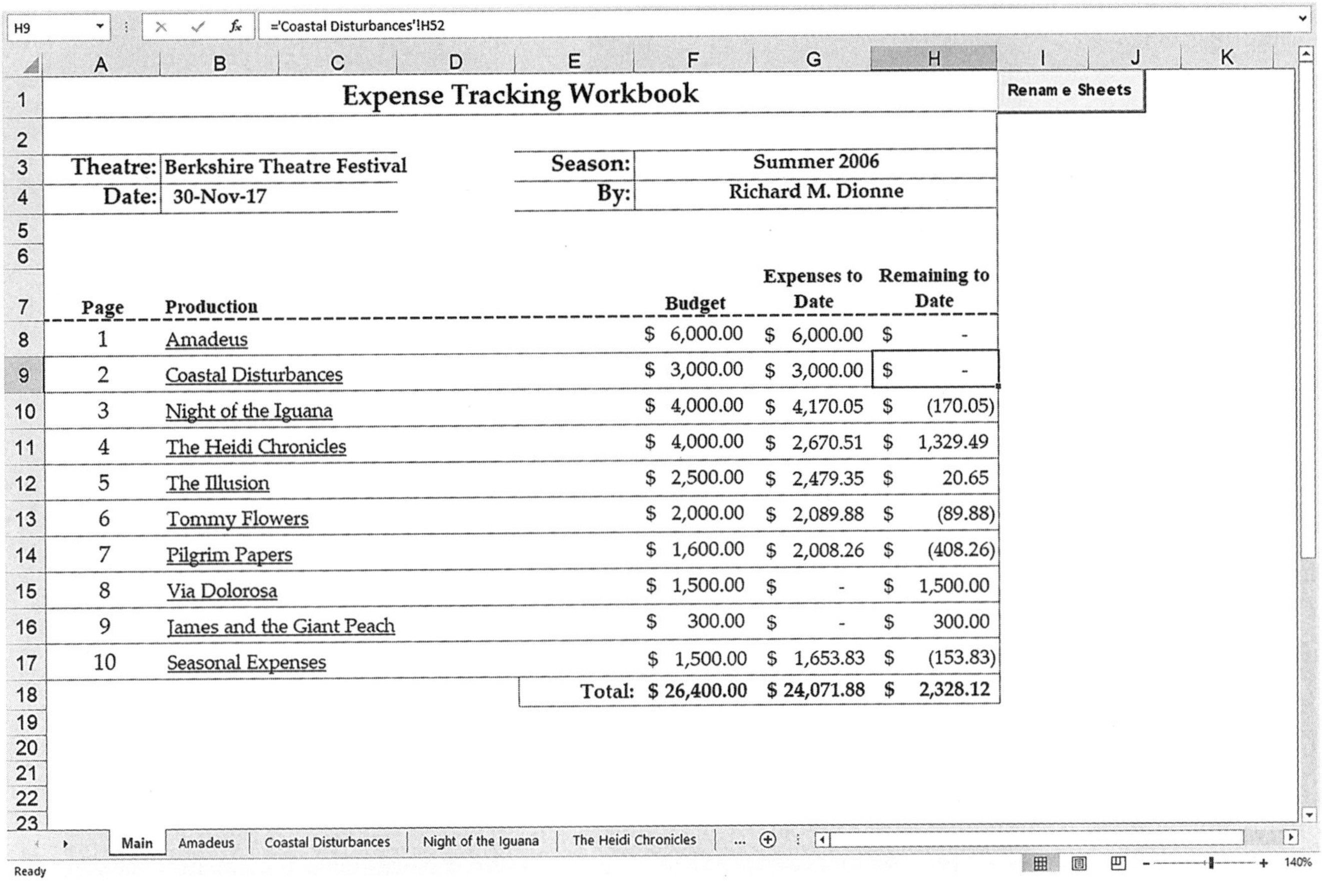

H9 | ='Coastal Disturbances'!H52

Rename Sheets

Expense Tracking Workbook

Theatre: Berkshire Theatre Festival | Season: Summer 2006

Date: 30-Nov-17 | By: Richard M. Dionne

Page	Production	Budget	Expenses to Date	Remaining to Date
1	Amadeus	$ 6,000.00	$ 6,000.00	$ -
2	Coastal Disturbances	$ 3,000.00	$ 3,000.00	$ -
3	Night of the Iguana	$ 4,000.00	$ 4,170.05	$ (170.05)
4	The Heidi Chronicles	$ 4,000.00	$ 2,670.51	$ 1,329.49
5	The Illusion	$ 2,500.00	$ 2,479.35	$ 20.65
6	Tommy Flowers	$ 2,000.00	$ 2,089.88	$ (89.88)
7	Pilgrim Papers	$ 1,600.00	$ 2,008.26	$ (408.26)
8	Via Dolorosa	$ 1,500.00	$ -	$ 1,500.00
9	James and the Giant Peach	$ 300.00	$ -	$ 300.00
10	Seasonal Expenses	$ 1,500.00	$ 1,653.83	$ (153.83)
	Total:	$ 26,400.00	$ 24,071.88	$ 2,328.12

Main | Amadeus | Coastal Disturbances | Night of the Iguana | The Heidi Chronicles | ...

Figure 8.2. Spreadsheet with multiple worksheets and summaries for several projects

Additionally, each worksheet contains a running tally of the available funds after every purchase. (This kind of expense tracking is what is generally referred to as single-entry bookkeeping.) Additional data beyond that indicated above can also be recorded for each expense by adding additional columns to the spreadsheet.

What data to include in each expense record (i.e., each row of the spreadsheet) depends, as mentioned earlier, on what information will need to be reported or analyzed during the life cycle of the project (or for future purposes, including as a reference tool for the budgeting of later projects). Some projects may call for tracking expenses specific to nodes in a work-breakdown structure or tasks in a Gantt chart. Others may require less specific data. Fortunately, with the level of computing power available to most people working in live entertainment, setting up tracking spreadsheets with a significant level of depth of detail is relatively straightforward. In fact, in some cases, it is best to assume that a far greater level of detail is required and set up spreadsheets appropriately; it is far easier to ignore extraneous data than it is to try to reconstitute missing data later, when it becomes unexpectedly important.

In addition to a worksheet for each individual budget line, the example from Berkshire Theatre Festival includes a summary worksheet. This worksheet comprises summary data for each budget line being tracked, and each record includes

- Budget line (number, name, or both)
- Budget amount
- Expenses to date
- Remaining funds to date
- A total each for budget amount, expenses to date, and remaining funds to date

Where the worksheets for each budget line provide detailed information on expenses made in that line, the summary page provides a bigger-picture perspective. This big-picture perspective might include a summary of all expenses for all projects within a functional area (as shown in the example). This can prove especially helpful, for example, when considering whether potential over-budget expenses for a project might be able to be balanced against a project that might have gone under budget within a functional area, or if a cost might be shared across multiple projects in a functional area. Conversely, this big-picture perspective might provide a project-wide summary across all functional areas related to one specific project; this can be useful when considering reallocating budgeted expenses across functional areas for a project, or when considering whether costs might be shared across functional areas within a project.

In some theatres, a common practice is to allow managers of functional areas to spend money they saved on a production project for shop improvement purchases. This often places a premium on "being under budget," and can incentivize short-changing a project. Functional areas should have separate "seasonal" or "shop" expense budgets, and project funds should be spent only on project-specific expenses.

Issues of variance and control, like these, are explored more fully in chapter 9. However, consider the example from Berkshire Theatre Festival, above; on the summary page, it is clear that some projects have run over budget while some remain under. This might be a good opportunity to consider whether the scenery for the productions *Amadeus*, *Night of the Iguana*, and *The Heidi Chronicles* might be expected to come in under budget, and whether some of those funds might be able to cover the overages on *Coastal Disturbances*, *Pilgrim Papers*, and *Tommy Flowers*. The ability to respond to expenses beyond those that were expected is directly related to the ability to observe those unexpected expenses and to see the whole picture containing them.

Progress Tracking

Anyone reading this has probably experienced it at least once: the dreaded "thermometer" progress bar that never fills as a laptop operating system updates or a large folder of files copies from one hard drive to another. Frustrating as it is to watch, however, not knowing the status of that progress would be even worse. In many ways, tracking project progress is similar: it can sometimes be painful to recognize how little progress has been made, but it is far better to know that progress—however slow—is happening at all. More importantly, knowing when progress is lagging behind what is expected or required for successful completion of a project gives managers an opportunity to respond decisively to the situation.

The simplest method of tracking progress is a running tally of nodes from a work-breakdown structure or tasks from a Gantt chart that notes when they need to be completed, and whether they have been completed. This list can be updated daily, weekly, or even hourly, depending on the project and the reporting needs of the manager.

A more comprehensive and detailed picture of progress can be gained by updating a Gantt chart or precedence diagram. (Most software applications that allow for the creation of Gantt charts or precedence diagrams provide some means of inputting progress-tracking information.) Gantt charts or precedence diagrams should be updated with progress information at a frequency that matches the level of resolution of the chart. For example, a project with a Gantt chart set up for a resolution of half-day increments might need to be updated daily or every half day, where a project with a chart set up with weekly increments would likely only need to be updated weekly.

Updating progress on a Gantt chart or precedence diagram provides detailed information to a project manager not only about whether the project is running on schedule, but also about what parts of the project are running ahead or slipping behind (or, as unlikely as it might be, running exactly on schedule). Having this level of detail gives managers the ability to respond to variance and to make changes to remain on, or get back on, schedule.

Typically, progress in a Gantt chart or precedence diagram looks similar to one of the temperature progress bars mentioned above, often seen when copying digital files or updating an operating system. The colored block representing the duration of work for a task or node on a Gantt chart simply gets filled in as work progresses, while the node representing a task or work package in a precedence diagram gets shaded or colored. See, for example, the Gantt chart (figure 8.3) that shows a portion of the project "Crimes of the Heart," and indicates ongoing progress on multiple tasks.

In this example, Robby has been assigned to the task "cut pieces" for the porch brackets; Michael has been assigned to "attach," "fill and sand," and "send to paint." The rest of the day crew has been assigned to the task "porch spindles." According to the progress tracking on this chart, Robby and Michael have completed all of their tasks, while the day crew has only completed about 33 percent of the "porch spindles" task.

Reporting

Tracking information is only useful if it is available to those who need it. This process is known as reporting—sharing

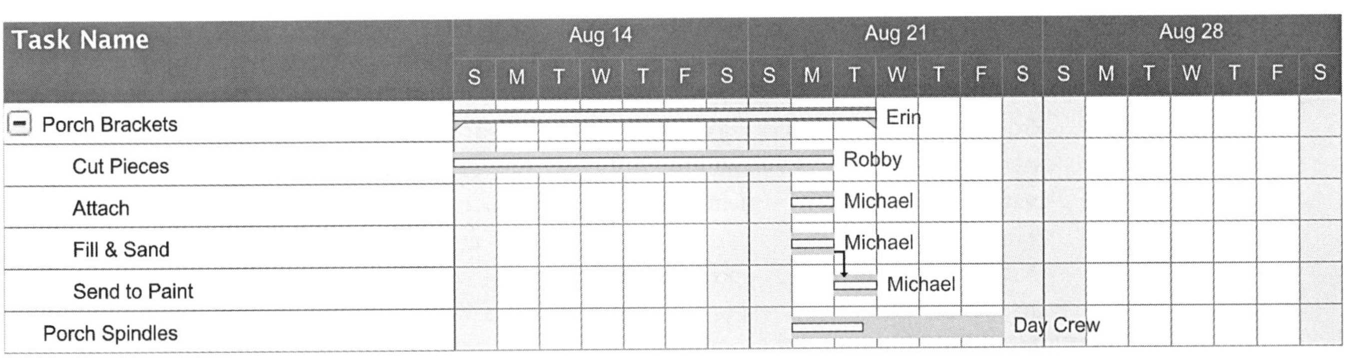

Figure 8.3. Tracking Gantt chart for *Crimes of the Heart*

information with other members of the team. Different types of projects have different methods of reporting. A typical live-entertainment project will have some version of rehearsal reports, production meetings, milestone reviews, and performance reports.

Rehearsal Reports

One of the most familiar progress-reporting methods in live entertainment is the rehearsal report (figure 8.4). These are typically released after every rehearsal, and report to the team progress on the portion of the production project led by the director. It seems silly to describe it this way, in some sense, but this is an important paradigm to understand if one is to be successful in any live-entertainment endeavor: the overall performance is still under development during the rehearsal process as the director and the performers come to grips with the story being told or the performance being created. This often means that the scope of many elements of the production may change during this process—sometimes in small ways, but sometimes in large ways. The rehearsal report is the primary means of communicating and documenting these changes in scope for the rest of the team, and to initiate discussion of their possible ramifications. (Managing changes in scope will be discussed in more detail in chapter 9.)

That changes in the scope of a production can happen throughout the rehearsal process can be frustrating for many members of the production team. Partially this is because some directors may see their role as being able to demand changes to scope, regardless of the impact on time and cost, and partially because some designers and technicians *imagine* that this is how some directors see their role. Regardless of these assumptions, demands beyond available resources mean that scope needs to change or more resources need to become available. This happens through discussions among members of the team, generally led by the production manager

Production Meetings

Progress and expense tracking are only useful when information about progress is available to and used by members of the team; regular progress reporting makes that happen by providing opportunities to share information to the rest of the team. Progress reporting is ongoing, throughout the life cycle of the project, through regular updates and through milestone reviews. Progress reporting can be informal, "check-in" kinds of events, or it can be more formalized, with documentation and organized visual presentations. Whatever the method, it provides other team members, project managers, and often stakeholders updates on the status of progress.

The traditional regional theatre production process has evolved a weekly progress-reporting structure: the production meeting. An efficient weekly production meeting will generally consist of three major components: progress reporting, expense reporting, and an opportunity to address questions and concerns that have arisen as the project has progressed. Some production meetings are organized around functional departments, with each providing progress and expense reports and addressing questions and concerns before moving

TO: R. Jones, R. Dionne, D. Flook, R. Starks, D. Taylor, R. Crow, K. Behren, S. Wynn, R. Lee, T. Fier, B. Sanders, R. James, J. Kunkel

FROM: **Dani Taylor**, *Stage Manager*

Purdue Theatre

Arms and the Man

Rehearsal Report # 4

Sunday, August 28, 2005

GENERAL:

Justin Karr has joined the Arms and the Man cast.

ATTN: Taylor, Kunkel Lee, Riley, Hadgikosti, Milliken, Mehringer, Karr

.

6:35pm: Begin rehearsal
6:38pm: Read Through Act I
7:05pm: End Read Through, Discuss
7:09pm: 5 min break
7:15pm: Walk Set
7:27pm: Block Act I
8:09pm: 10 min break
8:19pm: Back, Continue Blocking Act I
9:27pm: 5 min break
9:32pm: Back, continue Blocking Act I
10:30pm: End of Rehearsal, Cast dismissed.

- Is it possible to get a push broom and dust pan for the classroom?

Next Rehearsal: Monday, August 29, 2005, 6:30pm in PAO 2164

Publicity Photos are Monday at 5:00pm in the Experimental.

SOUND:

- When may we be able to record the actors for Act I (Nicola, Catherine, Louka, Officer)? Thanks.

LIGHTING:

No notes, thanks!

SCENIC:

- Has the placement of the electric bell been determined for Act III? Thanks.

COSTUMES:

- Is there a concern with a saber for the Russian Soldier, or will he still be able to have one? Thanks.

PROPERTIES:

- Is it possible to get a larger rehearsal Ottoman, thank you?

Thanks!
Dani Taylor
Stage Manager

Figure 8.4. Example of a rehearsal report

on to the next. Others are organized to go around the room and provide progress and expense reports for each department and addressing questions and concerns once the "business" reports have all been presented. While these can tend to be informal (depending on the organization), it is beneficial to be as specific as possible while remaining concise.

> It can be tempting—especially for early-career team members or team members new to a team or organization—to shade the truth during these reports. In an effort to appear to be doing well, a team member may elect to de-emphasize or minimize the reality of slippage on the part of a project for which he or she is responsible. A project manager should be mindful of this and generate an environment that promotes and rewards honest reporting. Any project will inevitably see slippages, whether due to mistakes, errors in planning, or circumstances beyond anyone's control. Reporting of slippages should be met with an attitude toward solving the problem, rather than recrimination for presumed failures.

Progress Reports

Progress reports at their most simple are a comparison of "where we expected to be" and "where we are"—what work was expected to be completed on a project by the date of the report, and what work was accomplished. Implicit in this information is a sense of whether the project has experienced any slippage—whether it is on time, ahead of schedule, or has fallen behind in any way. Team members should be encouraged to be specific and as accurate as possible during this report, and to make some attempt to make near-term projections: If the project is behind, will it remain behind? Is there a reason it might fall further behind? Will there be an opportunity to get back on schedule?

Ideally, a progress report should be accompanied by variance and control options to be weighed by team members, particularly by those who have a stake in the issue. (Chapter 9 examines variance and control considerations in more detail.) As any control options will inevitably impact the relationships among cost, time, and scope, the team member making control proposals should be prepared to estimate the impact to each of these areas for each option, and to discuss them in detail with stakeholders.

Consider the example from *Crimes of the Heart*, above. If we were generating a progress report at the end of the week of August 21, and progress-tracking information indicated that the "porch spindles" task was only 33 percent complete (as indicated in figure 8.2), we would be behind our planned schedule. When presenting this progress report, we should also present pertinent information about factors contributing to the delay on this task (that most of the day crew called out sick on varying days during the week, as the crew fell ill to the twenty-four-hour flu), and what impact this slippage will have on the project as a whole (in this case, that the day crew's upcoming tasks leave room for one member of the crew to continue manufacturing porch spindles without impacting other progress).

Expense Reports

Expense reports, like progress reports, compare the amount that was expected to be spent by this point in the project against what has been spent. In a perfect world, a project should see little-to-no variance between a well-executed, bottom-up estimate, and day-to-day recording of expenses. This is never true, of course—material and labor costs tend to fluctuate over time, or errors are made requiring the purchase of more material than was expected. Whatever the reason, actual expenses often vary from projected expenses. This difference will result in the project—or parts of the project—being over or under budget. As with progress reports, expense reports should be accompanied by an estimation of the impact any variances—or projected variances—will have, and by any proposed control options to be weighed by team members and stakeholders.

For example, a costume shop manager on a production of *Arabian Nights* may have gone fabric shopping with a designer and determined that at current pricing, it's unlikely he'll be able to obtain the fabrics required for the amount budgeted. The impact of this will mean a reexamination of cost, time, or scope:

- *Cost.* The designer may need to select less expensive options for other parts of the production, or the producer may decide to provide additional funds to cover the more expensive fabrics.
- *Time.* The costume shop manager and the designer may elect to go with a less-expensive fabric that will, unfortunately, result in spending more time on construction or during cleaning and maintenance (i.e., a stretch fabric instead of a nonstretch, or a fabric that can only be dry-cleaned).
- *Scope.* The designer may need to consider simplifying the design to require less fabric, or a less-expensive fabric—one that may be synthetic rather than natural, or less vibrantly dyed, or that has a different drape than had been hoped for.

These options impact the overall quality of the project, and their impact would need to be discussed with any relevant stakeholders. Consequently, the costume shop manager should be prepared to discuss the details of each option, their impact, and the ways in which they each address the over-budget concern.

Questions and Concerns

No matter how detailed reporting is, and no matter how comprehensive the documentation of the scope of a project, there are always questions and concerns that arise as a project's life cycle progresses. Directors realize they aren't clear which direction a door opens on the set; they discover they need the table farther from the sofa to permit the staging being developed in rehearsal; the costume designer finds shoes that are perfect for the lead actress that simply cannot be rubberized to be safe on the high-gloss floor. Whatever the questions are, they come up and need to be addressed.

Sometimes these questions and concerns are resolved quickly through responses to rehearsal reports or simple email or phone communication. Other times, issues cannot be resolved in these ways; typically, that is because the questions and concerns raised will have a direct impact on the scope of the project (and by extension on the cost and time required to complete it). Discussions of scope often require a more in-depth conversation, because they are conversations about changing the expectations of the project. Discussing these concerns in a production meeting usually ensures that any stakeholders and anyone with authority to make decisions about cost, time, and scope should be in the room and available to make those decisions. (Changes in scope are often documented using change requests, discussed in chapter 9.)

Production Meeting Reports

Production meetings are the site of many decisions related to the time, cost, and scope of a project as well as for the distribution of authority and responsibility for its different aspects. It is important to document and share any changes with the rest of the team to avoid confusion later, and so that there's a record to refer to if disagreements or confusions crop up. A project manager should generate a production-meeting report (figure 8.5) after each production meeting, detailing the decisions and changes made during that meeting. This can either be formal or informal; it is generally simplest to copy a meeting agenda, write in any decisions made related to each agenda item, and then distribute it to the team.

Milestone Reviews

Chapter 7 examined the concept of milestones: key moments in a project's life cycle, typically at which specific deliverables are expected from the team, and at which specific amounts of resource and labor expenditures should be expected. Milestones provide opportunities to quantitatively measure progress against expectations, by comparing what has been spent and what has been completed against what was planned to have been spent and completed. Milestones present key opportunities to review progress, at what are sometimes called—quite creatively—"milestone reviews."

As pointed out previously, a typical theatre production process (common in summer-stock and regional theatres) comprises some familiar milestones:

- Initial design meeting
- Preliminary design deadline
- Final design deadline
- Costing/budget due
- First fittings
- Final fittings
- Load-in begins
- First technical rehearsal
- First preview
- Opening night
- Strike

Each of these milestones has a set of deliverables associated with it, and progress on the project can be measured by assessing the level of completion of those deliverables. For example, at the final set design deadline, the set designer is expected to deliver a set of drawings, perhaps a model, color elevations, and other materials necessary for understanding the scope and vision of the set design. (Typically, these deliverables are delineated in his or her contract.)

Milestone reviews should be held as each of these milestones approach to allow for sharing of deliverables and a review of progress. They provide a bird's-eye view of project progress for all members of the team. Often, some of these milestone reviews have special meetings assigned for them—e.g., the final-design presentation and budget meeting. At other times, these reviews get folded into regular weekly production meetings. Whether held as a special meeting or as part of a regularly scheduled meeting, milestone reviews should focus on big-picture

Crimes Of The Heart Production Meeting Report **09/07/2016**

Department Check-Ins

Scenery • $2,179.96 out of $2,900 spent (updated since last meeting) Paint • $358.93 our of $650 spent (updated since last meeting) • Nearly everything that has been built has been painted Props • $500 out of $500 spent Lighting • $389 out of $500 spent • Hang went well; focus is this weekend	Sound • No money spent • Load-in last week; ready for calibration this Thursday and level set on Saturday Costumes • $713.26 out of $1,000 spent • Haircuts and second fittings this week Stage Management • Fire on stage information given to Production Manager

New Business

ALL: Paper Tech to be Next Friday → Possibly earlier on

Scenery:

- Load in notes → meeting to happen with **Scenic Designer** about observations not problems (update: occurred and items resolved)
- Mallet seating miscommunication → there are now seats in the moat because reserved seats were sold there; Mallet moved to reserved seating this summer; because of this change **Costume Designer** will provide undergarments for those actors wearing shorter outfits
- Expectations for "working set" → the set is not fully complete, but it will have the important items (i.e. working doors, stairs, etc.); roof truss may not be there for Focus → **Scene Shop** builds tonight (09/07), **Paint** has it ready by Friday (09/09) = It will be ready by Tuesday (09/13); because of this **Lighting** will need dark time next week

Props:

- Trash can is under the sink
- **Scenic Designer** will meet with **Prop Master** to discuss set dressing, item placement, and will prop hunt

Lights:

Figure 8.5. One page of a production-meeting report

progress and the ability to meet expectations at each milestone.

For example, a common concern leading up to the lighting-focus milestone is what scenery will be available to focus lighting *on*. In an ideal world, earlier in the project life cycle (during conversations concerning scope and estimating/scheduling) deliverables for focus should have been determined in coordination with the lighting designer, the set designer, the technical director, and any other stakeholders who might be involved (this may often include the stage manager and director, for reasons made clearer below). These might have included the following deliverables:

- All of the built scenery structures, including hanging elements that might directly impact focus
- Furniture, placed as determined through the ground plan and the rehearsal process
- All of the lighting fixtures hung and circuited, with data cables run as needed
- Completed channel patch at the control console
- A lighting crew comprised of master electrician, assistant master electrician, and four electricians, each comfortable with heights and experienced at focusing lighting fixtures

At a production meeting before the focus is scheduled to happen, the project manager should request a milestone review for the focus, asking for an update on the agreed-upon deliverables. This would include reports from the technical director, prop master, and master electrician on the status of each, any variance from the expected deliverables, the ramifications of any variances, and proposed controls to minimize the impact of those variances. For example, the following may be reported:

- All of the scenic structures will be installed as planned, though some may have only base coats of paint treatments.
- The furniture will be required in rehearsal during focus, but stage management can spike furniture placement on the stage prior to focus.
- All of the lighting fixtures will be prepped as expected.
- The patch will be completed as planned.
- The lighting crew will be comprised of the planned number and experience of electricians.

As with production meetings, milestone reviews that happen as independent meetings should be reported back to the team. Any decisions made about time, cost, scope, authority, or responsibility should be documented and shared.

Performance Reports

As much as it may seem like it, a live-entertainment project doesn't end at opening night. While it may enter a new phase of its life cycle, a live-entertainment project continues until closing and strike. After opening, most of the effort of team members is focused on maintaining the quality of the production during the run. This means facilitating and completing ongoing repairs and maintenance to scenic elements and costumes, brushing up on tempo, motivation, staging, and cue pickup for the performers, changing burned-out gels or refocusing fixtures that have dropped—that sort of thing.

Some organizations can assign people to the project team whose sole responsibility is this kind of maintenance work: wardrobe staff, deck carpenters, deck electricians, and others. For other organizations, these maintenance tasks revert to appropriate functional departments, or may even be the responsibility of the designer, or a single staff member. (As discussed in chapter 3, these decisions should generally happen early in the project definition phase of the project life cycle.) Regardless of who holds the responsibility for seeing to maintenance and repair tasks, the performance report (figure 8.6) is the way these concerns get documented and reported.

Performance reports outline issues related to a specific performance and are usually distributed immediately following it. These might include everything from details about the weather, the number of patrons, patrons' response to the performance, actor notes, and repair and maintenance notes. Reports are typically distributed to key stakeholders and those team members who have decision-making authority over and responsibility for key elements of the production (typically, scenery, lighting, costumes, sound, direction, musical direction, and video, among others).

> Responding to written reporting is an important part of production-team communication. When giving a report during a meeting or otherwise face to face, it is easy to determine if an issue or a concern has been understood and acknowledged. This is not the case for written reports that are distributed either on paper or via email. Consequently, it is essential for team members with responsibility and authority over issues raised in written reports to, at the very least, acknowledge that an issue has been understood.

Summing Up

Qualitative Tracking

Qualitative tracking methods generate a sense of progress, of quality, and of completion of scope, sometimes referred to as having a "thumb on the pulse" of the project. Two major means of getting a feel for the progress of the project are a weekly shop meeting and a "shop-walk" inspection review.

Shop Meetings (Weekly Progress Review)

A weekly meeting to discuss progress, questions, and concerns within each functional shop or area of authority and responsibility for a project. The primary goal is to get a sense of the project beyond what quantitative reports of measurable progress can reveal.

"Shop-Walks" (Inspection Reviews)

Shop-walks, or inspection reviews, provide an opportunity for project managers to observe progress first-hand, to examine quality and scope.

Quantitative Tracking

Quantitative tracking methods measure progress against expectations in terms of resources expenditures and adherence to predicted schedules.

Expense Tracking

Expense tracking is a means of recording and tallying every expense in a project, typically in a ledger or spreadsheet. The

Metamorphoses

PURDUE THEATRE

DATE Thursday April 21, 2005

TIME 8:00 pm

PERFORMANCE # 7

RUNNING TIMES:

	UP	DOWN	TOTAL
(STATUES)	8:05	8:08	3MIN
SHOW	8:08	9:41	93MIN
TOTAL			1H. 36M

WEATHER Rainy and Cool

HOUSE COUNT 126

HELD FOR Audience

PERFORMANCE NOTES:

The Audience tonight was very responsive to the show, and it seemed as if Kevin Lambert had friends in the house because he was a smash hit. Some usually tense moments in the play were countered with laughter tonight, but the actors were not negatively affected.

The roles usually played by Joe Quadres were played by Kevin Lambert during tonight's performance and he did a superb job with no noted problems.

TECHNICAL NOTES:

COSTUMES:
-Could you please wash the prop towels in the girl's dressing room? Also, if there are any white prop costume towels left in the hall, would you place them in the dressing rooms? Thank you.
-Steven Potts' white basic tunic is shrinking. Is there any way to fix this? Thank you.

PROPS:
-Thank you for fixing the jump rope. However, gold paint got on the black back of the jump rope and it is now visible in the house. Could the back of the rope be touched up? Thank you.

ADMINISTRAVTIVE NOTES:

Adjudication will be this Saturday following the performance. Please be at the Experimental by 9:45pm so that we may start as quickly as possible. Thank you.

Kevin Lambert will take over Joe Quadres' roles for tomorrow's performance.

THANKS!
Caitlin
STAGE MANAGER

Figure 8.6. Example performance report

level of detail of expense records depends directly on the level of detail required for reporting and variance control. Some organizations will expect extremely detailed expense tracking, to the level of tallying expenses specific to each node or task in a work-breakdown structure; others will expect less detail.

Progress Tracking

Progress tracking is keeping a running tally as to when nodes and tasks from a work-breakdown structure are completed. As with expense tracking, the level of detail is dependent on the level of reporting and variance control required. Often a Gantt chart can be used to indicate how much of each node or task is completed (with either printed percentages or with temperature-bar-style graphics).

Reporting

Rehearsal Reports

Rehearsal reports are written documentation of discoveries made by the director during the rehearsal process. Often these discoveries impact cost, time, and scope, and need to be further discussed by members of the team to determine how the overall project is affected by them.

Production Meetings

Regular (usually weekly) production meetings provide an opportunity for team members to share updates on progress and expenses, and to discuss questions and concerns that might impact cost, time, and scope, as well as authority and responsibility for various aspects of the production.

PROGRESS REPORTS

Progress reports are a comparison of where we expected to be and where we are: what work was expected to be completed on a project by the date of the report, and what work was accomplished.

EXPENSE REPORTS

Expense reports compare the amount that was expected to be spent by this point in the project against what has been spent.

QUESTIONS AND CONCERNS

Questions and concerns raised during the life cycle of a project often impact the overall production, whether in terms of cost, time, or scope, or in terms of authority and responsibility for certain parts of the production. Discussing these concerns in a production meeting usually ensures that any stakeholders and anyone with authority to make decisions about cost, time, and scope should be in the room and available to make those decisions.

PRODUCTION MEETING REPORTS

Production meeting reports summarize decisions made during production meetings related to cost, time, and scope of the project as well as distribution of authority and responsibility among team members, and should be distributed promptly after a production meeting has been held.

Milestone Reviews

Milestone reviews are opportunities to discuss big-picture progress as related to specific project milestones. On many production projects, milestones might include dates such as design deadlines, budget meetings, final fittings, load-in, focus, first technical rehearsal, and opening night. Milestone reviews can be either separate specific meetings or included as part of regular production meetings, and should be followed up with written documentation of decisions made in the same manner as production meetings.

Performance Reports

Performance reports are written documentation of ongoing repair, maintenance, and upkeep needs for every aspect of a production, from actor performances, to staging, to scenery, costumes, props, and many other elements.

9. Variance and Control

In some ways, the work of recognizing when a project is diverging from the planned progress, and dealing with the ramifications of that divergence, is one of the hardest parts of managing a project. It is easy to want to believe that once the hard work of planning the project has been completed, things will run smoothly. It is inevitable, however, that things will go awry. Tracking and reporting progress and expenditures throughout the life cycle of the project can help managers recognize these variances, and once recognized, they can be addressed through control measures that minimize their impact on the overall project.

German military strategist Helmuth von Moltke said, "No battle plan survives contact with the enemy." This is as true for project management as it is for military strategy: every plan, once put in motion, will inevitably become increasingly less accurate and reliable. Errors happen, assumptions are incorrect, and reality asserts itself. If variance, then, is inevitable—if there will need to be effort expended to develop control measures throughout the life cycle of the project—why spend so much effort developing a plan at all?

There are a lot of reasons to develop an initial project plan, to go through the steps of making estimates, of developing build schedules and plans, of defining the scope and determining the makeup of the team. The most important reason is to establish at the outset whether a project is feasible, whether it can even be accomplished. The second most important reason is that without a plan, every step of the process becomes an improvisation—and improvisation takes significant mental energy, has unpredictable costs, and, often, unreliable results.

However, improvisation can be flexible; it is quick, can be agile, and can provide outside-the-box solutions in the heat of the moment. What improvisation lacks in efficiency it makes up for in its usefulness for responding to changes in a plan. The flexibility of improvisation is one of the key elements of responding to variance. The best managers balance the efficiency of planning and tracking with the ability to be flexible and improvisational when the project changes, evolves, falls behind schedule or looks to be in danger of running over budget.

Topics covered in this chapter:

- Variance
    - Current variance
    - Predicting variance
- Control
- Managing change
    - Promoting discovery
        - Initiating a change request
        - Measuring impact
        - Reviewing impact
        - Approving or rejecting change

Variance

Chapter 8 presented methods for tracking and reporting project progress. One of the main purposes of tracking and reporting progress is to identify variance. Variance is defined as the difference between where the project is currently and where the project should be. In expense-tracking terms, variance is often discussed in terms of a project being under or over budget; in scheduling terms, variance is often discussed as slippage or acceleration. (There is some disagreement in project management circles here; sometimes "slippage" refers to any deviation in the progression of the project when compared to the schedule. Positive slippage means a task is behind schedule, and negative slippage means a task is ahead of schedule. This is counterintuitive, but think of it this way: slippage defines how far a project has fallen behind schedule: positive slippage—larger numbers—means a project is further behind. In this text, slippage refers to running behind schedule.)

As mentioned in chapter 8, tracking reveals any variance in expenses and schedule at a fixed point in time. This information is important in and of itself, but less so than knowing whether the project will hit all of its milestones for a timely delivery. Unfortunately, tracking will only reveal the end result of the project when the end of the project life cycle has been reached—far too late to make any decisions to effect change. However, when current variance reporting is coupled with future variance *predictions*, an inference of the results of any variance can be drawn, and control methods developed to assure a project reaches the end of its life cycle on time, on budget, while meeting the scope and quality expectations defined at the outset of the project.

This process is not unlike driving a car to a destination that is a good distance away—perhaps visiting parents, heading home from college, or driving to a long-planned vacation getaway. Imagine a day trip to a destination that is about five hundred miles away. A driving plan for that trip might look something like the following:

8:00 A.M.	Start driving, at approximately seventy miles an hour
12:00 P.M.	Eat lunch and get gas
1:00 P.M.	Start driving, at approximately seventy miles an hour
5:00 P.M.	Arrive at destination

After driving on the interstate for about two hours, traffic starts to get worse, and speeds slow to about fifty-five miles per hour for about thirty minutes. At 10:30 A.M. the total distance driven will be approximately 167 miles; the plan called for having traveled about 175 miles by that time. The project has started to slip. Anyone who has driven on a trip like this will know that just because the drive took a little longer due to some traffic doesn't mean the arrival time will be significantly delayed (if it's delayed at all): it will likely be possible to make up the time by taking a shorter lunch break.

Combining current variance ("I ran into some traffic that slowed me down") against predicted or future variances ("News reports indicate traffic will only be worse farther along my route") allows for an educated prediction of the overall variance of the completion of the project.

Current Variance

Current variance refers to any deviations from the expected expenses and schedule to date. Current variance is easily revealed by comparing project tracking to estimates and projections at any given time throughout the life cycle of the project. For example, consider the scenic schedule and tracking information for the date February 27 during the production of *Rabbit Hole* (figure 9.1).

According to the schedule, the following deliverables should have been completed:

- Kitchen platform
  - Build stud walls
  - Build custom platforms/triscuits
  - Build masking flats
  - Get stock triscuits
  - Cut/lay out floor
  - Cut/lay out facing
  - Paint floor
  - Paint facing
- Bedroom platform
  - Build stud walls
  - Build custom triscuits
  - Build masking flats
  - Cut floor
  - Lay out floor (for paint)
  - Cut facing
  - Lay out facing (for paint)
  - Paint facing

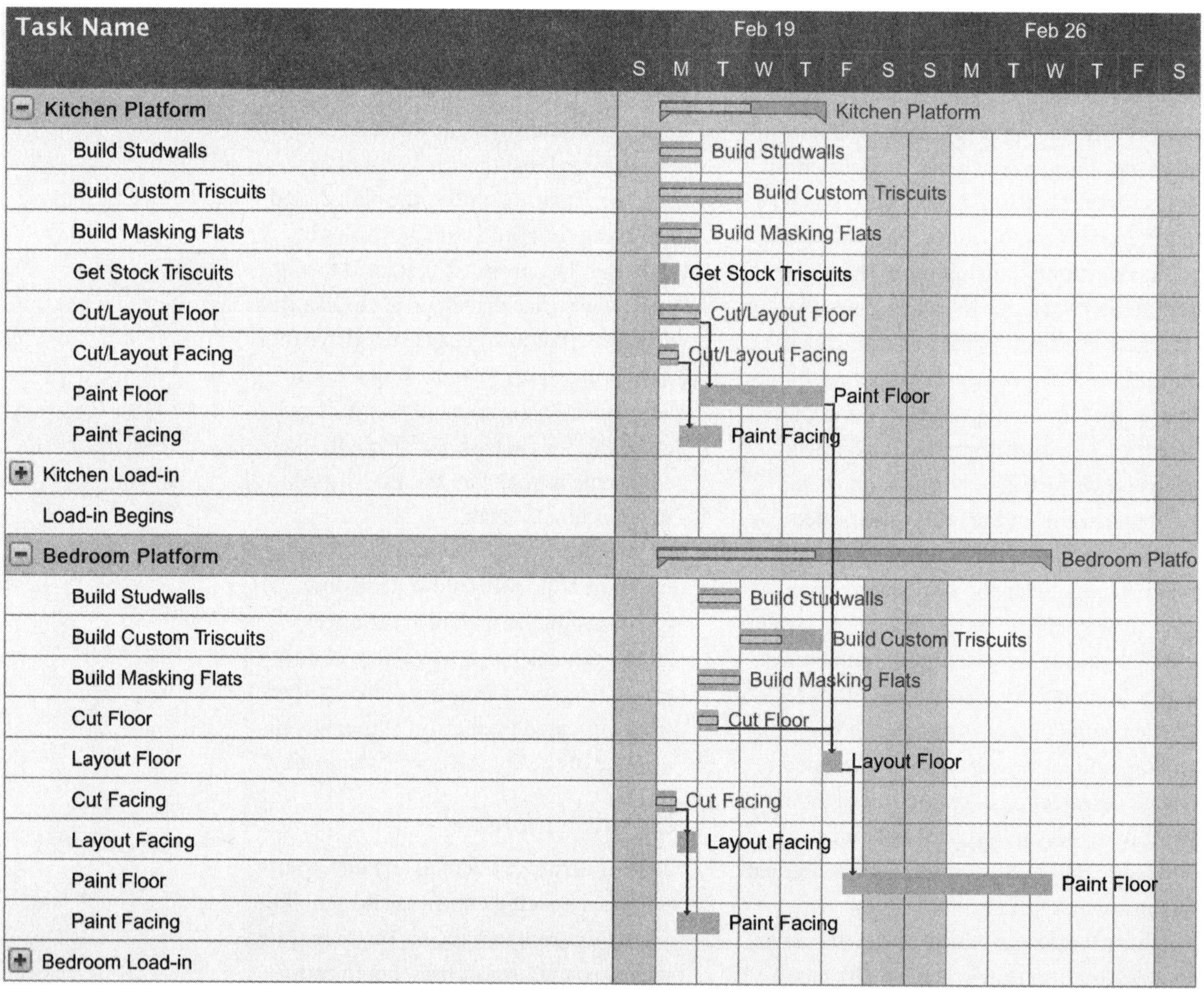

Figure 9.1. Scenery progress tracking for *Rabbit Hole*

The following should all be under way, but not yet completed:

- Paint floor (bedroom platform)

According to the tracking records, however, by this date, the following tasks have not started:

- Kitchen platform
  - Get stock triscuits
  - Paint floor
  - Paint facing
- Bedroom platform
  - Lay out floor (for paint)
  - Lay out facing (for paint)
  - Paint facing

The task "build custom triscuits," which should be completed, has been started but not completed. This reflects a variance in the build schedule for the production.

Consider another example: the costume shop manager for a production of *Amadeus* has indicated that on the first Sunday of the costume build, the designer and costume shop manager plan to make a trip to purchase fabrics in Chicago. They plan to spend $1,500 of the $2,000 budget on fabric purchases, to obtain all the fabric required for the costumes being built for Mozart, Salieri, Emperor Joseph, Constanze, and Katherina. (The remaining funds will be used for accessories, alterations, and the like.) However, after the shopping trip, the costume shop manager reports that they spent all the $1,500, but were unable to find suitable fabrics for one of Katherina's dresses. This represents a variance in expenses: materials for all the built costumes should have cost $1,500, but the shop manager will need to spend more than that if they intend to build all of Katherina's dresses.

Predicting Variance

Determining future variance, much like making estimates during the planning phase of a project, relies on a manager's ability to make predictions about cost and progress in the future. Future variance is a prediction of how factors that are either beyond a manager's control, or that hadn't previously been foreseen or anticipated, will likely impact costs, quality, or progress of the project going forward. Predicting future variance can easily be confused with efforts at controlling current variance; however, they are not the same. (Control efforts are discussed later in this chapter.)

Predicting variance requires being aware of information from a variety of sources, and making judgments about how some of that information may impact costs and progress in the future. It is part science and part art. For example, consider the lumber market immediately following Hurricane Katrina in 2005. In some parts of the country, the combination of rebuilding after the hurricane and rebuilding efforts overseas in the aftermath of the conflicts in Iraq and Afghanistan led to a reduction in domestic stocks of plywood panels in the United States. This further led to an increase in the price of plywood sheets in some parts of the country. Recognizing the impact the rising prices would have on ongoing projects is an example of predicting future variance.

Not all examples of predicting variance require devastating meteorological phenomena or global military and political efforts. A stitcher inadvertently sewing over his thumb on a Friday afternoon will have an inevitable impact on his or her ability to produce quality work in a timely manner in the coming weeks—a predictable future variance, to be sure.

Discovering that a method for routing mortar grooves in sheet goods for a brick façade will look far too squared off and fabricated to satisfy the designer's desire for an aged brick wall is another example of predictable future variance.

Monitoring for the possibility of future variance in time, cost, scope, and quality goes hand in hand with project tracking and determining current variance. Small amounts of current variance can be predictors for future variance. Consider, for example, that progress tracking reveals that every light that Johnny the electrician has focused in the hour after lunch has taken him about a minute or two longer than those he focused in the morning. It is not too significant a logical leap to predict that the rest of the lights he will need to focus that afternoon—thirty in all—will cause the focus call to run at least thirty minutes longer than planned.

Predicted future variance, when combined with accurate measures of current variance, provides an overall picture of the progress of the project, and can predict whether the totality of the project will be over or under budget, on time or delayed, or fail to meet quality and scope expectations or exceed them. It is this overall picture that is most essential for managing the project, because the estimation of overall project variance determines the need for control measures, what those measures will need to address, and how they will address them.

Control

Control, in a project planning and management context, refers to efforts to manage and mitigate the impact of variance in an ongoing project. Control measures can be direct (current) actions or compensatory (future) actions, and usually involve balancing the interrelated facets of time, cost, scope, and quality. Perhaps the biggest determination for a project manager when controlling variance is deciding when to step in and attempt controls. In any given situation, a manager could step in and take immediate, direct action as soon as variance is recognized to address the issue. Alternatively, he or she could wait to see if variances will resolve themselves. (Inevitably, every task in a project will have some variances, and often—if they are small enough—these variances cancel each other out.) Or he or she could take compensatory action by adapting parts of the project still to come, to address current or predicted variances.

Unfortunately, there is no simple checklist to determine when to intervene and take corrective action on a project. Every situation is different, and each situation will require a unique point of intervention. There are some questions to consider, however, that can provide insight into when to intervene.

- *How large is the variance right now?* A large variance at any single point in time in a project's life cycle probably requires immediate intervention. For example, finding out at the lunch break of a one-day lighting hang that the electrics crew has only completed the work they expected to complete in the first hour is something that should be addressed immediately. (In fact, this variance would beg the question, "Why wasn't the potential for this variance predicted earlier," which is a different—but no less important—problem to address.)

Conversely, a small variance probably doesn't require immediate intervention, but should be monitored, as the project progresses, for its impact on the totality of the project. Consider, for example, discovering that the cost of 2 × 4s has increased by ten cents per sixteen-foot board, resulting in an overall increase in the estimated expense of 2 × 4s for the project by fifteen dollars, out of a budgeted expense for the entire set of four thousand dollars. A variance this small can be observed for a while; perhaps 2 × 4 costs will drop again, or costs of other materials will be lower than anticipated down the line.

- *Does the variance stem from a systemic issue, or is it the impact of a one-time event?* A one-time event that impacts a project might not require immediate intervention, whereas a systemic one probably does. For example, consider a scenic build in which a carpenter read the plans incorrectly, and managed to face the back of a flat frame with lauan instead of the front. This will likely put the project behind by a couple of hours as the facing is removed and replaced on the correct side. (It will probably also result in additional material expenses to replace lauan sheets that can't be reused.)

  If this happened once, there's probably no need to make an immediate correction. An experienced carpenter will be mortified by her error and, odds are, it won't happen again; she will probably work hard on her own to make up for the time lost. However, if it happens more than once, this likely reflects a systemic problem. Perhaps the drawings are unclear, or this carpenter needs additional supervision or training, and in order to prevent additional setbacks in the construction process, a corrective intervention should be made quickly.
- *Will the variance grow over time?* If there is good evidence to predict that small variances will continue to occur, piling up over time, it makes sense to intervene sooner rather than later. For example, consider the scenic treatment of a faux marble column for a set—the first of many on stage. If the quality of the paint treatment is significantly less than what the designer expected, it would be a good idea to take corrective action early to ensure the remaining columns are painted in a more acceptable way.

Determining how to intervene is just as important as determining when. Do you take direct action, or do you take a compensatory action, impacting the future life cycle of the project? This is not the same as making an immediate control intervention or waiting until a later time; this is about what kind of corrective controls to put in place. For example, consider the example of the scenic paint treatment of the columns.

Clearly, an immediate intervention is required to address concerns about the quality and scope of the paint treatment on the columns. A direct control action might comprise discussing with the scenic charge and designer the concerns about the paint treatment on the first column, and ensuring understanding of goals and how they might be met. A compensatory action might be deciding to discuss with the lighting designer how those columns might be lit onstage, and highlighting them less when the time comes in order to de-emphasize the paint treatment.

Consider another example, from earlier in the chapter: the costume material expenses for a production of *Amadeus*. In the example, the costume designer and shop manager spent more on fabric for the costumes for Mozart, Salieri, Emperor Joseph, and Constanze, leaving none of the budgeted amount available for material for Katherina's costume, which they predict will cost an additional three hundred dollars, putting the costume expenses over budget. A direct action might be to approve the overage, and to obtain additional funds from the producer to cover the additional costs. (This is not a likely intervention, but a possible one.) A compensatory or future action might be to determine that of the remaining five hundred dollars in the budget, two hundred dollars will be allocated for materials for Katherina's costume and those expenses must be two hundred dollars or less. Any additional accessories or alterations must cost less than the remaining three hundred dollars.

Balancing the need to control variance against the tendency to micromanage is essential. The last thing a project manager wants is to have team members infer a lack of trust in them, which is often what results from micromanagement. It is important to allow team members to retain authority over those aspects of the project over which they've been given authority. In the best scenario, a project manager will facilitate a conversation with the necessary stakeholders and provide guidance toward developing an acceptable control action.

Once it has been determined when and how to intervene, developing the control intervention remains. Just as the interrelated facets of cost, time, scope, and quality informed the planning process, these facets are the areas that can be most directly affected by control measures. The control intervention, then, comprises methods to adjust those facets to minimize, reduce, or remove the impact of variances in the project.

When developing a control action, consider that each of the four facets that define the production—cost, time, scope, and quality—can be examined and adjusted. Consider the following:

- *Would additional money make a difference?*
  Obviously, this can only happen if more money can be made available. In many situations—particularly not-for-profit summer-stock and regional theatres—this is often not possible. However, it may be possible to, as the saying goes, "steal from Peter to pay Paul"; some tasks or elements of the project—or even other projects within the organization—may be running under budget and can be borrowed from. Or, elements of a project might be considered useful enough to justify capitalizing the cost over multiple years, or spreading the cost over multiple projects.
- *Can materials not yet purchased be replaced with materials that cost less?*
  Reducing future costs, or absorbing current overages in future expenses—is a straightforward idea. It boils down to accepting that because the project spent more now, it will have less to spend later. Inevitably, the decision to use lower-cost materials results in the potential

for lower-quality work, however, and the impact of this should be clearly determined and discussed.

- *Would additional time make a difference?*
  It's not uncommon for major construction projects to run well past their deadline—buildings are completed late, roads open later than planned. However, in live entertainment, this is rarely possible, as opening night is usually a fixed date, with paying customers expecting to see a performance. However, the deadlines for different parts of the production might be altered or adjusted. Perhaps most of the set can be ready for focus as planned, but the hanging picture frames suspended over the set can't go in until after focus, for example, or the wigs won't arrive until second dress rehearsal. Adjustments like these will likely impact the work related to other tasks on the project (i.e., the electricians may have to touch up focus after the installation of the picture frames), and this should be accounted for during any discussion of extending deadlines as a control measure.
- *Would additional labor make a difference?*
  Can labor be shifted from one part of the project to another? This will depend, of course, on the impact of reducing the labor available for other parts of the project. Sometimes, the impact will be negligible (especially for tasks not on the critical path); sometimes it will be significant. Occasionally, additional labor can be brought from outside; however, this typically represents a greater expense, an additional variance that will need to be compensated for.
- *Can the expectations of quality be flexed?*
  Reducing the quality expectations of a task or project should be considered one of the last resort options for controlling variance. However, reducing quality expectations for some tasks within a project can be an effective way of reducing the cost or time required to complete that task. Consider, for example, black masking fabrics hanging on curtain rods in the back of the set, which are never seen by the audience—they simply mask any light that might leak to the audience. They were budgeted as an eighteen-ounce black commando cloth, with a pocket on top (to receive a curtain rod) and bottom (to receive a chain weight). It might be possible, however, to replace the commando cloth with eight-ounce duvetyne (a lesser fabric), for example, and to forgo the pocket and chain weight on the bottom (which will result in a less clean look—but which an audience will never see).
- *Can the overall scope of a task or the project be altered?*
  If reducing expectations of quality should be one of the last measures considered when controlling for variance, reducing the scope of a project or task should be *the* last. This means, essentially, changing the expectations of the design in what might be significant ways. The most drastic example of this option for controlling variance is to determine that a specific unit, task, or element must be cut from the show: for example, the false

proscenium—which was being built last on the schedule—must be cut because previous cost overruns mean the materials can't be purchased and have the project remain within budget. However, modifications to scope that have a smaller impact on the production are also possible: for example, swapping out working door latch sets and strike plates for dummy knobs and bullet catches, or not adding pockets to pants constructed for a specific character.

It can be tempting to imagine that control measures are straightforward relationships between the kind of variance and the element of the project to control to correct that variance. However, controlling variance is rarely as straightforward as it seems. Predicted cost overruns can be controlled by changing the budget of the production, or by finding less expensive materials—either for the tasks that are running over budget, or by making changes to other tasks to reduce their materials costs. Sometimes, however, adding additional labor to a task can *also* reduce materials costs, by allowing for the use of different materials (like, say, larger sheet goods that can only be maneuvered by multiple people). Examining the scope and quality of the project can also result in reduced expenses: Might a lower-quality fabric that looks just as good but costs less be used? Can the shop forego building a full underdress for this character, even though the original budget had included it? Developing effective control strategies often requires compromising the balance among cost, time, scope, and quality, and should be done with the input of the relevant stakeholders.

Control measures, once enacted, change the original plan. These changes should be plotted to the end of the project's life cycle. Any tracking that happens after enacting changes should be compared against the revised plan to determine variance. This may seem obvious, but it can be easy to neglect revising the project plan to reflect control measures, particularly in live-entertainment projects. Productions tend to be quick and have short life cycles, and it can be tempting to assume that the project-long impact of control changes can be remembered and accounted for on the fly. This temptation should be avoided, both to ensure there are no cascading variances due to misremembered (or even forgotten) changes to the plan, and to

An important concept to consider here is something called "scope gap." Scope gap refers to those situations when different teams or groups on a project—or even the project team and the client—all think someone else is responsible for part of the project. Consider, for example, an "on air" light box for a production set in a radio station. The props master may believe the scene shop is building the box while the technical director believes the props artisan is, and all the while the electrics shop is waiting to get their hands on it to electrify it and connect it to the lighting system. This is scope gap, and can often be the cause of variance on a project. Clear discussions about scope during the planning phase of a project can eliminate a lot of scope-gap issues; however, when they do come up, change orders (see below) and clearly reassigning responsibility for those elements missed previously can usually clear up the issue quickly.

provide an accurate record for project review later (discussed in chapter 10), and for future project planning.

Managing Change

In a project manager's ideal world, change wouldn't happen; once the project's scope was defined and the plan developed, the project would move forward, variances would be controlled, and, at the end of the timeline, the project would be delivered as planned. Unfortunately, that's not always the case—and that is especially true with live-entertainment projects. In fact, in many ways, a live-entertainment project should be managed to actively *anticipate* and *encourage* change.

"Change," in a project management setting, has a specific meaning. It is different from variance, described previously, and from the ways a project plan is altered to accommodate them. "Change," in this context, refers to decisions made to adjust the totality of the scope of the project as the project progresses. In a more typical construction-industry project or many commercial-theatre projects, this might include deciding that the flooring for an entrance lobby should change from vinyl to ceramic tile because the client prefers it. Another example might be a situation in which the client would prefer the stairwell to the second floor to run along the east wall instead of the west wall.

In a live-entertainment project, change like this often comes out of the rehearsal process. While it isn't uncommon for many of the design elements to have been finalized and approved by the time rehearsals start, the rehearsal process is as much about discovering how to tell the story as it is about "practicing the play." Consequently, the director may see reason for the scope of the design elements to change during the process in response to what is happening in rehearsal.

For managers and team members who are more comfortable with a rigid, waterfall approach to the production process (as described in chapter 1), scope change during the process of completing the project can present a challenge. Schedules were developed based on an approved design; expense plans were generated based on that design and on existing budgets. Changes to the scope of the project—whether small or large—can leave plans and schedules in tatters, and team members feeling unsure about their ability to complete the project in a timely and financially responsible manner.

However, change like this is essential to the production process. The rehearsal process—unlike other elements of the project—involve people and stories about people. The human element of the production process is what makes each production different, unique, and worth producing. Consequently, the changes discovered and introduced during the rehearsal process should not simply be managed, but actively encouraged. And the management of the project should include methods and processes that provide that encouragement.

Promoting Discovery

As mentioned in chapter 8, the rehearsal report and the production meeting are key elements of promoting discovery during the production process. In many ways, the purpose of the rehearsal report is to provide a means for initiating a change in scope based on the discoveries being made in the rehearsal process. The time set aside during production meetings to discuss changes in scope also provides a venue to examine and approve any changes requested during the process. Occasionally, these changes are initiated by team members managing variance in the different aspects of physical production, but often they are initiated by discoveries made in rehearsal.

It is not uncommon for production team members to perceive scope change requests as dictates, or for some directors and designers to deliver them as such (often a practice that evolves from many experiences with production team members being resistant to change). A key to promoting discovery is mitigating both responses and encouraging a collaborative approach to discussing scope-change requests. One way to do this is by clearly establishing, at the outset of a project, that changes in scope should be expected and are, in fact, desirable. Another is to put in place a change management process that ensures that all members of the team can be assured that impacts to time, cost, and quality that result from change requests will be considered changes to their areas of responsibility. Every team member needs to be confident that changes in the scope of the project that arise during the project's life cycle are represented as changes to the plan.

What does this mean? In a traditional project-management model, a client must submit a written change order whenever he requests an alteration to the scope of the project. The change is then examined for its impact on the project: Will the change result in increased costs? Will the client pay those costs or must the contractors absorb them? Will the change result in a difficulty in completing the project on time? Will the client or customer accept a delayed delivery? What adaptations will need to be made to the project plan to accommodate the change request? The answers to these questions determine the ability of the contactors to make the change, and are included in a written record, usually signed by representatives of the project team and the client, along with the final determination of whether to make the change. The change process is outlined at the outset of the project; client, stakeholders, and project team members all know that all change requests will be measured against the impact on the project from the beginning.

Most live entertainment production processes don't begin with an explicit discussion of the change process. Instead, they rely on every team member's understanding of "accepted practice," that change requests are often initiated in rehearsal reports and discussed at production meetings. However, the assumption that all team members are on the same page about how change requests will be handled often leads to the kinds of frustrations discussed above. Better, instead, to outline clearly the change request process by clearly stating the following:

- How change requests will be initiated
- How the impact of change requests will be measured
- How the impact of change requests will be reviewed and discussed
- How change requests and accompanying project-plan changes will be approved and documented

An organization or project's change-approval process can be very formal, very informal, or somewhere in between. What is essential is that it be clearly defined. Consider the process outlined below, which might be considered somewhere in the middle between a formal and an informal process.

Initiating a Change Request

Depending on the scale of the change, change requests should be initiated through a note in the rehearsal report. If the perceived impact on the project would be relatively small, or the change is simply described—for example, adding a pocket to a pair of trousers, moving furniture placement, or changing the placement of a sound cue—the change request should be related in detail in the rehearsal report. If the perceived impact of the change would be larger, or if the change is complex or detailed enough to warrant it, the report should request a discussion of the issue at the next production meeting, or a separate meeting prior to the production meeting, if time might be a factor in making a decision.

> It should be clear that initiating a change request—by including it in a rehearsal report, or by discussing the change in a separate meeting or a production meeting—does not qualify as approving the change request! Initiating the request is only the first step in the process.

Change requests should include enough detail about the change to determine the impact on the project. For smaller changes, this may entail only a small amount of information; for example, an added pocket should be on the left-hand side, in the front of a character's trousers, and large enough to fit the notepad the character is carrying, which measures two inches by four inches and is only about a half-inch thick.

Larger changes, however, may require a far more detailed revision to measure the impact on the project. Consider, for example, a director who has just finished working through the exposition in act 2, scene 2 of *The Tempest*, in which Prospero relates the backstory of his fall from power, their arrival on the island, his discovery of Caliban and Ariel, and the identities of the mysterious passengers recently shipwrecked on their island. During rehearsal, he's determined that this is a lot of words without a lot of action, and, contrary to his initial estimation, those words aren't as compelling without some visual component to support them. Consequently, he'd like to add a dumbshow—actors miming some portion of his exposition, as if he's magically painting a picture for his daughter, Miranda. To weigh the possibility of adding this to the production, a number of questions have to be answered, among them:

- Will the actors be new actors, or actors already in the production?
- How will the actors be costumed? What will those costumes look like?
- Where will the dumbshow take place on stage?
- Will this require additional scenery? If so, what will it look like?
- Will any additional scenery need to be shifted/moved during performance? If so, how will this happen?
- How should this moment be lit?
- If the dumbshow is a kind of magical conjuring, should there be a sound element to support this?

The answers to these—and any other relevant questions—need to be provided so that the rest of the team can examine how this change might be implemented, and the impact that implementation might have on the plan for the project as a whole. The more detail that can be provided at this time, the more accurate the projections of impact are likely to be. It may take some time to develop the detail needed for extremely large or complex changes; in such a situation, creating a timeline for that development with clear deadlines that provide enough time for measuring the impact of changes on the project is essential.

Measuring Impact

Once a change request has been submitted—with as much relevant detail provided as possible—the team members with authority and responsibility over the parts of the project that would be affected should begin measuring the impact of the change request on the project. This can be considered a two-part process: What will be required to implement the changes requested, and how will the acquisition of necessary materials and allocation of necessary labor affect the overall project?

Just as with controlling variance, measuring the impact of change is easiest when a comprehensive and detailed plan for the totality of the project exists. For example, a costume shop manager weighing the possibility of adding a pocket to a character's trousers can quickly determine if there are tasks in the costume construction plan with any slack in the schedule, and estimate whether a stitcher from one of those tasks can accept the responsibility for adding a pocket without extending his currently assigned tasks past their deadline. If so, then the change will have minimal impact on the project.

Team members with responsibility for measuring the impact of change requests should create documentation that can demonstrate the impact of the request on the project (figure 9.2). This should be similar in form and function to the cost estimates and build schedules or Gantt charts normally provided during planning for the project, discussed more fully in chapters 5, 6, and 7.

Reviewing Impact

Similar to the project approval meeting discussed at the beginning of part 4 of this book, the documentation generated while measuring the impact of a change request should be presented to and discussed with relevant stakeholders. Typically, these stakeholders will include the director, the producer, the production manager, and any of the team members with authority over and responsibility for elements of the project impacted by the requested change.

At best, a review of the impact of a change request will reveal little or no impact on the project. Often, for smaller changes, this is exactly what happens. For larger changes, however, an in-depth conversation about the merits of the requested change balanced against its impact is required. Many times the impact of a change request can be lessened by adapting other parts of the project to accommodate it. For example, the scope or quality of later tasks in a project can be lessened, less expensive materials might be purchased, additional labor brought in, or more labor-efficient approaches considered. Additionally, the scope of the change can be lessened as well to make it more easily accommodated by the original project plan. As with controlling variance, balancing time, cost, scope, and quality for the requested change, other parts of the project, and the totality of the project can make the difference between a change request that can be fit into the project and one that cannot.

Change Request Form

Organization	Purdue University Theatre	Change #	3
Project Name	Blithe Spirit-Lineset Schedule	Date Submitted:	3/18/12
Requested By	Michael Banks	Date Reply Due	3/19/12

Description of Changes:

- Moving the Border on LS#16 to LS#14 (1'4" down stage).
- Lineset Schedule with Change:
    - LS#1: Legs (21' from CL), Border (22' trim)
    - LS#3: 1st Electric
    - LS#7: Chandelier
    - LS#8: Border (23' trim)
    - LS#9: 2nd Electric
    - LS#12: Legs (23' from CL)
    - **LS#14: Border (26' trim)**
    - LS#16: 3rd Electric
    - LS#19: 4th Electric
    - LS#24: 5th Electric
    - LS#28: Border (26' trim)
    - LS#31: 6th Electric
    - LS#33: Legs (21' from CL), Border (26' trim)

Justification:

Lineset 16 needed for an electric.

Impact:

Different available linesets for various areas.

Producer Approval: Joel Ebarb

Production Manager Approval: Rich Dionne

Director Approval: Larry Sommers

Scenic Designer Approval: Jessica Robertson

Lighting Designer Approval: Michael Banks

Technical Director Approval: Jeremy Jenkins

Figure 9.2. Change-order example from *Blithe Spirit*

> In practice, small change requests flow so quickly through the change protocol that a process hardly seems necessary. The temptation to skip any of these steps should be avoided, however, as it is important to develop a practice of discussing changes to the scope of a production in this way.

Approving or Rejecting Change

When all the repercussions of a proposed change have been discussed, team members and stakeholders must come to agreement about any compromises necessary for making a change possible. Every effort should be made by members of the team to realize the change; it is easy to assume that some compromises to time, cost, scope, or quality to accomplish a specific change request may be out of bounds based on the original project charter, but all such assumptions should be examined and deliberated. When discussion has come to a logical conclusion, a decision can be made about whether a requested change can go forward. Usually, this decision is self-evident: either the project plan can be adapted to accommodate the change, or it cannot.

After determining whether a change request can be approved or must be rejected, the results of the decision should be documented and recorded. Any approved change request is a change to the project—which, as discussed in previous chapters, is also an agreement among all the members of the team about time, cost, scope, quality, and areas of authority and responsibility. These elements define to what team members are being held, and to what they hold themselves accountable on the project. Consequently, all team members should be able to refer to the same set of expectations—and revisions to those expectations—at any time during the life cycle of the project. Providing written documentation of approved changes helps ensure this.

Change request approval documentation should include the following:

- The date the change was approved
- Any documentation of the change in scope requested (drawings, sketches, descriptions)
- Any agreed-upon changes to scope
    - Scope of the requested change
    - Scope of additional parts of the project
    - Scope of the overall project
- Any agreed-upon changes to future expense allocations
- Any agreed-upon changes to future labor allocations
- Any agreed-upon changes to schedules and deadlines
- Any agreed-upon changes to available resources and materials

These can be documented in production meeting notes, in notes following any separate meeting held to approve changes, or in a formal change order (figure 9.2).

Summing Up

Variance

Variance is defined as the difference between where the project is and where the project should be. Variance is often discussed in terms of a project being under or over budget; or as slipping behind schedule or accelerating ahead of schedule.

Current Variance

Current variance refers to any deviations from the expected expenses and schedule to date, and can be revealed through comparing detailed expense and progress tracking to planned expenses and project schedules.

Predicting Variance

Predicting variance is determining how factors that are either beyond a manager's control or that hadn't previously been foreseen or anticipated will likely impact costs, quality, or progress of the project going forward. Predicting variance can easily be confused with efforts at controlling current variance; however, they are not the same.

Control

Control refers to efforts to manage and mitigate the impact of variance in an ongoing project. Control measures can be direct (current) actions or compensatory (future) actions, and usually involve balancing the interrelated facets of time, cost, scope, and quality.

Managing Change

Change refers to decisions made to adjust the totality of the scope of the project as it progresses.

Promoting Discovery

Changes to project scope can cause anxiety, stress, and frustration for team members; a clearly defined method for managing change can reduce these effects and promote a culture that encourages discovery and development of the project through the rehearsal process.

INITIATING A CHANGE REQUEST

Any proposal to adapt, adjust, or alter the agreed-upon scope of the project initiates a change request. Typically, these should be in writing or recorded and documented for reference.

MEASURING IMPACT

Team members with authority and responsibility over the parts of the project that would be affected by a change should measure the impact of the change request on the project by determining what will be required to implement the changes requested, and how the acquisition of necessary materials and allocation of necessary labor will affect the overall project.

REVIEWING IMPACT

A change impact review is an in-depth conversation about the merits of the requested change balanced against its impact. As with controlling variance, balancing time, cost, scope, and quality for the requested change, other parts of the project, and the totality of the project can make the difference between a change request that can be fit into the project and one that cannot.

APPROVING OR REJECTING CHANGE

After determining whether a change request can be approved, the results of the decision should be documented and recorded. Providing written documentation of approved changes helps ensure that team members can refer to the agreed-upon changes in expectations.

PART IV
Closing Out the Project

A live-entertainment project isn't finished when the project opens, unfortunately. After the production has been rehearsed, teched, and opened, there is still the work of reviewing and archiving the project.

No project runs perfectly. All projects have moments of exceptional success, as well as significant setbacks. Team members and organizations only grow in experience if those successes and setbacks are examined and lessons are learned from them. Before declaring a production project completed, it is important for team members to look back at the project and reflect on what processes worked, what approaches to technical challenges were insufficient, and what distributions of responsibility and authority could have been more clearly communicated, for example. A project manager should develop methods for engaging in this kind of reflection as well as encouraging a culture of self-appraisal and growth.

The final step in closing out a project is archiving and recording the breadth and depth of the entire experience. This includes documenting the scope of the project and its objectives; the resources and time it required; the estimating, scheduling, tracking, and change-management processes; and the lessons learned from reflecting on the production process.

Chapter 10 explores methods for encouraging reflection on the production process and for archiving the production.

10. Project Closeout and Review

Closing out a project—which typically happens upon delivery of the materials agreed to during the project-definition phase of the project, but can also occur when a project has been deemed no longer viable—is an important part of the project life cycle. Unfortunately, it is one that can be all too often ignored or rushed, as the elation of project completion wears off and the pressures to turn to new and different projects come to bear. Attention paid to the closeout process ensures happy clients and stakeholders, provides documentation that can be useful for future projects, and gives insights into processes, policies, and procedures that worked well or that may need improving.

Topics covered in this chapter:

- Closing out the project
  - Deliverables: the punch list
  - Training and manuals: tech
    - Training best practices
    - Safety training
    - Risk-management: training for failure
    - Manuals and operating procedures
- Postmortem: reviewing lessons learned
- Project documentation and archiving

Closing Out the Project

For a "typical" project in a project-management context, the project ends at "delivery." This might mean the handing over of a completed building to new owners and tenants, for example, or the installation and setup of a working point-of-sale computer system. The end of a project in live entertainment can be a little harder to determine: the end of the project could be considered delivery of costumes, scenery, and other elements at technical rehearsals; it could be the often-magical threshold of opening night; or the project might be considered to be under way straight through until closing and strike. Each of these endpoints is somewhat arbitrary, and dependent on any number of factors, including the type of live-entertainment project, how contracts are written for various entities involved in the project, how staffing is managed and organized, and many others. Which of the three typical endpoints should define the delivery and closeout of the project should be determined during project definition, as discussed in chapter 2. Whichever one is chosen, the following should be considered when closing out the project.

Deliverables: The Punch List

The project definition delineates a clear set of items to be delivered at the end of the project (or, at least it should). Depending on the project end point, these deliverables may vary from including only completed scenery and costumes to including training for crew, performers, and operators. It should go without saying, but these deliverables should be delivered at the completion of the project. Traditional projects often follow a punch list approach to ensure all deliverable expectations are met.

A punch list is not much more than a list of deliverables and the tasks that must be completed according to the project definition, but which are not yet completed. This list is generated by the client, the project manager, and team members assigned responsibility and authority over items on the list. This typically ensures that small, niggling issues don't get overlooked in the rush to meet deadlines.

In live entertainment, official punch lists are uncommon; however, the notion of a list of notes to be addressed should be very familiar. In practice, the two are essentially the same; team members generate notes on those areas over which they have authority and responsibility and share them—usually during production meetings. The completion of these notes is typically the last step in completing the project—at least prior to opening night.

Training and Manuals: Tech

Many completed projects not related to live entertainment require specialized training or knowledge to use upon delivery. This is often true for many aspects of a live-entertainment project. The days (weeks, or even months) immediately prior to opening are usually comprised of an exhausting and comprehensive series of rehearsals most commonly referred to as "tech," short for "technical rehearsals." These rehearsals are, as one should expect, the time when all of the different elements of a production—lighting, sound, scenery, actors, costumes, projections, musicians, and more—come together for the first time. It is also the time when cast and crew become familiar with all of the technical elements of the production and trained on their use.

Many priorities demand time during technical rehearsals: costumes need to be seen under light and costume changes need to be rehearsed; lighting looks need to be established, lighting transitions finessed, and the timing of cues determined; the stage crew needs to be trained how to move or operate scenery and those shifts need to be practiced; actors need to become accustomed to projecting for the size of the space and adjust their staging to the realities of the set. As discussed in chapter 2, managing the balance of priorities during technical rehearsals can be challenging, and is best begun by reaching early agreement about how much time is needed for each task. However, any live-entertainment project will evolve: priorities will change leading up to and even during tech as team members learn more about what will be needed in terms of practice, training, and development of different aspect of the production. The project manager should be prepared to work with team members to adjust the tech schedule as these priorities develop.

Training Best Practices

Most good training practices follow three basic steps: I show you, you show me, you practice until you feel comfortable that you can consistently complete the procedure. For example, when teaching a crew member to operate a flown batten for the first time, a technical director (or deck carpenter, or other person responsible for training) should follow some version of the following process.

- Demonstrate:
  Check tension in operating line to check for an out-of-weight situation

Grasp rope
Check on stage for obstructions
Remove the lock ring and operate the lock
Check on stage for obstructions (again)
Pull rope in proper direction for desired movement with a hand-over-hand movement
Alternate checking rope for spike and stage for obstructions
Slow down movement/glide spike to the top of the lock
Operate lock and replace lock ring

- Observe the crew member perform the above procedure. Inevitably steps will be missed or done incorrectly; provide immediate feedback. Repeat this step until the trainer is confident the crew member can continue to practice unsupervised.
- Allow crew member to practice until it becomes second-nature.

Training in this way takes time, but is necessary for ensuring the quality of the production—and often to ensure the safety of cast and crew.

Safety Training

Live performance venues can be dangerous places. There is lots of electricity flowing through cables on and above the stage; there may be scenic units weighing multiple tons moving around the space at relatively high speeds; productions may include swords and other bladed weapons, blank-firing firearms, live flame, and atmospheric or pyrotechnic effects. Time should be set aside during tech to ensure cast and crew are aware of possible safety risks, and for proper training of anyone who might be at risk.

Proper training may include any or all of the following:

- *The use of proper personal protective equipment*
  Personal protective equipment (PPE) includes devices like earplugs, gloves, safety glasses, and harnesses. For example, a crew member operating a batten on a line set should wear gloves to protect his hands, or a crew member firing a blank-firing weapon offstage should wear safety glasses and earplugs. Fall-arrest harnesses are an important piece of safety equipment for actors involved in aerial/flying movement, and for both actors and crew members who might be working at heights. Anyone using PPE should be trained on how to wear it properly, as improper use of PPE can sometimes cause greater injury than not using PPE at all.
- *Safe operating procedures and practices*
  Blank-firing guns shouldn't be pointed at anyone, and should be kept locked up, and team members shouldn't play with prop swords backstage; these are examples of obvious safe operating procedures, but that they are obvious does not mean they shouldn't be clearly stated during tech. Other safe operating procedures are less obvious; for example, connecting an actor to a fall-arrest harness or firing pyrotechnics during a performance are moments in a live performance that each require a specific series of safety checks and opportunities to abort if safety thresholds aren't met. Cast and crew should be aware

of and comfortable with performing these procedures and practices.

- *Emergency response actions* Cast and crew should be made aware of what to do in the event of an emergency during a performance. What is the procedure if there is a fire? If power goes out? In some geographical areas and in some venues, hazardous weather conditions can arise. And, as uncomfortable as it may be to consider, live-entertainment events have been sites for violent acts. Team members should be trained in response procedures in advance—even if the likelihood of needing to use them is small—to avoid panic and mistakes if they do need to be used.

Risk Management: Training for Failure

When managing a complex live-entertainment project, it is tempting to assume that all elements of the production will work as planned, every night. However, one of the reasons live entertainment is compelling to so many is that every performance or event is different, and any number of things may happen to affect the performance—including elements failing to perform as designed.

Of course, team members work hard throughout a project's life cycle to ensure failure is highly unlikely. Aesthetic and technical designs, training, documentation, and maintenance procedures are all efforts at ensuring a consistent, quality experience. However, team members must recognize that even the best preparation can't rule out every possibility, and should plan appropriately.

Other texts discuss the principle of fail-safe design in far more detail than is possible in this chapter; suffice it to say that technical elements should be designed and constructed such that when failure happens it happens in a way that is safe, controlled, and planned. Time should be set aside during tech to explain and practice what happens when elements fail, even if they fail "as planned." Often, when an element fails it will have an impact on the rest of the performance, and the cast and crew need to be prepared for how to continue with the performance in order to provide the best possible experience for those attending the event.

Consider a performance of *Peter Pan*, when Peter is to fly around the Darlings' bedroom. The cast member who is to connect the actor's harness to the flying rig signals to the operator offstage that the harness could not be connected properly. Consequently, the operator knows not to perform the flying move. This keeps the actor playing Peter and the rest of the cast and crew safe from harm. However, the scene is somewhat dependent on Peter demonstrating that he can fly; how does the play progress, and how does the cast continue? The team must develop alternate staging for this situation during the tech process, provide time to practice it, and experience having to make the call in the moment to not run the flying effect and switch to whatever alternate staging has been developed.

Manuals and Operating Procedures

For some live-entertainment projects, operation and maintenance manuals should be delivered during tech and reviewed by those members of the cast and crew who need to be familiar with their contents to ensure understanding. The most common example of this type of documentation is the cue sheet, which lists things like a cue number (for reference and cue-calling purposes) and directions for how the cue is operated and what should happen on stage.

Additional documentation that should be delivered at tech might include maintenance and setup procedures that should happen pre- or postshow, or perhaps periodically during the run. For more complex parts of a project—for example, automated moving scenery—documentation of the basic operating procedures, electrical schematics, control-system drawings, and any other information necessary for understanding how the system functions should be included. Troubleshooting procedures are another especially helpful piece of documentation that can provide cast and crew with clear processes for dealing with problems.

Postmortem: Reviewing Lessons Learned

Many academic theatres—and some live-entertainment organizations of various types and sizes, as well—hold postmortem discussions once a production project has been completed. These discussions are typically informal, and, unfortunately, sometimes exist for backslapping and congratulating—as opportunities to point out successes. (This is not always because of a lack of willingness to examine the process honestly or to receive critique, but is sometimes due to the exhilaration that comes from completing the project at all.)

An in-depth examination of the project and the production process is necessary for an organization to grow and for team members to improve their skills for the next project, however. This starts with developing a culture that encourages self-reflection and the practice of giving, receiving, and acting on critique, and is extended by setting out a procedure for postmortem evaluation for team members to follow. Developing the culture is an ongoing process, one that requires modeling by project managers and team leaders. Developing a procedure for team members to follow during a postmortem project review is a little more straightforward.

A consistent procedure and clear guidelines for how to participate in a postmortem can help team members reflect more deeply on the successes and failures of the project process. It can also help forestall one of the biggest dangers in holding regular postproduction evaluation discussions: the tendency for them to become little more than gripe-fests and complaint sessions. While honest reflection and critique are important to growth, critiques that devolve into complaints and finger-pointing do little more than lower morale, raise frustrations, and alienate team members from each other. Postmortem guidelines should make it clear that while tensions may be high and emotions may be piqued, respect and a commitment to growth and improvement is the goal of the discussion, not blame or scapegoating.

Team members should come to postmortem discussions having already done some reflection prior to meeting as a group. Ideally, they should come to the discussion having given thought to how their performance impacted the project. Some questions for team members to consider:

- What did they personally do well?
- What did their team do well?
- How did they (and their team) contribute to the project's success?
- How did other's (and other team's) work contribute to their (and their team's) success?

- In what ways can they personally do better?
- In what ways can their team do better?
- In what ways could they improve on their (and their team's) contribution to success of others (and their teams)?
- In what ways could other team members' and their teams' contributions be improved?
- Which project processes were impactful to the project's success? Which detracted from the project's success?
- Was the project's scope clearly defined?
- Were project deliverables (and quality expectations) clearly communicated?
- Was the organizational structure of the project clear?
- Was the organizational structure of the project appropriate to the project? Why or why not?
- How were changes to the project's scope handled? Were these responses effective and appropriate?
- How were variances from the project plan managed? Were these responses effective and appropriate?

The list of questions above begins with examinations of each team member's own contributions, and then expands outward to less personal and bigger-picture facets of the project's management. Structuring questions in this way typically has the effect of preparing team members to be accepting of critique by preparing them to be self-reflective before being critical of others on the team.

Undeniably, receiving critique can be difficult. It should come as no surprise that in these meetings—especially following difficult or problematic projects—emotions can run high. Team members should be reminded before and during postmortem discussions about rules governing behavior. Decorum and politeness should be understood as a baseline expectation. Participants should be discouraged from talking over each other or invalidating the emotional claims of others.

The content of postmortem project evaluation discussions should be recorded. Any issues that arose during the production process should be noted, as should any suggestions for improvements. These notes can be used to develop better working practices and project procedures for the future. Notes from the meeting

"Postmortem" is a Latin phrase meaning, literally, "after death," that refers to the medical examination of a dead body, but is also commonly used (in theatre and elsewhere) to refer to an examination of something after it has occurred—in this case, examination of the production and the production process after the show has been "killed" at strike. Like many aspects of theatrical tradition, it is somewhat tongue-in-cheek, and reflects both the importance of reflecting on a project as well as the reality that some production processes are painful and consequently need to be reflected upon in order to prevent similar effects in the future. For some, waiting until after strike to have these discussions can mean too much time has elapsed to have a specific and accurate conversation about the process; some organizations, for this reason, hold postmortems after tech or immediately following opening night.

should be distributed to all participants, and copies should be included with the archival documentation of the project.

Project Documentation and Archiving

Frankly, this should be the shortest part of this text, because this important part of the closeout process is stated in one simple statement: *document and archive everything about the project.*

Every part of the project should be archived, from initial decisions about project scope, to last-minute control responses to variances as deadlines approached, and the hand-off of deliverables at the completion of the project. Every decision, small or large, that happened along the life cycle of the project should be documented. The project isn't just the deliverables (which, for most live-entertainment projects, is the show—which almost always has a limited run and in the end is an experience that disappears once the production closes); the project is the process of getting from vision to realization on stage.

For many theatres, documenting and archiving the project serve a somewhat practical purpose. It is not uncommon to revive productions, to remount them, or even to move them to other venues. (For example, many Broadway productions start at other, smaller venues, and evolve from those projects.) Documenting and archiving the project make remounts and moves far easier, as it is nearly impossible to progress through the entire process from start to finish and recreate every choice and decision.

Archived project documentation also provides information useful for other, future productions. Analogous material and labor estimates rely on previous experiences. The formulae used in parametric estimates can only be derived from actual data from previous projects. Evaluating the work of team members on previous projects provides insight into their developing skill sets and levels of experience. Examining previous organizational structures and project teams, and how effective they were at achieving a project, can help determine choices for future productions. Having all this information accessible is a must for any project manager.

What does "save everything" mean in practice, however? Frankly, it would be impractical to save every artifact from the production process. Scenic models are large, bulky, and sometimes fragile; it's impossible (and probably against copyright laws and union rules) to videotape every rehearsal and performance. Instead of saving every artifact, focus instead on archiving those items that provide insight into the fundamental aspects of any project: scope, quality, time, and cost. These might include artifacts like costume renderings and set-design plates; it might include photographs of finished costumes and the completed set, a light plot and digital file of the cues, and a stage manager's prompt book with cues and staging. These all describe elements of the scope of the production project and the quality expectations of various parts of the production. Cost estimates, build schedules, and production-meeting notes should also be included, as they provide insight into cost and time requirements for the production.

Exact methods and procedures for documenting and archiving a project will vary by organization and project. Some organizations have climate-controlled archive rooms chock-full of materials from previous production projects; others have little more than a shelf for scenic-design models and binders. Any storage procedure or method should provide for relatively easy access, however; file boxes stored in the loft of an old barn won't be accessed very often, and are therefore useless for providing insights gleaned from previous project experiences.

Digital storage can be an exceptionally effective alternative to analog file boxes. Not only do digitized files take up less physical space, they can be organized, sorted, and searched more easily. Consider a database or other storage solution that allows for keyword or hashtag searches, so projects can be marked for easy reference later. Artifacts from a production of *The Importance of Being Earnest*, for example, might be tagged with the name of the play, the period, the venue, budgeted funds for different aspects of the production, length of production process, and other keywords that might make for easy searching later when developing budgets, analogous or parametric estimates, or weighing scope and quality considerations for future productions.

Summing Up

Closing Out the Project

Deliverables: The Punch List

A punch list is a list of deliverables and the tasks that must be completed for each deliverable to be considered done. In live entertainment, official punch lists are usually communicated as "notes lists." The completion of these notes is typically the last step in completing the project prior to opening night.

Training and Manuals: Tech

The days (or weeks, or even months) immediately prior to opening are usually comprised of an exhausting and comprehensive series of rehearsals most commonly referred to as "tech," short for "technical rehearsals." These rehearsals are the time when all of the different elements of a production come together for the first time, and when cast and crew are trained on the technical elements of the show.

TRAINING BEST PRACTICES

Demonstrate the process, observe the crew performing the process to ensure they do it correctly, and have the crew practice the process until it becomes second nature.

SAFETY TRAINING

Train cast and crew on the use of any required personal-protective equipment (such as gloves, earplugs, and harnesses). Train them on safe operating procedures and practices for dangerous equipment and effects (such as moving scenery, pyrotechnics, and firearms). Train cast and crew on emergency procedures (such as what to do in the event of a fire, power loss, or dangerous weather conditions).

RISK MANAGEMENT: TRAINING FOR FAILURE

Explain to the cast and crew what happens when elements fail, even if they fail "as planned." Practice with the cast and crew how to continue with the performance in order to provide the best possible experience for those attending the event.

MANUALS AND OPERATING PROCEDURES

Deliver any maintenance and setup procedures that should happen pre- or postshow, or perhaps periodically during the run. Provide documentation of the basic operating procedures, electrical schematics, and control-system drawings for understanding how a system or effect functions. Provide troubleshooting procedures with clear processes for dealing with problems.

Postmortem: Reviewing Lessons Learned

A postmortem is a project review and evaluation process designed to learn lessons from the project and to improve team members and organizational processes.

Project Documentation and Archiving

Recording, documenting, and archiving project processes, decisions, and work provides information useful for future project work. Archive those artifacts that give insight into time, cost, quality, and scope of work for the project.

Index

Rich Dionne is an assistant professor and a faculty technical director in the Department of Theatre in the Patti and Rusty Rueff School of Visual and Performing Arts at Purdue University. He has published articles in *TD&T* and *Stage Directions*. He has served as the production manager at the Shakespeare Theatre of New Jersey and as the technical director for the Berkshire Theatre Festival, Alpine Theatre Project, Weston Playhouse Theatre Company, and Dorset Theatre Festival.